I0114625

THE GREEN ~~NEW~~ REAL DEAL

THE GREEN ~~NEW~~ REAL DEAL

American Energy, National Security, and a Better Plan for the Environment

BY BILL HERRINGTON

The Green Real Deal: American Energy, National Security, and a Better Plan for the Environment

First Edition: 2023

ISBN-13: 978-1-959677-12-3 (Paperback)
ISBN-13: 978-1-959677-11-6 (eBook)
ISBN-13: 978-1-959677-13-0 (Hardcover)

Published by Defiance Press & Publishing, LLC

Bulk orders of this book may be obtained by contacting Defiance Press & Publishing, LLC. www.defiancepress.com.

Public Relations Dept. – Defiance Press & Publishing, LLC
281-581-9300
pr@defiancepress.com

Defiance Press & Publishing, LLC
281-581-9300
info@defiancepress.com

TABLE OF CONTENTS

PART III: A BALANCED ENERGY PLAN FOR OUR FUTURE

"Beware of false knowledge; it is more dangerous than ignorance."

– George Bernard Shaw

INTRODUCTION

OCTOBER 16, 2016

It was just before noon, and the sidewalks of downtown Houston were packed with people on their lunch breaks. Rising above the typical urban noises of Metro buses and jackhammers were shouts in near-perfect cadence.

From my office at the Wells Fargo Tower, I made my way along Main Street until I came upon a peculiar demonstration several blocks away. I curiously approached the growing crowd.

About fifty protestors were marching and carrying colorfully painted signs, some of which looked professionally made, that read, "People before Profits" and "No More Pipelines."

Before that day, I had never paid much attention to protests or protestors against fossil fuels and the pipelines that transport them. I'd thought of fossil-fuel protestors as a minor, fringe element of society, people disconnected from the realities of modern-day life. And for me, the need for reliable energy was a modern-day reality.

My involvement in the energy industry began over forty years ago in Harrisburg, Pennsylvania, with a summer job replacing a section of a historic pipeline. From that humble start, my career in the energy finance business steadily progressed over many years. In the ensuing four decades, I worked in the banking industry, financing and investing in virtually every aspect of the energy business, primarily in Louisiana and Texas.

My perception of protestors changed that October morning as I listened to the echoes of chanting.

A leader shouted, "No D-A-P-L!"

The group immediately responded in rhythmic unison, "Water is life! Keep it in the ground!"

They were protesting the Dakota Access Pipeline, which was slated to carry crude oil from North Dakota's Bakken oil fields to Illinois. The leader of the group repeatedly bellowed the chant from a megaphone, reminding me of a marine drill sergeant exhorting his assigned boot camp recruits. Overshadowing them loomed one of Houston's tallest skyscrapers, which housed the offices of Energy Transfer Partners, the Dallas-based oil and gas company that owned the pipeline.

As the epicenter of the global energy industry, Houston is home to forty-six hundred energy-related firms.[1] Approximately two-thirds of integrated oil companies and the country's largest pipeline operators have offices in the Bayou City, providing hundreds of thousands, if not millions, of direct and indirect jobs. Because so much of Houston's GDP is tied directly to oil and gas, local protests against the industry are rare.

I looked around at the bystanders gathered beside me. They seemed as perplexed as I was. There had been widespread media coverage of protest activities where the pipeline was under construction in North Dakota, but no one expected the protestors to make their way down in force to Houston, Texas. I wondered who could have organized and financed such a passionate and prepared gathering.

But my confusion wasn't just about the distance the protesters had traveled or who had paid for the organization of the event. It was more

1."Energy," Greater Houston Partnership, https://www.houston.org/why-houston/industries/energy.

personal than that. The activists were protesting an industry that I knew very well, one that had provided the first real job I ever had. And the protests disturbed me.

It may not have been obvious by my suit and necktie, the requisite uniform of a corporate banker, but I had not forgotten my work as a common laborer on a pipeline forty years earlier. In those days, wearing jeans and steel-toed boots, I had driven over a thousand miles with a friend from my hometown in Louisiana to join a pipeline construction crew in Harrisburg, Pennsylvania. I was an inexperienced teenager hoping to earn a few bucks to cover college expenses, but I walked away with so much more from the summers of 1979 and 1980.

I was introduced to a genuine, American-made industry and the hardy men who built it. I participated in painstakingly laying pipe in the ground with meticulous care for the environment. My unique experience allowed me to see the pipeline construction business from the inside out, leaving me with an indelible respect for the work ethic of pipeliners and for the necessity of the industry.

For decades, I proudly carried my pipeline laborer experience as a memorable badge of honor. I appreciated the pipeline industry as a good, solid backbone of the United States, ensuring the necessary energy for our modern way of life, providing national security, supporting our strong economy, and providing stable careers for countless Americans and their families. I respected that pipelines and the products they transported were less threatening to the environment than nuclear, a competing energy source. So, I was confused by the depiction of the industry as evil. The protestors said pipelines were harmful to the environment, were bad for Americans, and should be eliminated from the United States.

I turned from the protest with a sense of anger, sadness, and frustration and drifted back toward the Wells Fargo Tower, the sounds of the protestors trailing off behind me. My four decades of confidence in an industry were shaken. I thought, "How have attitudes toward energy changed so quickly and so dramatically?"

The protest activities led me to objectively reexamine my understanding of the industry and the protestors, as well as what may have changed over the years. It was a years long journey that involved mining personal experiences, national historical accounts, and piles of news articles, research, and investigations.

Since that day in 2016, protests against the fossil fuels business have only grown and accelerated globally. Protestors are now demanding an immediate retreat from fossil fuels in favor of a transition to renewable or "green" energy. The consequences of abandoning some of the most powerful forms of energy (fossil fuels) for some of the weakest and least reliable (renewables) are rarely discussed.

And the protests are working.

Wall Street investment banks are avoiding the industry. Some commercial banks are refusing to finance fossil fuel projects. The World Bank has denied financing requests from undeveloped countries to build natural gas pipelines. During Joe Biden's presidential campaign in 2020, he declared that on day one of his presidency, he would require companies to disclose their greenhouse gas emissions and climate-related financial risks. In his first year, he'd work to require polluters to bear the full cost of their climate pollution. And he'd direct his EPA and Justice Department to pursue these cases to the fullest legal extent, holding corporate executives personally accountable, including jail time.

The energy transition has been set by politicians across the globe as the only way forward for human civilization. These green politicians have the loudest voices and have drowned out any commentary on the positive impact that fossil fuels have had on our country's economic and national security.

FEBRUARY 24, 2022

Then Russia invaded Ukraine.

It was a wake-up call to America and the world that Russia is a threat. It is a threat that has been ignored and dismissed for at least the last decade: the obsessive, singular, all-in stance in favor of renewables has rendered Europe's economy and national security vulnerable to Russian President Vladimir Putin, one of the world's most vicious leaders. And America is in danger of making the same catastrophic energy mistake as Europe.

As an example, Germany has pursued a much-celebrated path of phasing out fossil fuels and nuclear energy in favor of renewables, a national green policy referred to as *Energiewende*. The problem is that Germany began phasing out its own coal and nuclear energy plants before replacing this energy with renewable sources. Instead, Germany relied on Russia, Germany's arch enemy in World War II. In 2021, Russia supplied more than half of the natural gas and about a third of all the oil that Germany burned to heat homes, power factories, and fuel cars, buses, and trucks.[2]

After the Russian invasion of Ukraine, when Germany joined the NATO alliance in establishing sanctions against Russia, Russia threatened to terminate the shipment of natural gas to Germany through its Nord Stream pipeline. In response, Germany's top union official warned in 2022 that entire industries are in danger of permanent collapse—including the aluminum, glass, and chemical industries—which could lead to widespread social and labor unrest.

German Chancellor Olaf Scholz declared his regret over his country's decision against investing in energy infrastructure as a means of national security. He said the energy lesson Europe has learned the

2. "Sorry Zelenskyy, Germany's Hooked on that Russian Oil and Gas," Politico, last modified March 17, 2022, https://www.politico.eu/article/why-is-it-so-difficult-for-germany-to-say-no-to-russian-energy/.

hard way is to be prepared for a situation like this. Indeed, an experience from a ruthless Putin may prove to be a cruel lesson during the long, cold German and European winter.

Despite the foolish mistake of overly relying on Russian oil and natural gas, Chancellor Scholz is correct. If there is any silver lining to the attack on Ukraine, it's this: Putin may have prematurely invaded Ukraine and unwittingly provided a timely impetus for an energy course correction in the United States and in other democracies around the world.

Our country has been mesmerized by a cult of climate alarmists. They seem incapable of comprehending the most basic facts of energy production and dependence: energy is like oxygen, and it's unacceptable to run out.

The Green ideology of climate alarmists makes it taboo to ask four basic questions:

1. How can the West eliminate the two most powerful forms of energy (nuclear and fossil fuels) and replace them quickly with the two least reliable types of energy (solar and wind)?
2. Why is it acceptable to focus on the environmental risks of fossil fuels while ignoring the environmental risks of renewables, including the destruction of forests and land?
3. Why is the West reducing its reliance on fossil fuels and nuclear while Russia and China are expanding theirs?
4. Why are only the consequences of global warming explored without considering the consequences of the absence of fossil fuels?

Environmental activists are paving a disastrous ideological path. It started in earnest in 1979 when they last "saved the world" by shutting down new U.S. nuclear power plants after the Three Mile Island nuclear accident near Harrisburg, Pennsylvania. I remember protestors marching in front of the White House yelling, "Two, four, six, eight, we don't want to radiate!"

But the 1979 environmental protests against nuclear energy had a paradoxical impact. Pulling back from the most powerful form of energy known to man sent the U.S. and the world on a path of dependence on the *second*-most powerful form of energy: fossil fuels. Now, those fossil fuels—coal, oil, and natural gas—are the same fuels that environmentalists now claim are a looming existential threat to humans.

On one hand, the U.S. was politically unable to pursue a nuclear future; on the other hand, we were running out of conventional oil and gas. That's when it became necessary to develop sources of fossil fuels from Russia, the Middle East, and others around the world.

Thankfully, American ingenuity has remained at work. Along the way, we've enhanced our own fossil fuel resources through new technologies of deepwater drilling, directional drilling, liquefied natural gas (LNG), carbon capture, and hydraulic fracturing (also known as frac'ing, fracing, or fracking). These technological improvements restored our position as the world's leading supplier of fossil fuels.

And Russia feels vulnerable.

At least half of Russia's economy depends on fossil fuel production. Its grip on Europe is threatened by the U.S. reemergence as a domestic energy superpower and a European supplier.

How is Russia countering this threat?

It's utilizing a throwback tool from one hundred years ago during Vladimir Lenin's Communist regime: propaganda. Because of its dependence on fossil fuels, Russia is determined to undermine global perceptions of fossil fuels to protect its economic security and political influence around the world.

Russians are spreading disinformation and influencing protests about fossil fuels and pipelines around the globe. It's easy today with

Russia's state-backed news channel and with social media at their fingertips to spread lies like wildfire. The disinformation campaign is mobilizing environmental activists, American Indians, and ordinary citizens against an industry that's critical to our economic and national security. It is demonizing and threatening Americans whose jobs depend on a healthy energy industry.

Activists, supported by disinformation, insist the solution to greenhouse gas (GHG) emissions is not nuclear energy. It's not carbon capture. Nor is it natural gas as a bridge.

They say it's solar and wind energy.

Though the wind doesn't always blow, and the sun doesn't always shine, they claim renewables are reliable. Though renewables consume huge amounts of land, forests, and minerals, they tout renewables as clean and environmentally friendly.

I am not denying GHG emissions; they need to be addressed. But they should not be addressed at the expense of our economic and national security—and they don't have to.

What activists are not acknowledging is that renewables have their own problems. The dirty secret is that renewables involve massive mining for rare-earth minerals, most of which is controlled by China. They cause health and water issues for miners and citizens, and it's no easy task to dispose of batteries and other "renewable" waste materials.

And—as Germany has learned—the innate unreliability of renewables similarly spells disaster for U.S. national security.

Yet the attack on fossil fuels continues.

Europe has moved quickly toward less-efficient renewable energy, combined with Russian natural gas for "base load" power—the minimum amount of power it needs to maintain a stable supply for its electrical grid daily. Its countries are realizing the flaw of tethering the fate of their economic and national security to intermittent energy and a ruthless dictator.

With a U.S. president and Congress that have declared war on fossil fuels, we are not far behind. The United States is pursuing a path of energy inefficiency that threatens everyday working folks and our economic and national security.

Meanwhile, as America squabbles with itself, Russia is becoming richer through the increased production and sale of fossil fuels and becoming a global nuclear leader by designing modular nuclear reactors. China is also becoming economically stronger by building coal and nuclear plants which produce cheaper electricity.

The Green Real Deal explores the truth about Russia, China, and the energy policy we need to power the world. It offers a path for Americans who want to understand the climate change debate and determine a realistic energy policy for the United States. The book addresses:

- Why peace and national security won't exist without oil and pipelines
- The three faulty accusations behind American Indian protests against pipelines
- How environmental activists and "dark money" are weakening our nation and strengthening Russia and China
- Why Russia is spreading propaganda to destroy shale oil production and divide democracy
- The dirty secrets of "green" energy
- Why we quit nuclear power—and why it deserves a second chance
- An autopsy of the Green New Deal and what makes it dangerous
- The five tenets of a balanced path forward

We can address the threats of global GHG emissions *without* weakening the economic and national security of our great nation. If we want to remain strong, the United States needs to pursue *all* forms of energy for the foreseeable future, including fossil fuels with carbon capture, renewables, and nuclear energy.

ACKNOWLEDGMENTS

The Green Real Deal was made possible by the collaboration of many people. Thank you to my publisher, the Defiance Press team; my editor, Ella Ritchie; and those early readers who helped shape the book through their honest, constructive feedback.

PART I

THE WISDOM OF THE PAST

CHAPTER 1

NATIONAL SECURITY AND WESTERN DEMOCRACY

IT WON'T EXIST WITHOUT OIL AND PIPELINES TO MOVE IT

United States
1860s - 1940s

"It is an unfortunate fact that we can secure peace only by preparing for war."

– John F. Kennedy

IF ANYTHING POSITIVE CAN COME from the 2022 war between Russia and Ukraine, it may be the opportunity for a course correction and critical change in the energy policy of the West. In the intensity of battle and in the face of imminent danger, bold and creative ideas emerge that can alter the course of history. We saw it in World War II, and we can see it again.

In World War II, that critical change arrived in the form of an unlikely duo that traveled from East Texas straight to the heart of our conflict with Nazi Germany. The heroic pair unified thousands of people and rallied the private and public sectors along the way. They were credited with helping the U.S. defeat the evil, racist ideology of Adolph Hitler.

They were nicknamed "Big Inch" and "Little Big Inch." But they were not men. They were America's first long-distance interstate pipelines.

The "Inch" pipelines helped transport the more than seven billion barrels of oil consumed by the Allies in World War II, six billion of which were supplied by the United States. You wouldn't know it from the hateful campaigns lobbying against the industry today, but these pipelines did more than move oil and gas.

They helped win the war.

A RADICAL IDEA

EAST COAST
1942

When "Big Inch" and "Little Big Inch" emerged in 1942, the United States was facing a big problem. Congress had unanimously declared war upon Nazi Germany, but the strength of the U.S. military was in jeopardy. Its strength depended on oil—as does the strength of every military around the world today—but there were complications in delivering oil in time to defeat Hitler.

At the time, 60 percent of the world's oil was produced in the United States, mostly in Texas.[3] The preferred method of shipping the Texas oil to the northeast U.S. was by sea because it was cheaper and faster than by rail. There was one problem though: it was a terrible wartime strategy. German U-boats were patrolling domestic and trans-Atlantic routes and routinely taking target practice on our slow-moving tankers.

U.S. tankers were among the Germans' favorite targets. German captains delighted seeing our oil go up in great balls of smoke and flames, calling it the "American shooting season."[4] In the winter of 1942, seventy-four oil tankers were sunk or damaged—with no losses to the German U-boats. It was all part of Hitler's "Operation Paukenschlag," or Operation Drumbeat. The campaign was designed to cripple America's shipping industry in the first stages of the U.S. participation in World War II.

Unfortunately, Hitler's plan was working. The Germans easily discerned the silhouettes of American freighters and tankers against the glow of neon lights in our coastal cities, where communities refused to dim their waterfront lights for fear of losing tourists and business. The U-boats picked off U.S. targets within sight of passengers landing at New York airports and sunbathers on Virginia Beach.[5]

America was in an acute predicament. Ships were sunk, and nearly five thousand seamen drowned so that Americans could enjoy "business and pleasure as usual." Insurers refused to cover the remaining tankers. The problem was further magnified by the fact that the U.S. had earlier

---

3. Diana Davids Olien and Roger M. Olien, *Oil in Texas: The Gusher Age, 1895-1945*, (Austin, Texas: University of Texas Press 2002), pp. 220-221.

4. Nikola Budanovic, "Operation Drumbeat – U-Boat Happy Days On The USA East Coast," War History Online, September 27, 2016, https://www.warhistoryonline.com/world-war-ii/operation-drumbeat-u-boat-happy-days-x.html.

5. Michael D. Hull, "Operation Drumbeat's Devastating Toll on Allied Shipping," Warefare History Network, August 2014, https://warfarehistorynetwork.com/article/operation-drumbeats-devastating-toll-on-allied-shipping/.

sent fifty of its tankers to the United Kingdom in its fight against Hitler. When the U.S. eliminated oil transport by sea and focused on rail, a scarcity of suitable railcars contributed to delays and oil shortages.[6]

Both sides quickly realized that the victor of the Second World War would be determined by oil. Everything about modern warfare depended on the ability to supply and move petrol, including fighter planes, bombers, tanks, submarines, trucks, guns, machinery, and runways. For the Axis powers—Germany, Italy, and Japan—Hitler told Mussolini that their success was entirely contingent on his access to oilfields, and failure to acquire oil would mean defeat. For America and the Allied powers, the need was so dire that General George S. Patton prioritized oil over food.

"My men can eat their belts, but my tanks have gotta have gas," he said to President Eisenhower. In a letter home, he wrote, "My chief difficulty is not the Germans, but gasoline." When he ran out of fuel at the German border, he demanded that French producers airlift supplies from Normandy. The emergency supplies were delivered against all odds.

Fuel shortages shaped war tactics and civilian life around the world. In North Africa, German field marshal Erwin Rommel built intimidating "dummy tanks" mounted on Volkswagons to improve fuel efficiency and fool the enemy. In Japan, household supplies of spirits and vegetable oils were turned into fuel, and fighters were forced to fly directly at the enemy, their "kamikaze" missions making use of excess personnel and planes without the need to fuel return journeys. In the United Kingdom, fuel rationing resulted in a frenzy of wartime bicycling.

In the United States, two new fossil fuel plants were built to produce the synthetic rubber that was used for tires. Although the Japanese con-

6. "U-Boat Attacks Of World War II: 6 Months of Secret Terror in the Atlantic," New England Historical Society, last updated 2022, https://www.newenglandhistoricalsociety.com/u-boat-attacks-of-world-war-ii-6-months-of-secret-terror-in-the-atlantic/.

trolled 90 percent of the world's natural rubber supplies, the American plants ensured that the Allies never ran out of rubber. Meanwhile, the public was outraged with Secretary of the Interior Harold Ickes' measures, which included banning auto racing and non-essential driving, limiting speeds to thirty-five miles per hour, and encouraging "gasolineless Sundays." Blackouts along the coast were finally imposed, which saved countless lives of seamen.

Still, we needed more oil. American forces in Europe required one hundred *times* more gasoline in World War II than in World War I. And delays spelled danger for the free world: the future was decided by who arrived first. When logistical challenges in 1944-1945 delayed the Allies' path to Berlin by eight months, the Soviet Union captured East Germany, Poland, Czechoslovakia, Hungary, and Yugoslavia, all of which ended up as part of the great Soviet Empire.[7]

That's when Ickes proposed a radical solution. He recommended interior land-based pipelines that would safely transport oil from Texas to the Northeast, without the inherent perils of German U-boats and inclement weather.

It was a bold and attractive idea, but numerous challenges remained. One challenge was properly constructing pipelines to cross the twelve hundred miles between Texas and New York. Another challenge was the limitation on the amount of deliverable oil. Until the late 1930s, the largest pipe that was structurally suitable and commercially viable was about eight inches in diameter. This diameter could only deliver twenty thousand barrels per day, which was insufficient to meet demand.

But technologies were improving, and the pipeline proponents triumphed. When Ickes was appointed Petroleum Coordinator for National Defense and became the administrator of the Petroleum

7. "Oil and War: Ten Conclusions from WWII?" Thunder Said Energy, March 3, 2022, https://thundersaidenergy.com/2022/03/03/oil-and-war-ten-conclusions-from-wwii/?utm_source=rss&utm_medium=rss&utm_campaign=oil-and-war-ten-conclusions-from-wwii.

Administration for War, the government passed legislation enabling the acquisition of privately owned land and the construction of two pipelines essential for the war effort. "Big Inch" and "Little Big Inch" were born.

UNPRECEDENTED FEAT

TEXAS
1942 – 1944

The pipeline project was unprecedented in every way. When work began in June 1942, it was the longest, biggest, and heaviest undertaking of its kind. The project required sixteen thousand people, 725,000 tons of construction materials, and permission for the government to build across 7,500 parcels of land, three hundred of which invoked the right of eminent domain. It also required cooperation from both the public and private sectors. The pipelines were built and operated by War Emergency Pipelines, a nonprofit headquartered in Little Rock, Arkansas, with financing by the federal government and backing by some of the largest U.S. oil companies, such as Standard Oil and Shell.

The diameters of the pipelines were unprecedented as well, which is how they earned their nicknames. The "Big Inch" was a twenty-four-inch-diameter pipeline for crude oil, and "Little Big Inch" was a twenty-inch-diameter line that carried gasoline and other refined products.

Each pipeline was built in three phases, with construction beginning on "Big Inch." Crews used ditching machines and manual labor to dig trenches that were four-feet deep and three-feet wide. By utilizing specialized tunnels and trenches, they navigated remarkable obstacles during the construction. "Big Inch" passed under thirty-three rivers and two hundred creeks and lakes as well as more than nine hundred railroads and highway intersections.

Each day, between five and nine miles of the steel pipeline were lowered into position in the trenches, including miles of underwater piping. The larger pipes were so heavy that they required enormous caterpillar tractors equipped with counterweights. When the pipeline needed to curve, the crews invented a specialized piece of equipment, a bending machine, to curve the pipe. The pipes were then cleaned by pulling a workman with cloths through the inside before welding the parts together. Finally, the trench was back-filled, completing the process.

More than 237,000 tons of steel later, the construction of "Big Inch" was completed on New Year's Eve 1942. It stretched nearly 1,254 miles from Texas to Pennsylvania, where it branched into two segments to reach both New York and Philadelphia. On August 14, 1943, the first crude oil arrived at Phoenixville via "Big Inch," which began to carry up to 334,456 barrels a day.

Construction on "Little Big Inch" came next. It spanned 1,475 miles from Texas to Arkansas, where it joined "Big Inch" at a pumping station, and the two continued on parallel paths to New Jersey and Pennsylvania. In March 1944, the first refined product arrived via "Little Big Inch," which would provide 239,844 barrels of gasoline per day.

As we bolstered our oil supplies, we destroyed our enemies' supplies. The Allies deciphered U-boat codes and sank 30 percent of the German ships in one month alone. And Allied bombers began targeting Germany's fuel facilities. On what is known as "Black Sunday," more than seventeen hundred U.S. airmen carried out an unprecedented, low-level bombing raid on some of Germany's critical oil refineries.[8] By September 1944, Nazi air operations ran out of fuel and were incapacitated. Hitler continued issuing orders from his bunker, but his army slowed to a halt. His trucks were dragged by oxen in the final days of the war.

8. Katie Sanders and Mara Storey, "The US Military is Trying to Identify Dozens of Airmen Who Didn't Make it Home from a Daring Bomber Raid on 'Hitler's Gas Station,'" Business Insider, June 5, 2022, https://www.businessinsider.com/us-military-trying-to-identify-airmen-killed-in-ploesti-raid-2022-6.

Back in the United States, the completion of the dual pipeline project was celebrated as a feat unprecedented in scale in the history of pipeline construction. "Big Inch" and "Little Big Inch" were the longest and widest pipelines ever constructed—and each was completed in less than a year. The project earned praise as one of the greatest examples of public-private cooperation in American history. The cooperation between the U.S. government and American oil companies ensured our victory—by an inch.[9]

Spurred by the sense of urgency created by the Germans' sinking of American oil tankers, the United States had unleashed its ingenuity and resourcefulness in record time. Both pipelines were completed before the D-Day invasion at Normandy on June 6, 1944, increasing the delivery of oil and refined products by 35 percent.[10] In all, the United States provided 85 percent of the Allies' oil. Ships still transported barrels by sea to Europe in a risky transatlantic route from the northeast, but pipelines shortened the voyage and reduced the risks from German U-boats.

Without U.S. oil, we would not have won World War II. The Allied victory depended on the collaboration of the oil and gas industry and the government.[11]

"Big Inch" and "Little Big Inch" were a culmination of the resourcefulness and ingenuity of pipeline engineers. It was impressive, considering the humble beginnings and evolution of the pipeline industry in the United States.

---

9. "How the Permian Helped Fuel D-Day," Texas Oil and World War II, Black Mountain Sand, June 6, 2019, https://www.blackmountainsand.com/blog/texas-oil-and-world-war-ii/.

10. "Big Inch Pipelines of WWII," *American Oil and Gas Historical Society*. https://aoghs.org/petroleum-in-war/oil-pipelines/.

11. Keith Miller, "How Important was Oil in World War II?" History News Network. https://historynews-network.org/article/339.

THE FIRST DISCOVERY

PENNSYLVANIA
1859 – 1865

The logistical challenge to deliver oil to the American market existed before the German U-boats of World War II. It has persisted for more than 160 years—since August 28, 1859, to be exact. On that day the first commercial oil well was drilled by "Colonel" Edwin Drake in Titusville, Pennsylvania.

The "black gold" gushing from the ground was a serendipitous discovery for the United States. At the time, petroleum was used primarily for lighting. It was distilled into kerosene for lamps, replacing whale oil, which was by then becoming scarce. Petroleum was also used for salt production, literally paving the way for the first asphalt streets of New York.[12]

The drillers, who initially pumped the first oil into bathtubs, faced a predicament. How would the product be efficiently collected and transported to the rest of the country?

They formed a plan: the oil would be collected in converted whiskey barrels. These wooden barrels would then be loaded into wagons and pulled by teams of horses driven by hardy men called "teamsters." Of course, this was well before the formation of a labor union of the same name. The teamsters would cut new wagon trails from remote mountainous regions through dense forests and down to the rivers of Pennsylvania, where oil barrels would be loaded onto barges.

But transporting the oil by wagons posed a tremendous challenge. The dirt roads were sometimes filled with over a foot of mud, and the horses required feed as well as barns for shelter. Blacksmiths and a system of suppliers kept the teamsters, their wagons, and their sundry

---

12. Alex Wilson, "Our History of Petroleum Use," *Green Building Advisor, The Taunton Press,* https://www.greenbuildingadvisor.com/article/our-history-of-petroleum-use.

equipment running smoothly and efficiently. An entire network was developed to produce and transport oil from these inaccessible and mountainous areas.

It was dangerous work executed by hardened men. The work was also deadly for their beasts of burden, as the horses lost most of their hair due to oil buildup and freezing temperatures. The combination of the harsh conditions and maltreatment from owners meant that a horse's lifespan was short—only six months. In fact, the high mortality rate caused a shortage of horses, with more having to be brought in by rail from New York and Ohio.[13]

Despite the arduous conditions, hordes of prospectors journeyed to Pennsylvania a few years later, when the first oil gusher was established by Ian Frazier in 1865. The successful oil businessman had hired an "oil diviner" who predicted that his next set of riches was waiting near a creek in Pithole, a northwestern town that some suggest may have been named after the sulfurous emissions emanating from the holes and fissures in the ground along the creek. Sure enough, the prediction proved to be accurate. The *Titusville Herald* proclaimed Pithole as having "probably the most productive wells in the oil region of Pennsylvania."[14]

Pithole became a boomtown. At its peak, it was home to twenty thousand people and had fifty-four hotels and flophouses, three churches, one of the state's largest post offices, a newspaper, and a theater. But the young town also boasted other, less virtuous businesses like saloons, billiard parlors, and brothels—*lots* of brothels. These new businesses and services were marketed to the growing number of colorful characters who were seeking fortunes.

"Colorful" may be an understatement for the people attracted to

13. Darrah, William Culp, *Pithole, the Vanished City: A Story of the Early Days of the Petroleum Industry* (Gettysburg Pennsylvania: William Culp Darrah, 1972).

14. Douglas Wayne Houck. *Energy & Light in Nineteenth-Century Western New York: Natural Gas, Petroleum & Electricity*, (Gloucestershire: The History Press, 2014).

Pithole. The teamsters were "free spenders, heavy drinkers, brawlers, and worse." Flamboyant characters emerged, like a man named Ben Hogan. Ben was a barrel-chested, handsome cabin boy turned coastal pirate who spent his ill-gotten gains on gambling. When he arrived in Pithole, he moved from job to job as a card dealer, strongman in traveling acts, and prizefighter. According to his biographer, George Trainer, "Hogan's face is one which attracts the beholder, and it is extremely doubtful whether anybody would select its owner for a prizefighter."[15] But select him they did, because although he was only five feet eight and weighed 180 pounds, he had steely muscles and compact legs that gave him a competitive edge.

That is, until a popular prostitute named "French Kate" became his mistress and business partner. The two opened a brothel and dance house and made a small fortune together. But when Hogan unwisely gambled away their collective earnings, an infuriated Kate fired several shots at him with her pistol, ripping off a hunk of one of handsome Ben's ears before parting ways.[16]

The era of the oil-toting teamsters has been called one of the most profane periods of the Pennsylvania oil business. But the teamsters and their associated cast of flamboyant characters like Ben Hogan and "French Kate" were difficult to manage. The teamsters refused to work in bad weather and at times simply extorted enormous sums from their customers. At the time, oil was selling for about five dollars a barrel, three of which went to the teamsters for distribution.[17] Their virtual

15. George Francis Trainer, *The Life And Adventures of Ben Hogan: The Wickedest Man in The World,* Ben Hogan, 1878.

16. Samuel T. Pees, "Oil History," Petroleum History Institute, *last modified January 2002,* http://www.petroleumhistory.org/OilHistory/OHindex.html.

17. Uri Berliner, "Even Pickaxes Couldn't Stop the Nation's First Oil Pipeline," *All Things Considered,* NPR, Washington, D.C., WAMU, February 24, 2015, https://www.npr.org/2015/02/24/388729919/even-pickaxes-couldnt-stop-the-nations-first-oil-pipeline#:~:text=Courtesy%20of%20PHMC-,Tanks%20holding%20oil%20in%20Pithole%2C%20Pa.%2C%20in%201868.,it%20was%20an%20engineering%20marvel.

monopoly on the movement of oil out of Pithole was a growing source of frustration for the oilmen. The high transportation costs and frequent labor disputes caused oil producers to seek a better transportation solution.[18] Something had to change.

And a new industry was born.

PIPE DREAM
PENNSYLVANIA
1865

The first time the idea of a pipeline was mentioned in the bars and brothels of Pithole in 1865, the free-spending teamsters scoffed at such an outlandish "pipe dream." They also ridiculed the man behind it, a newcomer named Samuel Van Syckel.

Van Syckel was an oil merchant who simply wanted a dependable method to move his oil to market. Ignoring the jeers, Van Syckel obtained a $100,000 bank loan, an enormous sum in that day.

His pipeline was nothing like the experimental conduit that had been constructed a few years earlier: a one-thousand-foot channel built out of two wooden planks nailed together with a third plank closing the top. That conduit had leaked at the joints and wasn't durable enough to bypass the teamsters.

No, Van Syckel's pipeline was a new technology and legitimate threat to the teamsters. Under an engineer's close supervision, it was the first means of transporting oil that accounted for all of the engineering factors that mattered, such as distance, topographical relief, pumps, and rate of flow. The pipe was made of wrought iron, its fifteen-foot joints reinforced with lap welding. It crossed five miles of hilly terrain, some

18. Samuel T. Pees, "Oil History," Petroleum History Institute, last modified January 2002, http://www.petroleumhistory.org/OilHistory/OHindex.html.

parts above ground and some parts two feet underground. Although the pipe was narrow by today's standards—only two inches in diameter—the rate of flowing oil stunned the teamsters. With the help of four pumps, the pipeline delivered twenty-five hundred barrels of oil per day. And unlike the early conduit, mechanical problems were minor and easily fixed. Van Syckel's idea had become a reality.

The disruptive technology threatened the livelihood of the teamsters, who had long relied on a complex support network of working men and women. The teamsters were determined to thwart this new hazard to their cash flow. Sabotage, threats, and widespread violence erupted in Pithole. The teamsters rampaged, pulling up the pipe with chains and teams of horses and smashing the wrought iron with pickaxes.

The rampage didn't stop Van Syckel. By enlisting the help of the local sheriff and hiring a security team, the oil merchant prevailed, signaling the end of the teamsters' local monopoly.[19]

Van Syckel laid a second pipeline parallel to his first, and fellow entrepreneurs constructed others. A telegraph line arose along the same right-of-way, relaying complicated accounting information on the various buyers and sellers of the crude oil. The telegraph also signaled emergencies, alerting pipeliners on the other end to leakages or other problems.

Unfortunately, while the success of the pipelines took off, Van Syckel ran into bad luck. When his two business partners failed for other reasons and defaulted on their loans, the pioneer relinquished control of his pipelines to the bank.[20] Even so, his legacy remains. The oil industry owes its beginnings to the vision and perseverance of men like Van Syckel, whose pipeline was the first to deliver oil to a railroad.[21]

---

19. Berliner, "Even Pickaxes Couldn't Stop the Nation's First Oil Pipeline."

20. Samuel T. Pees, *Oil Creek Valley and Pithole, Pennsylvania, Guidebook,* not formally published, 2001.

21. John J. McLaurin, *Sketches in Crude Oil,* (Franklin, PA: Mount Pleasant Press: 1896).

Van Syckel not only inspired the men around him but also singlehandedly ushered in a new era of pipeliners, providing the foundation of an American industry that would change the world.

THE ERA OF PIPELINERS

It took time, but the teamsters eventually realized they could play a valuable role in getting oil to market. Instead of ripping up pipelines, they embraced the new technology and hauled pipe, equipment, and supplies to new construction sites. And they put some of the oil to good use themselves by abandoning their horses and relying on gasoline-powered trucks.

The work was mostly seasonal due to the Northeast's harsh winters, which caused the ground to freeze. But the seasonal work paid well, still affording an opportunity to earn a good annual income. It appealed to rugged men who craved adventure because it preserved the winter months for hunting, fishing, and time with family. It also appealed to criminals—not habitual criminals but those guilty of young, blind foolishness—though early pipeliners didn't question a man about his past if he worked hard.

It was blind foolishness, for example, that got a man named Shug Smith caught. Smith was a Cherokee Indian who had robbed a bank before making his getaway on horseback. It was the wrong century for that kind of getaway: automobiles and telephones were commonplace by then. After his conviction, Smith persuaded the governor of Oklahoma to allow him to serve on the front lines of the Army instead of in prison, a commitment he kept so well that he was pardoned when he returned home. He started his new life as a pipeliner, eventually becoming recognized as one of the best pipeline foremen of the era.[22]

Over the ensuing decades, pipelines expanded rapidly across Pennsylvania and into other oil-producing regions. Whenever a big strike occurred, pipeliners built a local or regional line down to the railroads and rivers, which would transport the oil to distant refineries. When the pipeline was finished, the pipeliners moved on to the next job, wherever it happened to be. Sometimes the next job was far away from their home. Because of the long distances, the men appreciated the lasting friendships that developed among them as they worked together in teams, or "gangs," a tradition that continues today.

Throughout this time, the long-distance hauling of oil was left to the railroad and shipping industries because pipelines remained short and relatively small—usually no more than eight inches in diameter.[23] But that all changed in World War II with the entrance of "Big Inch" and "Little Big Inch." In addition to fortifying the nation at a critical time, the two large, long-distance pipelines revolutionized the transportation of oil in the United States.

Following the triumph of the Allied forces, the pipeline industry faced resistance by activists—but they were not motivated by the environment. The pipelines originally allowed private companies to control oil transportation, and it was to that power that activists objected. By the late nineteenth century, Standard Oil controlled 80 percent of America's oil transportation markets, and reformers believed oil was too important to be controlled by just one private company. But by the time the issue became a subject of public policy, private enterprise and inadequate public policies on the state level had become precedents in

22. Willbros Group, Inc., *A Good Job on Time: A Portrait of Willbros Group, Inc.*, (Houston: Grover Printing, 2007).

23. Texas Eastern Transmission Corporation, *The Big Inch and Little Big Inch Pipelines: The Most Amazing Government-Industry Cooperation Ever Achieved*, (Houston: Texas Eastern Transmission Corporation, 2000).

the pipeline industry. Standard Oil eventually gave up some control of the industry after the government intervened, but little changed with how private industry made decisions about building and investing in pipelines.[24]

A fierce debate about pipelines erupted within the energy industry, too. Different camps argued over the best use of the two "Inch" pipelines. In one camp, the major oil companies believed that the pipelines should be converted for the transfer of natural gas, for which demand was rising rapidly. At the time, Texas oilfields were producing large quantities of natural gas, but without a method to transport it to the Northeast market, it was flared or burnt off uselessly into the atmosphere. The railroads and coal companies argued against this conversion because it presented additional competition and would likely lower demand for their goods and services. To prevent the transport monopolies of the larger corporations, the smaller oil companies favored the continued use of pipelines for oil. During the debate, a national coal strike was threatened, which only drew more attention to the need for natural gas.[25]

The Surplus Property Administration hired an engineering firm to determine the best solution for the pipelines, which was deemed the largest disposal of war-surplus property. The independent firm recommended that the pipelines be converted to natural gas transmission. A four-month lease with the Tennessee Gas and Transmission Company proved the feasibility of natural gas transmission, so the pipelines were auctioned.

In 1947, the Texas Eastern Transmission Corporation, which

24.Laura Clark, "Oil Companies First Built Pipelines in the 1860s; They've Been Contested Ever Since," Smithsonian Magazine, January 12, 2015, https://www.smithsonianmag.com/smart-news/americas-first-oil-pipelines-180953870.

25. Christopher James Castaneda, *Regulated Enterprise: Natural Gas Pipelines and Northeastern Markets, 1938-1954*, (Columbus: Ohio State University Press, 1993).

eventually became part of Spectra Energy, was declared the successful bidder on the pipelines. After purchasing them for more than $143 million, the corporation converted the lines to transport natural gas. Thus, the United States was changed through an "extraordinary" expansion of natural gas.[26]

It was a time of growth for the United States beyond just the pipeline industry. When World War II servicemen returned home, they brought a spirit of victory and prosperity partially due to the expansion of natural gas distributed through pipelines that influenced the economy. Major corporations consolidated into conglomerates, and the automobile industry quadrupled its annual car production. Housing was stimulated by affordable mortgages for returning servicemen. Families of the postwar baby boom spilled out into new suburbs, followed by businesses, highways, and television sets. Throughout the 1940s and 1950s, the postwar economy grew remarkably as Americans reveled in its position as the richest country in the world, fueled by prolific amounts of natural gas that made the American energy industry the envy across the globe.[27]

LESSONS LEARNED

As Americans faced the future, one resounding takeaway from World War II was this: fossil fuels were necessary for national security and global peace. Americans witnessed firsthand how oil, gas, and pipelines dictated wartime strategy. The ability to transport fuel dictated life or death. Wielding it meant winning, and limiting it meant losing. The map of the modern world reveals its impact; the spheres of influence

---

26. David A. Waples, *The Natural Gas Industry in Appalachia: A History from the First Discovery to the Tapping of the Marcellus Shale*, Second edition, (Jefferson: McFarland, 2012).

27. "The Postwar Economy: 1945-1960," American History, University of Groningen, http://www.let.rug.nl/usa/outlines/history-1994/postwar-america/the-postwar-economy-1945-1960.php.

we see today are based on wartime movements fueled by oil and gas.

Americans also recognized the fragility of American democracy. Our national vulnerability in the 1940s—and the critical need to protect our nation today—is not lost on people like Mitt Romney. In a 2022 speech, the Senator reminded his party of the extraordinary experiment that is the United States. Our democracy stands apart as unique throughout four thousand years of civilizations marked by the rise and fall of autocracies and authoritarian leaders. The contributions of the "Inch" pipelines to the war effort were notable because they preserved our freedom.

In time, however, the nation's confidence in fossil fuels was undermined by a growing awareness of sustainability. Americans became increasingly concerned by their ability to maintain their way of living. Not only were scientists projecting declines in the nonrenewable resources that powered the country, but the United States had become overly dependent on foreign oil along the way. There was also evidence that carbon emissions from producing fossil fuels were negatively impacting the environment, a concern that has become a primary issue today. As academics teach that oil and gas is a dirty and dying business, college students consider the environment and climate change top priorities in voting.

As the nation grappled with the problem of sustainability, the pipeline era gradually gave way to a new idea. Nuclear power emerged as a new technology that promised a better solution.

It was the beginning of the nuclear era.

Domestic poster from World War II. Courtesy of National Archives at College Park, Public domain, via Wikimedia Commons.

General George S. Patton in command of US forces on Sicily. Image in the public domain, via Wikimedia Commons.

Tanker *Byron D. Benson* on fire after being torpedoed by *U-552*. Courtesy of National Oceanic and Atmospheric Administration, Public domain, via Wikimedia Commons.

Tanker *R. P. Resor* burns off the shore of New Jersey after it was sunk by *U-578*. Courtesy of Wide World, Public domain, via Wikimedia Commons.

World War II image from the United States government. From archive.org: "When You Ride Alone You Ride With Hitler ! Join a car-sharing club TODAY!" by Weimer Pursell, 1943. Printed by the Government Printing Office for the Office of Price Administration.

Source: National Archives and Records Administration (NARA). Courtesy of Weimer Pursell, Public domain, via Wikimedia Commons.

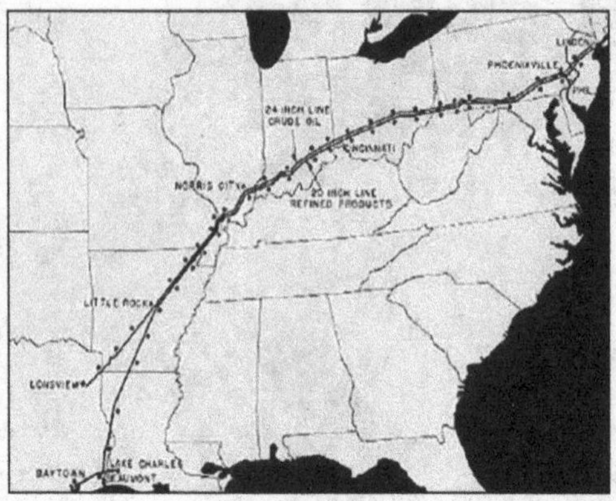

The Big Inch and Little Inch pipelines from Baytown and Beaumont, Texas, to Linden, New Jersey. National Archives and Records Administration (NARA) 208-LU-37C-1.

Big Inch pipe, welding using roll-weld method. Courtesy of John Vachon, Public domain, via Wikimedia Commons.

Workers on the Big Inch pipeline. Courtesy of John Vachon, Public domain, via Wikimedia Commons.

First carload of 24-inch seamless pipe for the Big Inch (July 17, 1942). Courtesy of Petroleum Administration for War, Public domain, via Wikimedia Commons..

Hoisting Big Inch pipe. Courtesy of John Vachon, John, Public domain, via Wikimedia Commons.

"Starting at dusk and using kerosene lamps and headlights, we tunneled under the railroad using twelve-inch casing, and then pushed eight-inch pipe through. We cleaned up the area and were gone by dawn," John recalled. "Two days later, they (the crew) returned to the crossing. The pipeline had been dug out, pulled out, cut and placed on the right-of-way in neatly stacked two-foot sections. It looked like neat stacks of cordwood."

All 56 crossings were completed in a single day, with the crews eating ham sandwiches and downing water, milk and Cokes while they worked around the clock.

Innovation at work: a pipe-bending machine takes on a 30-inch pipe at the company's shop in Houston, Texas, 1947.

47

Innovation at work: a pipe-bending machine takes on a 30-inch pipe at the company's shop in Houston, Texas, 1947. Courtesy of Willbros archives, the Williams family archives, The Williams Companies. *A GOOD JOB ON TIME: A PORTRAIT OF WILLBROS GROUP, INC. On The occasion of the company centennial anniversary* (Panama City, Panama: Willbros Group, Inc., 2007.

Illustration from the book *Sketches in crude-oil; some accidents and incidents of the petroleum development in all parts of the globe*, ... 3rd Edition. by McLaurin. Courtesy McLaurin, John J. (John James), b. 1841, Public domain, via Wikimedia Commons.

Holmden Street in Pithole, Pennsylvania, from First Street, circa 1866. Courtesy of Wikimedia Commons.

Activity around the United States Well, Pithole, Pennsylvania in the 1860s. Original Caption: "The United States Well at Pithole was struck Jan. 8th, 1865 and flowed 800 bbls per day." Courtesy of Frank Robbins, Public domain, via Wikimedia Commons.

Samuel Van Syckel. Courtesy of Ida Tarbell, Public domain, via Wikimedia Commons.

CHAPTER 2

THE NUCLEAR ERA

WHY AMERICA QUIT NUCLEAR POWER AND REFOCUSED ON OIL & GAS

Pennsylvania
1950s – 1970s

"Politics is more difficult than physics."

– Albert Einstein

PRESIDENT EISENHOWER FIRST PROPOSED the idea to harness nuclear power for energy. In his 1953 "Atoms for Peace" speech to the United Nations General Assembly in Manhattan, New York, he suggested that it was not enough to simply reduce the use of nuclear energy as a weapon; it should be repurposed and redeemed.

"Experts would be mobilized to apply atomic energy to the needs of agriculture, medicine, and other peaceful activities," Eisenhower said. "A special purpose would be to provide abundant electrical energy in the power-starved areas of the world."[28]

The idea was met with approval. Eisenhower set a new course that would resolve the problem of non-renewable resources and redeem the wartime research. The efforts initially focused on the atomic bomb were reoriented towards civil nuclear energy development to generate electricity.

Of the nuclear energy sources that had been produced and evaluated as part of the Manhattan Project, uranium had been selected and developed as the superior nuclear fuel for weaponry. Uranium seemed the most ready and plausible candidate for civil nuclear energy. In preparation for its new function, uranium received further attention and investment while the development of other fuels remained in relative infancy.[29]

The first commercial nuclear power stations began operating in the 1950s, and the nuclear power industry enjoyed rapid growth. It offered a new way to provide electricity that was economical, environmentally clean, and safe—and that loosened America's dependence on foreign oil.[30]

---

28. Michael Shellenberger, "If Nuclear Power Is So Safe, Why Are We So Afraid Of It?" *Forbes*, June 11, 2018, https://www.forbes.com/sites/michaelshellenberger/2018/06/11/if-nuclear-power-is-so-safe-why-are-we-so-afraid-of-it/#3df6f8866385.

29. "Outline History of Nuclear Energy," *World Nuclear Organization,* last modified October 2022, http://www.world-nuclear.org/information-library/current-and-future-generation/nuclear-power-in-the-world-today.aspx.

30. "The History of Nuclear Energy," U.S. Department of Energy: Office of Nuclear Energy, Science and Technology, https://www.energy.gov/sites/prod/files/The%20History%20of%20Nuclear%20Energy_0.pdf.

But in 1979, a nuclear power accident turned the fervor to fear, causing the nation to rethink its stance on energy.

THE ENERGY CRISIS
AMERICA
1970s

The development of nuclear power came at an opportune time when the United States was growing increasingly concerned over its dependence on foreign oil. In 1970, President Nixon lifted restrictions on oil imports when America's domestic supply began dwindling. Between 1970 and 1973, oil imports more than doubled, and America was more dependent on and vulnerable to foreign oil shocks than ever.[31]

During this time of anxiety in the United States, many people increasingly pointed to nuclear power plants as the answer to the energy crisis. The industry had grown rapidly throughout the 1960s and into the 1970s. It seemed the perfect solution for America's dwindling resources and its dependence on Middle Eastern oil, a dependence that was underscored by two defining foreign crises.

The first crisis erupted in 1973 when oil-producing nations imposed an embargo on the U.S. in retaliation for its support for Israel during the Yom Kippur War. The embargo strained the U.S. economy and quadrupled the price of oil per barrel. In a televised address to the nation, Nixon called it "an energy crisis." He urged the resourceful development of energy, and he appealed to people to voluntarily conserve energy or face mandatory rationing.[32]

---

31. Content throughout this section was derived from Meg Jacobs, "America's Never-Ending Oil Consumption," *The Atlantic*, May 15, 2016, https://www.theatlantic.com/politics/archive/2016/05/american-oil-consumption/482532.

32. Content throughout this section was derived from the Office of the Historian, Bureau of Public Affairs United States Department of State, "Oil Embargo, 1973–1974," https://history.state.gov/milestones/1969-1976/oil-embargo.

The national conversation suddenly changed from one of freedom to conservation. Amoco pulled images of the open road from its marketing campaign and replaced them with images of Johnny Cash saying, "Drive slow and save gas." *Time Magazine*'s front cover featured an automobile weeping from its headlights. Congress passed a speed limit of fifty-five miles per hour for highways, and some Democrats advocated for mandatory rationing.

The embargo was lifted in 1974, but the nation remained on edge about its energy dependence. When President Carter, a nuclear engineer, took office in 1976, he attempted to restore a sense of calm and control to the nation. Wearing a cardigan and sitting by a fireplace in a televised address, he encouraged people to conserve resources. He followed with a proclamation requiring that commercial, government, and most other public buildings set their thermostats no higher than sixty-five degrees in the winter and no lower than seventy-eight degrees in the summer.[33]

"We must not be selfish or timid if we hope to have a decent world for our children and grandchildren," Carter said. "We simply must balance our demand for energy with our rapidly shrinking resources. By acting now, we can control our future instead of letting the future control us."

But most Americans had no interest in changing their way of life. When the nation was rocked again by a second foreign crisis in 1979, the public dismissed Carter's call to drive less, carpool more, and use public transportation as acts of patriotism.[34]

33. Richard Halloran, "Carter Orders a 78° Cooling Limit For Public Buildings This Summer," *New York Times,* July 11, 1979, https://www.nytimes.com/1979/07/11/archives/carter-orders-a-78-cooling-limit-for-public-buildings-this-summer.html.

34. Jimmy Carter, "Energy and the National Goals—A Crisis of Conscience," July 15, 1979, 945, Miller Center of Public Affairs, University of Virginia, transcript and Adobe Flash audio, 32:59, https://millercenter.org/the-presidency/presidential-speeches/july-15-1979-crisis-confidence-speech.

"Carter, kiss my gas," retorted a popular bumper sticker.

This time, the crisis was the Iranian Revolution. The Shah of Iran, Mohammad Reza Pahlavi, fled his country earlier that year, and the Ayatollah Khomeini soon became the new leader of Iran. Iranian oil production was disrupted, and gasoline prices shot up to record levels.

Americans felt more than threatened by the sudden shortage; they were swept by panic. Anxious motorists rushed to fill their tanks before sunrise when long lines formed at gas stations. Many bought locks for their tanks to prevent siphoning. Drivers accused each other of cutting in lines for gasoline, and fistfights broke out at gas stations. One man was fatally shot, and another was stabbed to death. At a riot in Levittown, Pennsylvania, automobiles and gas stations were vandalized and set ablaze.

But while the United States was struggling with its energy crisis, it was unprepared for what would happen next. A nuclear power accident was about to introduce the nation to a completely new form of panic.

THE THREE MILE ISLAND DISASTER

THREE MILE ISLAND, PENNSYLVANIA
1979

In March 1979, Hollywood released *The China Syndrome*, a fictional film starring Jane Fonda, Jack Lemmon, and Michael Douglas. The movie dealt with the aftermath of a nuclear meltdown at a reactor outside of Los Angeles, a scenario that experts at the time scoffed at as implausible.

No one was scoffing when it nearly happened that same month at the Three Mile Island plant near Harrisburg, Pennsylvania. The plant was built on a small island in the Susquehanna River called Three Mile Island. Construction of the nuclear plant had begun in 1968 and was completed ten years later, when the second of two state-of-the-art nuclear reactors at the site came online to produce electricity.

That second nuclear reactor began to overheat in the early morning hours of March 28, 1979. A mechanical or electric failure had set off a series of actions and events that led to a partial meltdown, causing about half of the nuclear fuel to melt through its metal container. Trace amounts of radioactive gasses leaked from the top of the plant into the surrounding community. Water pumps designed to cool the radioactive fuel in the reactor core malfunctioned. The staff didn't realize the reactor was experiencing a loss of coolant and took a series of near-catastrophic actions that worsened the problem, further depriving the reactor core of critical water flow.

Local officials and the surrounding community became even more concerned when a large hydrogen bubble formed inside the reactor unit. They feared an explosion would release even larger amounts of radioactive material into the atmosphere. President Carter arrived at Three Mile Island to inspect the plant himself. He hoped his visit and his training as a nuclear engineer—which included dismantling a Canadian nuclear reactor while in the U.S. Navy—would calm local residents and the nation. By that afternoon, he and a team of experts agreed that the hydrogen bubble was not in danger of exploding.[35]

It was the most significant accident in the history of U.S. power plants, rated a five on the seven-point National Nuclear Event Scale. The area was declared an emergency site. Pennsylvania Governor Dick Thornburgh advised pregnant women and small children within a specified radius of the plant to evacuate the area. In days, 140,000 people left the area, most returning within three weeks.

The immediate crisis ended three days later when experts deter-

35. "Nuclear disaster at Three Mile Island," History.com, last modified March 31, 2019, https://www.history.com/this-day-in-history/nuclear-accident-at-three-mile-island.

mined the hydrogen bubble was no longer a threat. The subsequent cleanup effort would span fourteen years at a cost of over $1 billion. The damaged reactor was permanently closed and entombed in layers of concrete; radioactive fuel and water were removed from the reactor; and over fifteen tons of radioactive waste were eventually shipped to a nuclear waste storage facility in Idaho. Although two million people were likely exposed to small amounts of radiation, comprehensive investigations of people's health and environmental samples by well-respected government agencies and independent organizations have concluded that the release had "negligible effects."[36]

THE EPICENTER OF A WORLDWIDE DEBATE

Even with relatively good health reports, the near miss stoked the protests of activists and the fear of the general public. Public support for nuclear energy fell from an all-time high of 69 percent in 1977 to only 46 percent after the accident.

The Three Mile Island incident galvanized anti-nuclear activists in the United States. The social movement against the global nuclear arms race had emerged after the U.S. attacks on Japan in 1945 and strengthened in the early 1960s at the height of the Cold War. The nuclear disaster sparked high-profile protests around the country, including one in New York City in May of 1979 and another in Washington D.C. Bright yellow helium balloons rose over Pennsylvania Avenue while more than 65,000 young protestors marched on the Capitol, carrying a coffin with "dead" babies and banners that read, "No More Harrisburgs." A line of children linked arms and chanted, "Hell no, we won't glow," and "Two, four, six, eight, we don't want to radiate."

36. "Backgrounder on the Three Mile Island Incident," United States Nuclear Regulatory Commission, last modified November 15, 2022, https://www.nrc.gov/reading-rm/doc-collections/fact-sheets/3mile-isle.html.

They cheered on a lineup of speakers, including the governor of California at the time, Jerry Brown, who boomed, "Reliance on nuclear power is a 'pathological addiction, storing up for generations to come evils and risks that the human mind can barely grasp.'"

One after another, political activists stepped up to the microphone to protest the dangers of nuclear energy. Consumer advocate Ralph Nader claimed then-President Carter betrayed the people by appointing James Schlesinger as energy secretary, whom Nader accused of dismissing campaign promises and prioritizing the needs of energy producers over consumers.[37] Actress Jane Fonda demanded that Carter replace Schlesinger or face certain replacement in the next presidential election. Her husband, Tom Hayden, said Carter had a "nuclear energy mentality that is eclipsing and destroying his Christian philosophy." Former safety engineer Robert Pollard claimed the Nuclear Regulatory Commission "routinely put the financial interests of the nuclear industry ahead" of public safety. [38]

The United States found itself at a crossroads. The old, familiar fossil fuels and pipeline technology that helped win World War II clashed with new, risky nuclear technology that had initially promised a bright future for Americans. Amid the backlash from environmentalists and the concern over nuclear safety, the nuclear power industry declined in favor of fossil fuels.

This epic decision marked a turning point in the development of nuclear power and altered the course of history. Projects were canceled, and few new reactors were ordered. The price of uranium dropped, and

---

37. Warren Brown, "Nader Decries Schlesinger's Energy Policy," *Washington Post,* October 10, 1978, https://www.washingtonpost.com/archive/politics/1978/10/10/nader-decries-schlesingers-energy-policy/5a3a1539-26ca-47e1-868c-9a13e8eff9b5/.

38. Paul Valentine, Karlyn Barker, et al., "The Protestors," *The Washington Post,* May 7, 1979, https://www.washingtonpost.com/archive/politics/1979/05/07/the-protesters/b2ea631e-933c-4f07-b59e-e97bf1068b7e/?noredirect=on&utm_term=.5133ed6695b6.

oil companies that had entered the uranium field bailed. It was a disappointing end of a nuclear era that had seemed a promising solution to many of America's energy problems. [39]

In the wake of Three Mile Island, Americans resigned themselves to the critical need for conventional oil and gas to power the country—and the pipelines to move it. The U.S. refocused on better technology to develop and transport what was deemed to be a safer source of energy. This transition would be solidified by Ronald Reagan, whose first major political decision as president would be to lift all federal controls from domestic production and distribution of oil and gas. The long national era of energy regulation was over.

The return to oil, gas, and pipelines was a fateful decision, one that would be harshly criticized forty years later by environmentalists, including Jane Fonda, who would reemerge as a climate activist. Ironically, she and the environmentalists who had demanded a stop to nuclear power were the same environmentalists who would one day criticize the nation's return to oil and gas. Nevertheless, in the late 1970s, amid protests against nuclear energy, the nation recommitted itself to pipelines to transport crude oil, natural gas, and refined products like gasoline.

AMERICAN JOBS
HARRISBURG, PENNSYLVANIA
SUMMER 1979

It was during this period of recommitment to fossil fuels in the summer of 1979 that I found myself at the crux of the transition. The nation shifted its attention away from nuclear projects like Three Mile Island

39. "Outline History of Nuclear Energy," *World Nuclear Organization,* last modified October 2022, http://www.world-nuclear.org/information-library/current-and-future-generation/nuclear-power-in-the-world-today.aspx.

and back to fossil fuels and pipeline projects like "Big Inch" and "Little Inch." Of course, I didn't know it at the time. I was oblivious to decisions being made that would alter our nation's course.

All I knew was that a high school buddy had lined up a summer job for us and needed my help to get there. My carefree, adventurous friend and his brother had stranded their 1972 Cutlass in a cornfield after a night of too many Budweisers. Somehow my buddy talked me into driving more than 1,200 miles in my fuel-efficient 1978 Toyota Celica, from Louisiana to Harrisburg, Pennsylvania, to replace a section of pipe. He promised high pay and overtime.

"Like a summer vacation," he added for good measure.

But it wasn't a summer vacation. Nor was it just another summer job. I may have agreed to drive all that way purely for the high pay and overtime, but I hadn't realized the significance of the timing, the job—or of the pipe.

When we arrived at the Sheehan Pipeline Construction yard in Harrisburg, I learned I was fourteen miles away from Three Mile Island, the epicenter of the worldwide debate on nuclear energy and its promise to change the world. And I also learned I'd be working on part of the original Big Inch pipeline system, the unprecedented civil engineering effort that really did change the world by helping defeat the Nazis in World War II.

I experienced many things that summer that would stay with me the rest of my life, and the education began that first June morning when I had hoped to blend in with the other pipeline veterans. Unfortunately, my brand-new, unscuffed Red Wing boots and my Japanese car immediately exposed my status as a newcomer in the pipeline construction business. The veterans soon branded me a "greenhorn" and eyed me with skepticism.

I found out quickly that as harsh as the job was on the men, their treatment of each other was sometimes worse. In retrospect, I suppose being called a greenhorn wasn't nearly as bad as some of the nicknames the pipeliners doled out. The lucky ones, like me, only got a "y" added to their first names, so Bill became Billy. The unlucky ones were named something that exploited their weaknesses, like one Richard who unwisely confided to his buddies about his bedroom misadventures and became known as "Dead Dick." Very little was held sacred as they tested the mettle of young men. Their biting humor belied a serious need to know that they could rely on each other when the job became dangerous or difficult.

Whatever the case, among the motley crew, there was no one surlier than a fellow who had earned the unfortunate nickname, "Stubby." One of his arms had been severed a few inches below the elbow in an accident years before, leaving only a stub. Stubby was at least six feet six and probably weighed close to three hundred pounds, with a loud and dominant personality that made him impossible to ignore. And he was mean. I couldn't be sure if he had always been mean or if he had become that way due to his accident or his nickname. Even with only one good arm, Stubby was unmistakably the alpha male among hardened men, and there was no mistaking that he detested me. Or at least what I represented.

"What stupid sumbitch has the balls to drive a goddamned, job-killin' Jap car," Stubby bellowed across the yard that first June morning. All eyes turned to my Toyota Celica hatchback parked against the fence.

I quickly decided against confessing that I was the stupid sumbitch owner. To avoid further scrutiny, I wondered if I could somehow bury the car, or burn it and collect the insurance. Or disown it. Or at least hide it from Stubby and the other Pennsylvania union boys. But I had no such luck. I was destined to drive the "job-killin' Jap car" the rest of the summer. Stubby just shook his head in disgust and headed toward his American-made, Ford F150 pickup.

Stubby had exposed my greenhorn status to the veterans that first morning, and I loathed him for it. Trading places with "Dead Dick" would have seemed like a worthwhile exchange to me at the time. But there was no denying Stubby and I had something in common: at that moment, I didn't want to be there, and Stubby didn't want me to be there, either.

I didn't grasp the significance of what my car meant to Stubby. He had likely spent his entire career in the pipeline industry, and he had sacrificed an arm in the process. It didn't sit well with him that a young, inexperienced kid was taking a job from a union man. My "Jap car" was even more insulting. Building an American infrastructure as fundamental as pipelines was everything to men like Stubby.

Sometime later, I found out why Stubby thought my Toyota Celica was killing jobs—and that he was not alone in his disdain for "Jap cars." The United States had enjoyed unprecedented prosperity in the post–World War II era, a period dominated by ambitious war veterans who many would call America's "greatest generation." But by 1979, the American growth story was getting long in the tooth, and other countries around the world, particularly Japan, were catching up, winning, and taking American jobs.

Detroit's dominance in car manufacturing faded as smaller, more efficient Japanese cars became popular among consumers. However, "Jap cars" weren't popular with American workers, especially union members like Stubby. They scoffed at the smaller cars because of the emerging Japanese threat to U.S. manufacturing jobs, much like the teamsters who preceded them had scoffed at new technologies in Pithole, Pennsylvania.

It was a year of great anxiety for the workforce in Pennsylvania. In addition to the Japanese threat to their jobs and the chaotic wake of the

Iranian Revolution, none of the pipeliners felt comfortable drinking the water in Harrisburg. I had seen Three Mile Island all over the news and knew it was the worst commercial nuclear accident in U.S. history, but I hadn't counted on seeing the impact up close.

The pipeliners hauled their own Igloo coolers filled with water every day from their hometowns up north of Three Mile Island, grumbling about how "them 'sum bitches' screwed up that nuclear plant." The pipeliners who had worked on Three Mile Island were easily recognizable because they sported stainless steel belt buckles and custom barbecue pits, all crafted from the leftover stainless-steel metal that was used to build a nuclear plant. "They damned near poisoned the river," they added, referring to the beloved Susquehanna River, named by the Lenape tribe for its oyster beds, which zigzags 444 miles across the heartland of southeast Pennsylvania and is one of the oldest rivers in the world.

Amid the national problems and the slowing economy, I began to understand the concerns of the next generation, particularly that of the pipeliners in Pennsylvania. As Stubby and the rest of the union members saw it, I was taking a coveted job from a local and was announcing it to the world with my foreign car.

And I wasn't yet sure if the Pennsylvania boys were going to let me get away with it.

PIPELINE CLAN

I suppose in some ways they *didn't* let me get away with it. Throughout the next few weeks, I endured Stubby's relentless derision. It was clear that I was the low man in the pipeline hierarchy, deeply resented as the college boy who drove a "job-killin' Jap car."

I kept my head down, hauling twenty pound, five-feet-long planks of timber, or "skids," as a laborer. Laborers were a group of unskilled workers who were there to do the jobs that the other three skilled groups didn't want to do or weren't required to do.

The three skilled groups included:

1. **The International Brotherhood of Teamsters**, the guys who drove the trucks that had displaced the horse teams in the early years of the pipeline business, back when Samuel Van Syckel's outlandish "pipe dream" disrupted the industry in Pithole, Pennsylvania.
2. **The United Association of Plumbers and Pipefitters**, which included the pipeline welders and their welder helpers.
3. **The International Union of Operating Engineers**, the men who operated the heavy machinery, including Stubby. The men in these groups had learned specialized skills over many years and were paid well for their expertise.

My unskilled group, the **Laborers International Union of North America**, was the lowest paid of the pipeline crew. In 1979, that meant $8.56 per hour, which was still significantly higher than the federal minimum wage of $2.90 per hour. And because the seasonal work demanded sixty-hour workweeks, there was the added incentive of overtime whereby any work performed over forty hours earned "time and a half," or $12.84 per hour. It was exhausting work, but I focused on the fact that I was earning more than six or seven times my friends back home. Today, these unskilled workers make about $19 per hour and $27 for overtime hours.

It wasn't until a mishap when we were executing a stream crossing that I had the opportunity to turn things around with the rest of the crew. Stream crossings are a major challenge for pipeline contractors. The mechanical and engineering challenge is demanding due to the need to bend the pipe to exact specifications so that the pipe may be laid and buried below the riverbed. It is especially difficult to accomplish this task while satisfying regulations and remaining sensitive to environmental concerns.

Even in 1979, pipeline contractors were aware and respectful of environmental issues. "Leave it better than you found it" was the rule for stream crossings according to our spread boss. Stream crossings were so important to the entire project that the spread boss was typically on-site during the final placement of the finished pipe under the river. Most pipeliners are outdoorsmen and fishermen, so they equally understood the importance of incident-free stream crossings.

That day, our work was halted when a large strap attached to a crane was inadvertently lost in the river under an unstable section of pipe. No one was willing to take the risk of diving and finding the strap in the muddy, fast-moving water. The spread boss looked at me and the man standing next to me, Big Thomas, the only other new laborer considered as lowly as I was.

Thomas was a big Black guy dressed in overalls, about six feet two and about 240 pounds. He routinely picked up a skid in each hand, while the other laborers and I could only manage one skid at a time. His enormous hands appeared to be capable of easily breaking my 160-pound frame in two. But, as big as he was, he was a gentle man, and we became fast friends. His timid smile didn't quite match his powerful frame. And we had something in common: neither of us was a perfect fit on the pipeline spread. I was the southern boy who drove a "Jap car," and Thomas was the Black guy, and if you had dug down a foot or so below the general population of laborers, that's where you would have found Big Thomas and me as the newest greenhorn laborers. Innately, we both knew that we were second-class citizens in the Pennsylvania pipeline pecking order.

When the boss looked at him, Thomas's eyes widened, and he whispered to me, "Billy, I'd jump in, but I can't swim." He looked over at the spread boss and repeated in a loud voice, "Boss, I can't swim."

So, that left me, a greenhorn determined to prove myself, and I volunteered. For the second time that summer, all eyes turned to me. As scrawny as I was compared to Big Thomas, I was the least likely candidate for the job. But I had one thing going for me: I had grown up in Louisiana and was accustomed to diving into murky water.

Everyone watched as I searched for the missing strap and, after struggling a bit, returned it to the bank and the anxious spread boss. After failing to find a foothold out of the trench, a large, black hand reached down and pulled me out like a rag doll. No other laborers had volunteered to help, other than Big Thomas. Our budding friendship was sealed.

By then, I had made a few other buddies among the colorful characters on the pipeline. There was Ed, a teamster and father of two whose light-skinned arms and hands were speckled with sun damage from a lifetime of working on pipelines across the country. He laughed often, which caused his dentures to accidentally pop out sometimes, to his sheepish embarrassment.

And there was Gene the welder, a handsome, confident man in his forties, a modern-day Ben Hogan whose pipeline tales and comedic timing were legendary. Gene always managed to find amusement in the daily drudgery, like the afternoon he spotted a woman in "hot pants" watching the pipeliners from her backyard fence. He bet each of us twenty bucks that he could talk her into a bologna sandwich and a glass of milk, and twenty minutes later, he coolly sauntered back to collect his winnings. The next day, he negotiated bologna sandwiches for the rest of us.

NOT JUST A JOB BUT A CAREER

After my rescue of the strap in the stream, I was no longer singled out for daily inspection or hazing. Then it dawned on me: I had been facing an informal probationary induction into the pipeline business. Initially, I thought I had simply taken on a job, but I was gradually learning that it was much more than that.

I had been granted provisional membership in a privileged group. Not a team and not exactly a family, but more like a clan. Folks were united by an appreciation for a unique industry and were guardedly protective of its members. They didn't think of it as simply a job, but as a career. Respect had been earned among its participants over many years, some over multiple generations. Men were descended from fathers and grandfathers who worked in the original pipeline gangs in the early 1900s. Not college boys who drove foreign cars.

It seemed many men were flawed in some way. Stubby was missing his arm, and Ed was missing his teeth. Some men had criminal backgrounds. Even Gene, with his charm and confidence, had a flaw. On payday, he pulled me aside and quietly asked me to interpret the FICA deduction numbers on his paycheck. Gene had dyslexia and couldn't read.

Although their flaws differed, these men shared the desire and ability to work intensely despite their varied limitations. They worked up to eighty hours per week in one-hundred-degree temperatures many miles away from home. They instinctively understood it was dangerous work, as proven by the scars on their faces and the fingers and limbs missing from life-altering accidents. The pipeliners cultivated worthy members who watched for potential hazards to the rest of the clan and who were united in their aim to support their families.

Their aim has become increasingly challenging today as fossil fuels and pipelines are canceled in favor of "green energy" dreams. In 2020, for instance, then-presidential hopeful Joe Biden told unemployed fossil fuel laborers to learn to code to transition to a green economy: "Anybody who can throw coal into a furnace can learn how to program, for God's sake!" he said. It is a ridiculous solution—tone-deaf, one politician called it—for blue-collar workers who have dedicated their lives to developing their job-specific careers.

Biden isn't the only one offering unrealistic solutions. Vice President Kamala Harris encouraged workers to reclaim "abandoned land mines," a remark that highlighted the disconnect between career politicians and regular working folks.

The out-of-touch comments illustrate how much has changed since my days as a greenhorn. Pipeline and other oil and gas workers have been relegated to afterthoughts, mere collateral damage as politicians push their unrealistic energy agendas and unnecessarily destroy good jobs. Many workers are resisting the training programs, some in hopes that their industry will rebound, others because it's too daunting to learn a new skill late in life. They're frustrated by the arrogant thinking that they can "just go find another career."[40]

That was the sentiment expressed by business owners in South Dakota on the day President Biden was inaugurated in January 2021 when news broke that he had revoked the permit for Keystone XL, the fourth proposed phase of the Keystone pipeline system. A hotel owner choked back tears as she described the forlorn faces of pipeliners packing their belongings and heading home without jobs. And a truck-stop owner talked about the "nightmare" of dashed dreams for thousands of locals and workers. They all felt used, like pawns in the latest political tug-of-war pitting climate change against economic

40. Jennifer A. Dlouhy and Ari Natter, "Biden Assurances on Jobs Sting Like Insults in Mines, Oil Patch," Bloomberg, February 15, 2021, https://www.bloomberg.com/news/features/2021-02-16/miners-and-oil-workers-hear-insults-in-biden-talk-of-better-jobs.

development.[41]

The reality is that American workers will be hard-pressed to find a career like those in oil and gas. The industry has allowed people with few skills and no college diplomas access to pensions, vacation time, and middle-class incomes for their families. When the United States reemerged as the world's leading oil producer, entry-level oil workers earned an average of $76,000 per year for their manual labor. But their middle-class hopes and dreams are threatened by the relentless attacks on fossil fuels.[42]

Back in 1979, a career in the oil and gas industry was still promising. That's why I felt anxious when the job site treasurer asked me into his office a week after I found the missing strap. On the table was my union card paperwork that had been approved by the spread boss. I didn't know if the strap had anything to do with the boss's decision, but I didn't ask any questions and quickly signed the documents.

I emerged from the building and smiled. I was a card-carrying member of Local Union 158–Harrisburg, Pennsylvania, of the Laborers' International Union of North America. Finally, I was a bonafide member of the clan.

SIMPLE WISDOM

My last day on the job as a pipeliner in Pennsylvania was on a Saturday in mid-August, 1979. I was ready to go home.

---

41. Barnini Chakraborty, "After The Haulting Of The Keystone XL Pipeline, Two Local Business Owners Voice Their Concerns For Their Future," Pioneer Review, February 3, 2021, Ravellette Publications, Inc., http://www.pioneer-review.com/pioneer-review/after-haulting-keystone-xl-pipeline-two-local-business-owners-voice-their-concerns.

42. "Editorial: Biden Prefers Having Slaves Produce Oil," The Gazette editorial board, *Colorado Springs Gazette,* published August 16, 2021, updated September 19, 2022, https://gazette.com/opinion/editorials/editorial-biden-prefers-having-slaves-produce-oil/article_bc46795c-fc79-11eb-b865-63c56a2c51ab.html.

Our job that summer to replace a portion of the original Big Inch pipeline was essentially completed. All the sections of pipe had been painstakingly welded into place and positioned into the trench. The mounds of dirt on the side of the trench had been pushed by the dozer operators back into the earth from where it had been dug. Only one hole near the final tie-in remained to be filled.

Big Thomas, Ed, Gene, my buddy, and I leaned against our vehicles parked at the end of the line. My reviled Toyota Celica waited alongside the row of trucks for the twelve-hundred-mile trip back to Louisiana.

I gazed back up the mountain to observe the summer work that had been completed. The pipeline right-of-way stretched up the side of the mountain as far as the eye could see, following the curves of the seemingly endless hills of south-central Pennsylvania. Stubby, the lone dozer operator left on the job, was skillfully smoothing the earth back into place. Soon, new grass would sprout, and the land would return to its natural green.

I took a swig of imported northern Pennsylvania water from an Igloo and quietly watched Stubby smooth over the last mound of earth. No one said a word. We were all contemplating our work that summer, the relationships we had developed, and what lay ahead for each of us.

An approaching pickup truck crunched over gravel, and the spread boss got out and walked toward us, holding our paycheck envelopes. Stubby killed his dozer's engine and joined us.

"Hello, boys." Our spread boss admired the smooth earth up the row. "Looks good, fellas. Real good."

He began sorting his envelopes. Stubby got his first, claiming it with his one good hand. Then each of my laborer partners got theirs. Mine was the last envelope.

My spread boss said, "Billy, I'll be honest. I didn't think you were gonna make it when I first laid eyes on you. But you stuck it out and did a good job."

I smiled, opened my paycheck, and then grinned wider at the amount. It was a lot of money for an eighteen-year-old. All the money I earned would go toward expenses at Louisiana State University and getting a head start in adulthood.

When I looked up, my spread boss was already climbing back into his truck to deliver paychecks to the other tired men eager to get home. I turned and said goodbye to the crew. For the second time in our short friendship, Big Thomas extended his giant hand with a smile and good wishes. I held on and sincerely wished him the same.

As I headed toward my Celica, I glanced toward Stubby and gave him my regards. Stubby nodded. "Billy, you know Ford makes some really good trucks. And they're made right here in the USA." I slid into my hatchback and nodded back, smiling.

Forty years later, I think of Stubby's parting words when I climb into my Ford Expedition SUV. And I still remember the simple wisdom of a one-armed pipeliner.

When I see misguided pipeline protests and misinformation about the fossil fuel industry, I think of Stubby, Big Thomas, Ed, and Gene. The blue-collar workers on the Big Inch pipeline that summer of 1979 instilled in me a deep respect for the pipeliners, their American jobs, and their American industry.

THE LIFEBLOOD OF AMERICA

I must have passed the pipeliner test that summer because I was invited back the next year to work in the heartland of America, in Illinois, Iowa, and Nebraska. And although I worked alongside union pipeliners for only two summers, it was long enough for me to think like a pipeliner:

natural gas, pipelines, and Ford F150 pickup trucks were good. Japanese cars were bad. And nuclear folks were a bunch of 'sum bitches.' I held these views for forty years.

I had come to respect pipeliners as some of the hardest-working men I had ever encountered who deserved every penny of their high-paying jobs. I had also come to appreciate the pipelines that are carefully laid across America.

Today, there are more than two million miles of pipelines in the United States—the largest network of pipelines in the world—some of which are buried under our homes and streets.[43] The petroleum pumping through pipelines remains the lifeblood of industrialized countries. It creates lubricant for equipment and machinery. It generates heat and electricity for our houses and businesses, providing nearly half the energy used in the world.

U.S. oil is also indispensable in our transportation, including its use in laying runways, manufacturing synthetic rubber for tires, and distilling into gasoline. Fuels made from petroleum provide power for automobiles, airplanes, factories, farm equipment, trucks, trains, and ships. And thousands of everyday products depend on the widespread availability of petroleum, including cosmetics, carpets, detergents, toys, fertilizers, and toothpaste. Oil is so essential to our lives that if it didn't exist, it would have to be invented.[44]

The pipeline industry has come a long way since that first pipeline in 1865—and even since my stint as a pipeliner in 1979 and 1980. As the infrastructure has grown steadily and new technologies have emerged, America has been made more secure, the economy has been strengthened, and the nation has been more competitive in the international

43. "Where are Liquids Pipelines Located?" Pipeline 101, https://pipeline101.org/topic/where-are-gas-pipelines-located/.

44. *The World Book Encyclopedia*, CD-Rom Edition, 1997.

market. The United States has reemerged as a dominant oil producer, regaining its status as a global oil power and threatening the influence of the Middle East and the Russians.

It has all happened without much controversy. Laborers, welders, teamsters, and dozer operators have continued working on pipelines around the country without much fuss, just as the generations did before them.

That is, until 2016. And then all hell broke loose.

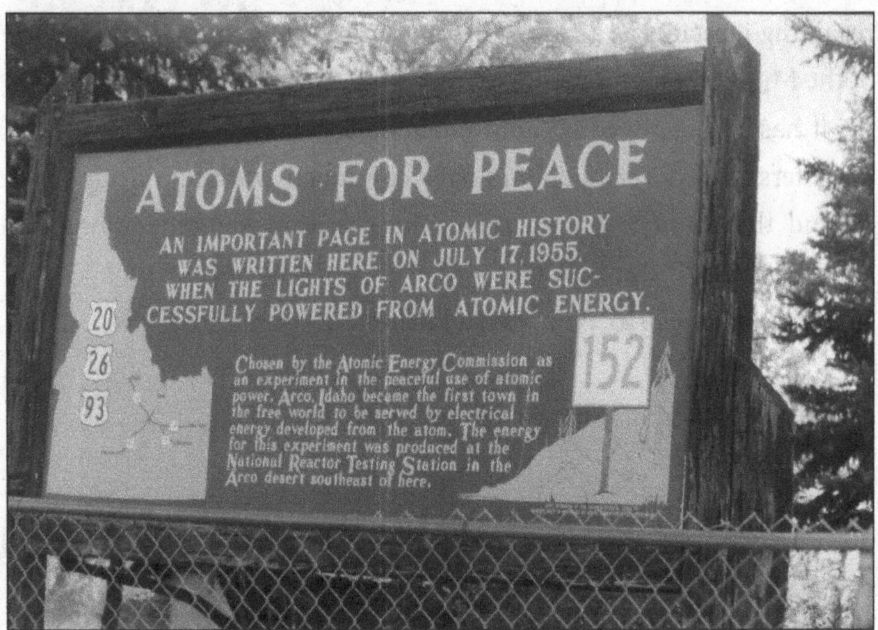

A sign from Arco, Idaho, "the first town in the free world to be served by electrical energy developed from the atom." Courtesy of David Wilson from Oak Park, Illinois, USA, CC BY 2.0, via Wikimedia Commons.

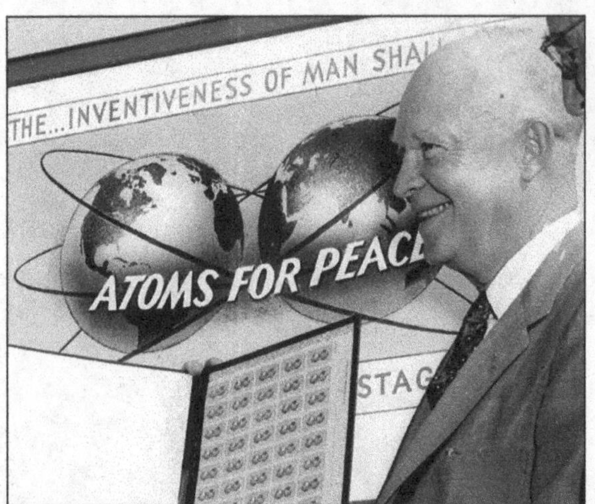

President Eisenhower receives an album of Atoms for Peace stamps. Courtesy of ENERGY.GOV, Public domain, via Wikimedia Commons.

For the Documerica Project (1971-1977), the Environmental Protection Agency (EPA) hired freelance photographers to capture images relating to environmental problems, EPA activities, and everyday life in the 1970s. David Falconer documented the fuel shortage in the west during the 1970s, as well as water pollution in the area at the time. Falconer took photos from April 1973 to May 1974 mainly across the states of Oregon and Idaho. Courtesy of David Falconer, Public domain, via Wikimedia Commons.

The Three Mile Island nuclear power plant near Middletown, Pennsylvania, which was the site of a March 28, 1979 power plant accident. Courtesy of Wikimedia Commons.

Anti-nuclear rally outside the Pennsylvania State Capitol in Harrisburg, Pennsylvania. Courtesy of National Archives and Records Administration (NARA), Public domain, via Wikimedia Commons.

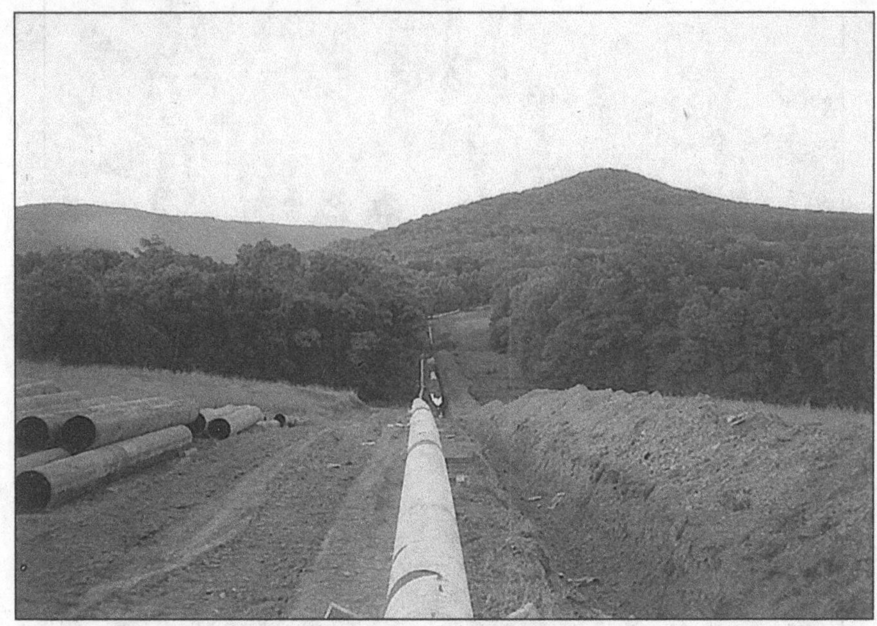

The replacement pipeline that Herrington worked on for Texas Eastern, the company that owned the Big Inch pipeline system. Courtesy of Bill Herrington.

Bill's friend, Tony Moore, whose father was the pipeline spread boss in Pennsylvania. Courtesy of Bill Herrington.

Bill Herrington and the infamous “Jap car.” Courtesy of Bill Herrington.

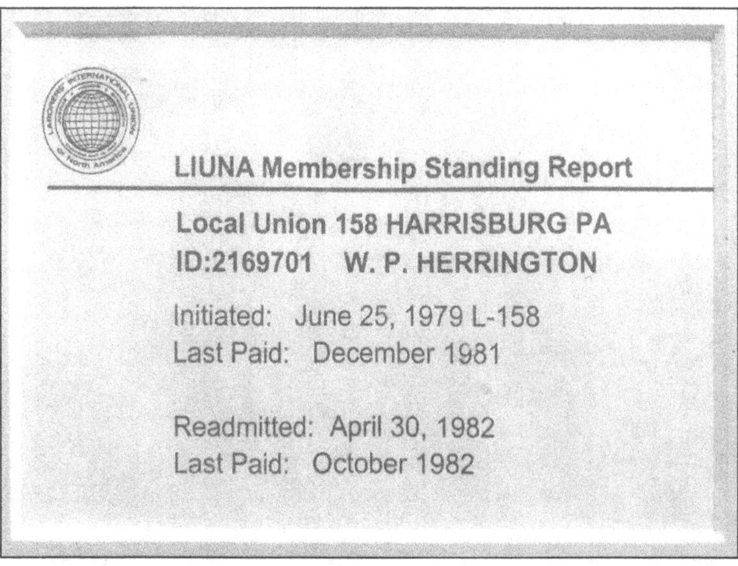

LIUNA Membership Standing Report

Local Union 158 HARRISBURG PA

ID:2169701 W. P. HERRINGTON

Initiated: June 25, 1979 L-158

Last Paid: December 1981

Readmitted: April 30, 1982

Last Paid: October 1982

Herrington’s Union Card. Courtesy of Bill Herrington.

PART II

THE FLAWED NARRATIVE OF THE PRESENT

CHAPTER 3

AMERICAN INDIANS AND THE POISONOUS BLACK SNAKE

THE DAKOTA ACCESS PIPELINE PROTEST IS BASED ON THREE FAULTY ACCUSATIONS

Standing Rock Reservation
Morton County, North Dakota
2016

"Sometimes the routes leading to feelings of anger are so convoluted and circuitous that it takes enormous skill to discern their original source, or fountainhead."

– Theodore Isaac Rubin, MD, *The Angry Book*

Early one morning, American Indians walked quietly through the plains of North Dakota. Others rode horses, their faces streaked with paint and their jaws clenched in determination as they neared the battlefront. Members from more than two hundred tribes were banding together against a common enemy, a collaboration the likes of which had not been seen since the Battle of Little Bighorn in 1876.[45]

But this wasn't 1876. It was 2016.

This wasn't the old-fashioned battle of rifles and archery led by Crazy Horse. It was a modern-day battle at a construction site, led by a new generation of tribal chiefs.

And the common enemy wasn't General George Armstrong Custer and the U.S. Cavalry. It was the pipeline industry and the Dakota Access Pipeline, a 1,172-mile pipeline that the American Indians scornfully labeled "the poisonous black snake."

A previously obscure industry was under siege and in the crosshairs of protestors and their supporters. It became a surprisingly fierce, wide-ranging war, one that attracted worldwide attention and galvanized international support for the American Indians, who could not have predicted the wild growth or the disturbing implications of the protest.

The protest escalated into violence that shocked even veteran reporters. As crowds crammed onto the construction site, people pushed, threw rocks and sticks, and set fires that led to restraining orders and hundreds of arrests.

Environmentalists fanned the tension by taking to social media and attempting to cut off support to pipeliners by publicly shaming and blacklisting banks that financed them. Celebrities responded by circulating petitions. Political leaders added to the fray by taking photographs of their own vandalism of the pipeline.

---

45. Jack Healy, "Occupying the Prairie: Tensions Rise as Tribes Move to Block a Pipeline," *New York Times,* August 23, 2016, https://www.nytimes.com/2016/08/24/us/occupying-the-prairie-tensions-rise-as-tribes-move-to-block-a-pipeline.html.

In the aftermath, the country's outlook regarding pipelines abruptly changed. It no longer seemed to matter that the pipeline industry was part of our nation's framework for 150 years and had served as the crux of the U.S. victory in World War II. It didn't matter that 2.6 million miles of pipelines were supplying energy across all fifty states. And it didn't matter that millions of American jobs were sustained by pipelines and natural gas products as our country was kept competitive and diversified. An opposition fueled by environmentalists gained a foothold in the minds of Americans.

MORTON COUNTY MAYHEM

One of the first signs of trouble began in Morton County, North Dakota, on August 10, 2016. As the morning sun rose over the prairie on the banks of the Missouri River, a pipeline crew arrived in pickup trucks at the construction site. Their day began just like it had countless times before, and they assembled and readied themselves for the work ahead, oblivious to the impending encounter.

But the crew was interrupted by a group of thirty or so other men. The men were American Indians who felt they had been pushed far enough. They demanded that the pipeliners halt construction.

"If you continue your work, you will be hurt," one of the men warned, brandishing a knife attached to his hip. Another protestor chained himself to a fence to impede the progress. The alarmed pipeliners had no choice but to shut down the construction site and to notify law enforcement.

The crew was woefully unprepared for the confrontation. Protests were not new to the pipeliners, but the intensity of the threats was greater than in previous incidents—as was the number of people. By that afternoon, the group of thirty American Indians swelled to one hundred, some of whom threatened the pipeliners and demanded that they leave.

The next day, the protestors showed up again, this time numbering close to two hundred people. Over forty law enforcement officers monitored the protest and maintained the peace. But as the crowd grew, the protestors became more unruly. One man wielded a knife and refused to cooperate with law enforcement. When he was confronted, he jumped a fence and ran toward the contractor's equipment. Other protestors also refused to cooperate, tearing down barricades and blocking pipeliners from entering or exiting the job site.

On the third day, the number of protestors had grown to 350, including the chairman of the Standing Rock Sioux Tribe, Dave Archambault, and Tribal Council member Dana Yellow Fat. Archambault had earlier excused all Standing Rock Tribal members from work that day to show up for the protest. Protesters formed lines to block the entrance, and exiting vehicles were damaged by thrown objects. Eighteen protestors were arrested for their part in the unlawful activity, including Archambault and Yellow Fat.

Despite the arrests, threatening language persisted and even escalated throughout the days and weeks ahead. "Force will be met with force!" an American Indian protester yelled, while claiming the situation was akin to a declaration of war.

As the crowds grew, those familiar with the pipeline industry were puzzled at the charged protest, including Cory Bryson, a local business representative for the Laborer's International Union. As a pipeliner of more than ten years, Bryson had seen opposition in the thirty-two years his own father had worked as a pipeliner, but he had never seen anything at this level. It seemed like a war against the workers, who faced violence and lost wages due to shutdowns. They endured vandalism such as smashed windshields and gas tanks clogged with dirt.[46] After one laborer was beaten up at a gas station on his way to work, they began traveling in groups and avoiding wearing company branding.[47] Bryson received an anonymous email showing a photo of himself, his wife, and his three small children that read, "We hope you enjoy burning in your home with your children."[48]

For more than a century, thousands of working-class pipeliners like Bryson have worked to construct the millions of miles of pipelines across America. It has been a well-established industry with a vibrant history, one that had been applauded for creating jobs, dramatically expanding the industrial revolution, and helping to defeat Hitler in World War II. But the American Indian protestors were unmoved by the long history of the pipelines, and a meeting was scheduled between Dakota Access representatives and the tribal chairman of the Standing Rock Sioux Tribe at the time, Dave Archambault II, to discuss the reasons behind the protest.

THREE FAULTY ACCUSATIONS

Archambault laid out the three allegations made by the American Indians against DAPL, the pipeline that had been planned for years by a Texas-based company called Energy Transfer Partners. They wanted to stop the thirty-inch-diameter pipe from moving half a million barrels of crude oil daily across 1,172 miles, from the booming Bakken shale oil fields in North Dakota to Patoka, Illinois.

46. Kevin Sullivan, "Voices from Standing Rock," *The Washington Post,* December 2, 2016, https://www.washingtonpost.com/sf/national/2016/12/02/voices-from-standing-rock/?noredirect=on&utm_term=.b0c328984eb3.

47. Bronte Wittpenn, "'It Turned into a War': Pipeline Workers Thrown into the Middle of Protests," *Billings Gazette*, November 20, 2016, https://billingsgazette.com/business/it-turned-into-a-war-pipeline-workers-thrown-into-the/article_4b255cea-443e-5ecf-a33b-a48a8c54b034.html#1.

48. Sullivan, "Voices from Standing Rock."

However, Craig Stevens, a spokesman for the Midwest Alliance for Infrastructure Now Coalition, worked to set the record straight. He exposed each allegation as a misleading statement, propaganda, or outright falsehood.

Sacred land

First, the tribes argued that building the pipeline, which would run under Lake Oahe, would "desecrate sacred waters and make it impossible for the Tribes to freely exercise their religious beliefs," in violation of the Religious Freedom Restoration Act.[49] In a statement, Archambault said,

> "Several of our Lakota and Dakota relatives have had visions and dreams. They have been visited in a spiritual sense and have been told that there is a black poisonous snake trying to come among us. Our instructions say snakes are good – they serve a great purpose in the web of life. Our elders and the elders before them have given us wonderful teachings and a beautiful way to live and co-exist with all that is; however, the black poisonous snake we are being warned about does not come from the Creator. It is man-made and the creature is made from nothing but greed."

But the pipeline does not cross sacred American Indian land.

Stevens pointed out that the path of the pipeline, which had been decided two years earlier, did not enter the Standing Rock Sioux Tribe's reservation. The portion under scrutiny was on private property, not previously undisturbed land.[50]

The map revealed that the route of DAPL was approximately

49. *Standing Rock Sioux Tribe v. U.S. Army Corps of Engineers*, No. CV 16-1534 (JEB), 2017 WL 2573994, June 14, 2017.

50. Craig Stevens, "On the Dakota Access Pipeline, Let's Stick to the Facts," *The Hill*, September 21, 2016, https://thehill.com/blogs/congress-blog/energy-environment/296926-on-the-dakota-access-pipeline-lets-stick-to-the-facts.

ten miles above the northernmost boundary of the Standing Rock Reservation. The reservation covered an expanse of more than 3,500 square miles and was home to 8,200 people, but it was evident that the pipeline would not cross their sacred land. The path of the DAPL was nearly identical to the path of an existing pipeline that crosses Lake Oahe and that has been operating safely since 1982, a pre-existing energy corridor in which electricity transmission lines and the Northern Border natural gas pipeline already lay.

Kelcy Warren, the CEO of Energy Transfer Partners, a second-generation pipeline welder who grew up welding with his father, confirmed the facts on *PBS Newshour*. DAPL was not on tribal lands at all—only private lands.[51,52]

Proper consultation and study

Second, the American Indians pointed to regulations requiring federal agencies to "consult with Indian tribes when they attach religious and cultural significance to a historic property regardless of the location of the property," according to a committee that oversees historic preservation on behalf of Congress. The regulations state, "A local tribe is not supposed to be hustled in at the end for a rubber stamp, but included throughout the process as a collaborative body."

The tribe felt these regulations had not been met. However, the project involved the input and oversight of archaeologists, the state of North Dakota, and the federal government. It was reviewed and approved by a state agency whose sole mission is to identify, preserve, interpret, and promote the heritage of North Dakota and its people. The

51. "Telling Fortunes: No. 18: Kelcy Warren," *Texas Monthly*, September 15, 2013, https://www.texasmonthly.com/list/telling-fortunes/no-18-kelcy-warren/.

52. *PBS News Hour*, "CEO behind Dakota Access to protesters: 'We're building the pipeline,'" PBS, November 16, 2016, https://www.pbs.org/newshour/show/ceo-behind-dakota-access-protesters-building-pipeline.

pipeline's route was also approved by the State Historic Preservation Office, which determined that no significant sites were affected. The state's chief archaeologist confirmed that due diligence under existing regulatory law and regulation was properly completed.

In his *PBS Newshour* interview, Warren said the Army Corps of Engineers gathered input from all concerned and made suggestions on any necessary deviations in the route. The route was not determined in a vacuum by Energy Transfer but only after great consultation with the Army Corps of Engineers, whose offer of consultation had allegedly been declined by the Standing Rock Sioux.

Former district chairman Robert Fool Bear of Cannon Ball, located a few miles from the protest's epicenter, said the Standing Rock Sioux Tribe could have attended hearings two years earlier to make their concerns known but they had not. Bryson concurred. He had heard no protests at any of the public hearings held prior to the construction of DAPL. Of the fifty or more people who attended public hearings in 2014—including landowners, residents, legal staff, and representatives of Energy Transfer Partners—he said none were representatives of the Standing Rock Sioux Tribe.[53]

The thorough review process was what made the protests "fundamentally unfair," according to the American Federation of Labor and Congress of Industrial Organizations (AFL-CIO). It is the largest federation of unions in the United States, made up of fifty-five national and international unions representing more than twelve million active and retired workers. The organization believes that community involvement in the construction and location of pipelines is important; it also believes that it's unfair to hold union members' livelihoods and financial security "hostage to endless delay" once the review process is complete.[54]

53. Wittpenn, "'It turned into a war': Pipeline workers thrown into the middle of protests."

54. "Unions Weigh in on the Dakota Access Pipeline," New Labor Foruym, CUNY School of Labor and Urban Studies, September 2016, https://newlaborforum.cuny.edu/2016/09/30/unions-weigh-in-on-the-dakota-access-pipeline.

Water supply

The tribe said the pipeline would cross Lake Oahe, a large reservoir of the Missouri River, which is the source of drinking water for the Standing Rock Reservation. In an official statement, Archambault said, "To poison the water is to poison the substance of life. Everything that moves must have water. How can we talk about and knowingly poison water?"[55]

The protest boiled down to the claim that the Dakota Access Pipeline would poison the water and destroy Native American lands. But it wasn't true. DAPL didn't threaten the water supplies of the Standing Rock Sioux Reservation.

Warren explained that the pipeline was being built to safety standards that far exceeded government requirements, including new, extra-thick steel pipe laid 150 feet below the surface of Lake Oahe. In the unlikely chance of a leak, automated valves would shut down the pipe, containing the small section in danger.

The American Indians said their 2016 protest was about protecting their water and lands, but one by one, their three allegations against DAPL were debunked.

The pipeline did not cross sacred land.

The project did receive proper consultation and approval.

And DAPL did not threaten water supplies.

The DAPL protest was a fraud. Along the way, the protest and the related unlawful activities stifled an industry and its high-paying jobs.

---

55. Dave Archambault II, "Aug 16, 2016 - Statement from Standing Rock Sioux Tribal Chairman on the Dakota Access Pipeline," Last Real Indians, August 15, 2016, https://lastrealindians.com/news/2016/8/16/aug-16-2016-statement-from-standing-rock-sioux-tribal-chairman-on-the-dakota-access-pipeline.

A COMPLICATED RELATIONSHIP

The hostility didn't suddenly boil over with DAPL and the three allegations. Angst had been simmering between American Indians and the U.S. government for generations, before the Battle of Little Bighorn.

Back in the 1800s, settlers and American Indians clashed repeatedly, resulting in much bloodshed and in the designation of hundreds of reservations, or lands managed for the benefit of tribes recognized as American Indian. Most American Indian land is effectively held in trust by the United States, and federal law still regulates the political and economic rights of tribal governments, periodically defining and redefining their role through various laws and court decisions. These legalities cast American Indians in the role of government wards, with the right to be consulted on matters that concern them but without the right to make decisions.

This relationship regarding land rights is at the root of the frustration today. The American Indians' long-standing desire to control their lands is the real reason behind the objection to DAPL.

Archambault believed the construction of DAPL was yet another example of a greedy land-grab, and he pinned the blame directly on the U.S. government. He said his reservation was one of the ten poorest places or counties in the United States, caused by the greed of U.S. lawmakers and their policies.

However, not all American Indians blame the U.S. government for the use of pipelines. In fact, not all members of the Standing Rock Sioux Tribe itself even backed the protest of DAPL. Most of the protestors were not even Standing Rock Tribe members. According to Fool Bear, many tribes weren't part of the protest because they felt it was reversing decades of collaboration and cooperation between the indigenous American tribes and the oil and gas industry.[56]

56. Richard Nemec, "Native Americans and Energy Projects – High Stakes in the Ground," *Pipeline and Gas Journal* 244, no. 6, (June 2017), https://pgjonline.com/magazine/2017/june-2017-vol-244-no-6/features/native-americans-and-energy-projects-high-stakes-in-the-ground.

AMERICAN INDIANS PRODUCE OIL AND OWN PIPELINES, TOO

The collaboration and cooperation are perhaps the most complicated truth of all: not only do some tribes support oil and gas companies, but they are some of the country's largest producers of oil and gas in the industry. Many even own pipelines.

One example of an American Indian who is benefitting from the oil and gas industry is T. J. Plenty Chief. His company, Red Road Trucking, transports oil and gas supplies, including drill pipe, gravel, and water for drilling and production activities. Plenty Chief supports a family of ten with his trucking company and claims that truck drivers can earn as much as $90,000 a year.[57]

He's not alone. A tribal council that accepts and encourages pipelines and oil and gas production is the Mandan, Hidatsa, and Arikara Tribes, together called the MHA Nation. The MHA Nation is on Fort Berthold Reservation, just 150 miles northwest of the Standing Rock Sioux Tribe, alongside the same Missouri River. The reservation lies in the heart of the Bakken oil formation. Years earlier, the MHA Nation decided that oil production was financially worthy of any risks the industry posed to the environment.

"We are in this oil play already," said Edmund Baker, the tribal environmental director. "We want to be able to do it responsibly. We want to be able to do it competently. We want to show other tribes it can be done."

Today, tribal members of the MHA Nation live on top of the oil pipelines that transport the Bakken crude. More than four thousand miles of pipelines with more than fourteen hundred operating oil wells intersect Fort Berthold Reservation. According to the MHA, the

57. Amy Sisk, "While One Tribe Fights Oil, Another Cautiously Embraces It," *Inside Energy,* November 22, 2016, http://insideenergy.org/2016/11/22/while-one-tribe-fights-oil-another-cautiously-embraces-it.

oil industry provides a way for its fifteen thousand tribal members to become self-sufficient. Since just 2008, they have benefitted from nearly $2 billion in revenue. Other tribes make even more.[58]

But while some tribes have worked to benefit from the oil and gas industry, the Standing Rock Sioux worked to oppose it. It gained national and international attention, growing to levels that surprised even the leaders of the tribe.

Soon, a new group of protestors joined their cause, and they brought with them unexpected consequences.

58. Amy Sisk, "Upstream From Standing Rock, Tribes Balance Benefits, Risks of Oil Industry," Morning Edition, NPR, Washington, D.C.: WAMU, November 24, 2016, https://www.npr.org/2016/11/24/503212965/upstream-from-standing-rock-tribes-balance-benefits-risks-of-oil-industry.

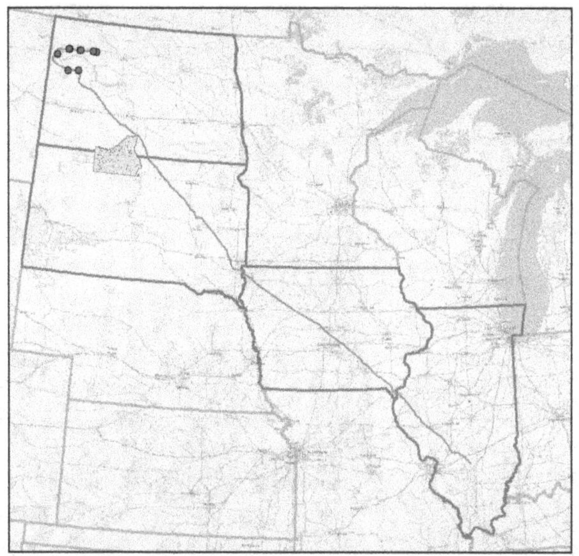

A map showing the Bakken pipeline (Dakota Access Pipeline) and the Standing Rock Sioux Reservation. Courtesy of NittyG, CC BY-SA 4.0, via Wikimedia Commons.

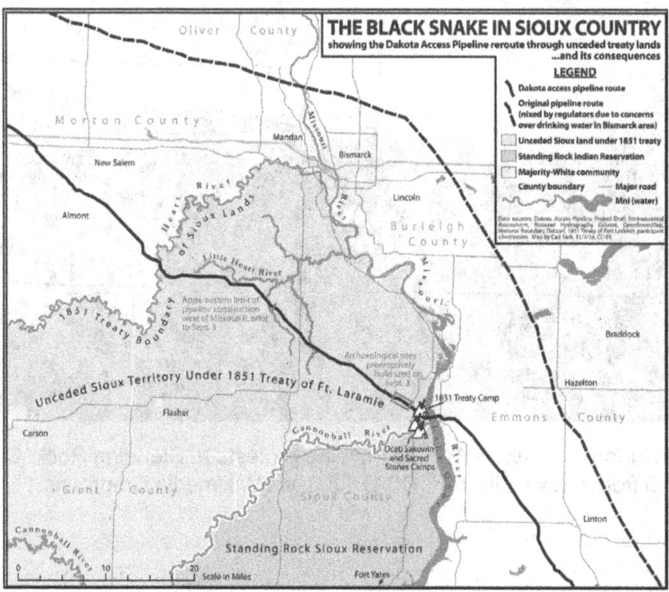

Dakota Access Pipeline reroute. The dotted line shows the original route of the pipeline; the solid line shows the actual path after the pipeline was rerouted. Courtesy of Carl Sack, CC BY 3.0, via Wikimedia Commons.

Flag flown during the Dakota Access Pipeline protests at Standing Rock. Courtesy of Becker1999 from Grove City, OH, CC BY 2.0, via Wikimedia Commons.

Dakota Access Pipeline Native American protest site, on Highway 1806 near Cannonball, North Dakota, August 15th, 2016. Courtesy of Shane Balkowitsch, CC BY-SA 4.0, via Wikimedia Commons.

People protesting the Dakota Access Pipeline with signs and banners. Courtesy of Pax Ahimsa Gethen, CC BY-SA 4.0, via Wikimedia Commons.

Floris White Bull, Hunkpapa Lakota - Cochiti Pueblo, was instrumental in the Standing Rock protests against the Dakota Access Pipeline. Courtesy of Shane Balkowitsch, CC BY-SA 4.0, via Wikimedia Commons.

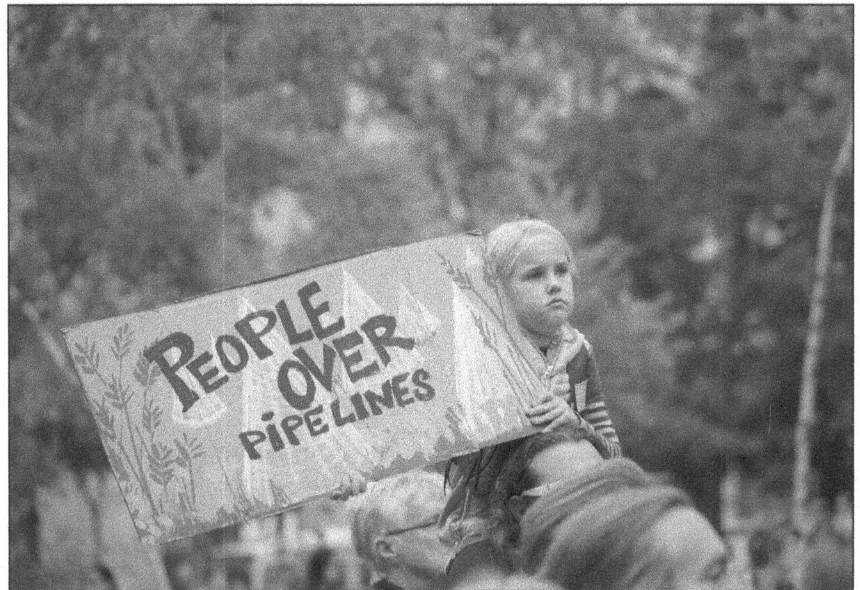

St. Paul, Minnesota, September 13, 2016. This was one of the solidarity rallies happening around the world this day to show support for the protests against the Dakota Access Pipeline. Courtesy of Fibonacci Blue from Minnesota, USA, CC BY 2.0, via Wikimedia Commons.

The old Four Bears Bridge spanning Lake Sakakawea/Missouri River seen from Crow Flies High view point, Fort Berthold Indian Reservation, North Dakota. Courtesy of Naawada2016, CC BY-SA 4.0 via Wikimedia Commons.

CHAPTER 4

DARK MONEY AND THE BUSINESS OF ENVIRONMENTAL ACTIVISM

THE AGENDA AND FUNDING BEHIND THE U.S. ENVIRONMENTAL MOVEMENT

"The empty vessel makes the loudest sound."

– William Shakespeare

MADNESS. THAT'S WHAT ROBERT FOOL BEAR called the Dakota Access Pipeline protest less than two months after it began in August 2016. The former reservation district chairman was irked by the crowds who streamed through his reservation from all over the world.

American Indian leaders may have welcomed the growing attention on the protest at first, but once troubling issues surfaced, the situation deteriorated. Outbursts of violence and illegal activities erupted, forcing legal authorities to act at taxpayers' expense. Protestors set up a permanent camp, forcing residents to drive miles out of their way to avoid roadblocks. Millions of pounds of garbage teetered in tall piles, threatening the very land that protestors claimed to be protecting.

The situation rapidly worsened, but not because of the residents of Cannon Ball. Nor was it because of American Indians. The DAPL protest had spun out of control largely because of a new player who had entered the scene: environmental activists. They came armed with a green agenda to replace fossil fuels with less-powerful, less-efficient energy sources that weaken our nation.

THE KEY TO THE OPPOSITION

It wasn't the first time activists arrived on the pipeline scene. They appeared in 2014 during permitting negotiations for another pipeline: the Keystone Pipeline System.

Known simply as Keystone, the oil pipeline system is owned by a Canadian pipeline giant, TransCanada Corporation. The first three phases of Keystone were completed between 2010 and 2014 without much controversy, and the system began transporting oil from the Western Canadian Sedimentary Basin in Alberta, Canada, to refineries in Port Arthur and Houston, Texas, as well as Patoka, Illinois. But things changed for the fourth proposed phase: the "Keystone XL."

Keystone XL was slated to start in Canada, just like the three previous phases. But Keystone XL would take a more direct route to Steele City in Nebraska. Nebraska Governor Dave Heineman had already provided approval, and both chambers of the U.S. Congress passed a bill approving the construction of the pipeline in January 2015. It would enter the United States at Morgan, Montana, and then move on to Baker, Montana, where American-produced oil would be added to the pipeline. The route would continue to South Dakota and then through the Sandhills of Nebraska.

It was with the Sandhills that the troubles began for the Keystone XL and the unsuspecting Canadians at TransCanada. Nebraskans were concerned about the impact of the pipeline on the complex ecosystem in that region. With a mixture of grass prairies and sand dunes, the Sandhills are unsuitable for agriculture and unattractive to farmers. As a result, the unspoiled area hosts a large array of plant and animal life, with its ponds and lakes also replenishing the Ogallala Aquifer, which in turn feeds other creeks and rivers.

A spokesman for Keystone provided facts to reassure Nebraskan residents. He explained that thousands of miles of pipelines had been crossing the Ogallala Aquifer without incident for years. However, a wall of opposition had already formed.

One of the principal organizers of the opposition was Jane Kleeb, an activist from the rural town of Hastings, Nebraska. She joined forces with American Indians and other environmental groups who eagerly entered the fray, like Greenpeace, the Sierra Club, and Friends of the Environment. She successfully grew the small political fight on the prairie into a national series of at least 750 protests around the country. Several tribal leaders from the U.S. and Canada were arrested for protesting outside the White House, claiming that Keystone XL posed a risk to sacred sites and threatened water supplies.

As the conflict over the Keystone Pipeline expansion reached a fever pitch in 2014, Cyril Scott, president of the Rosebud Sioux Nation, declared, "We are outraged…We are a sovereign nation, and we are not being treated as such. We will close our reservation borders to Keystone XL. Authorizing Keystone XL is an act of war against our people."

Despite the earlier government approval, the liberal political fallout became too much. President Obama vetoed the Keystone XL authorization about a year later, arguing that the final decision rested with the executive branch of the government, not with Congress. Whereas Americans in 1942 celebrated the record one-year construction of the "Big Inch" pipeline, environmentalists and American Indians whooped with joy for a very different reason. In one year, they had successfully shut down a project worth billions of dollars, one that had been painstakingly planned since 2008.

The Keystone XL project remained indefinitely delayed during the Obama administration. It was revived by President Trump but then canceled by President Biden in the first days of his administration. The Canadian Energy Research Institute estimated that building the pipeline would have provided twenty thousand shovel-ready jobs and an additional 179,000 American jobs by 2035.[59] Instead, thousands of pipeline laborers, welders, truckers, machinery operators, suppliers, contractors, and others were out of work.

The successful campaign against Keystone meant big things for Jane Kleeb, who earned the nickname "Keystone Killer." She was soon elected as chair of the Nebraska Democratic Party to "spur the development of a political movement beyond the pipeline."[60] It also meant that

59. Afshin Honarvar et al., "Economic Impacts of New Oil Sands Projects in Alberta (2010–2035)," *Canadian Energy Research Institute (CERI),* June 2011, https://www.ceaa.gc.ca/050/documents_static-post/59540/81969/Appendices_-_Part_20.pdf.

60. Madeline Ostrander, "This Keystone Activist Is Bringing the Tactics That Defeated the Pipeline Into the Democratic Party," *The Nation,* July 1, 2016, https://www.thenation.com/article/this-keystone-activist-is-bringing-the-tactics-that-defeated-the-pipeline-into-the-democratic-party.

the American Indians were now equipped with a successful blueprint for organizing opposition to pipelines. And they had found a new partner in their opposition: environmental activists.

The battle was on. Together, activists and American Indians were poised to successfully oppose pipelines. Their next opportunity presented itself just two years after Keystone with the Dakota Access Pipeline.

A BLUEPRINT FOR SUCCESS

The opposition to DAPL may have started one morning with a group of just thirty American Indians. But with the blueprint provided by Kleeb, the leaders of the Standing Rock Sioux Tribe knew what it would take to grow their local, grassroots protest at the construction site into an international, environmental call for action.

One of their first strategic decisions was to brand their opposition. They adopted the name "Water Protectors," a caring expression that resonates with passionate protestors. Archambault teamed up with other leaders who identify as "Water Protectors," men like James Iron Eyes, a member of Standing Rock Sioux, and Chief Harry Goodwolf Kindness, an official of an advocacy group called American Indian Movement. In remarks seeking to appeal to a broader base of opponents, American Indian Movement Official Chief Goodwolf Kindness said, "This pipeline affects everybody, not just the Indian Nation. It's no different than somebody putting it right in downtown Los Angeles." The environmentalists cheered on the cause of their new American Indian friends.[61]

61. "American Indian tribes unite to protect Missouri River from pipeline," *Capital Journal,* published Aug 28, 2016, updated Sep 24, 2019, https://www.capjournal.com/news/american-indian-tribes-unite-to-protect-missouri-river-from-pipeline/article_118989ee-6d97-11e6-9942-2b418a1fb0bd.html#comments.

The ingenious moves worked. In just three days, the crowd of protestors grew from 30 men to 350 protestors—and it didn't stop there. As activists swarmed to the cause, the protest garnered national and even international attention. NBC News reported that up to four thousand protestors from several countries, as well as members of three hundred other American Indian tribes, have ultimately protested at the site and in neighboring communities. In fact, the protestors established an entire community of tepees and trailers in the hills of the Standing Rock Sioux Reservation near the construction site. The miniature settlement was complete with a cafeteria-style kitchen, dining facility, school, and an area where tribal members conducted sacred rituals and maintained a perpetual fire. Some protestors even hunkered down and stayed throughout the harsh North Dakota winter.

The crowds excited and encouraged the organizers of the opposition. "We haven't gone anywhere, and we're just building momentum," said Joye Braun, a Cheyenne River Sioux tribal member who helped oppose both Keystone and DAPL.[62]

And build momentum they did—with an amazingly sophisticated social media marketing campaign. They created the hashtag #defund-DAPL to punish the supporters and funders of Energy Transfer Partners, DAPL, and other pipelines. They also identified thirty-six banks that provided financing to pipeline construction companies and encouraged the public and local municipalities to close accounts at these banks in favor of eco-friendly banks and credit unions. It was an ironic move, considering that American Indians are among the largest oil producers and pipeliners in the country and that they rely on some of the blacklisted banks. American Indian tribes and individual mineral

62. Will Parrish and Sam Levin, "'Treating Protest as Terrorism': US Plans Crackdown on Keystone XL Activists," *The Guardian,* September 20, 2018, https://www.theguardian.com/environment/2018/sep/20/keystone-pipeline-protest-activism-crackdown-standing-rock.

owners received $975 million in disbursements from energy production in 2021 alone.[63]

The social media campaign also circulated emotional images to draw support beyond the construction site. The strategy attracted Hollywood celebrities like Oscar-winning actor Leonardo DiCaprio, who lent his support on Twitter by announcing that he is "standing with the Great Sioux Nation to protect their water and lands." He linked to a petition urging the U.S. Army Corps of Engineers to stop the construction of the Dakota Access Pipeline. The heartfelt campaign didn't inform supporters that the pipeline didn't actually cross American Indian land.

The campaign attracted significant political candidates eager to join the fight. Jill Stein, the Green Party presidential candidate in 2016, accused the pipeline industry of destroying the planet. Stein said in a statement that she supported Indigenous leaders fighting the "greedy" fossil fuel industry. She accused the other 2016 presidential candidates, Donald Trump and Hillary Clinton, of supporting corporate destruction of communities for profit. Stein hoped that North Dakota authorities would press charges against the "real" vandalism of bulldozing sacred burial sites and the unleashing of "vicious attack dogs" instead of focusing on the resistance by tribal members and other protesters.

As Stein made accusations of vandalism, she committed her own act of sabotage. In a photograph taken of the smiling candidate, she squatted on the ground with a can of spray paint and scrawled an anti-pipeline message on a bulldozer: "I approve this message." She was oblivious to her offensive breach of respect for the equipment as well as for the men who worked to build the pipeline. She seemed equally oblivious to the implications of her decision to dine with Russian President Vladimir

63. "Interior Department Announces FY 2021 Disbursements, Providing Important Funds for States, Tribes and Conservation Initiatives," Office of Nautral Resources Revenue (ONRR), U.S. Department of the Interior, November 23, 2021, https://www.onrr.gov/about/public-affairs#:~:text=lands%20and%20waters.-,View%20press%20release%20document,-30.

Putin at a 2015 event celebrating the tenth anniversary of the news outlet Russia Today (RT)—when it was later revealed that Putin used RT to undermine American energy.[64]

I can't be sure what nickname the pipeliners assigned to Ms. Stein after the vandalism incident, but I imagine it wasn't very flattering. As it was, Stein was arrested and pled guilty to charges of defacing property at the Dakota Access site, for which she was ultimately given probation.[65]

With the help of outspoken environmental activists like Stein, the American Indian leaders succeeded in their mission to raise furor over the construction of DAPL. But unexpected complications have emerged from the hasty alliance between the two groups.

THE PARADOX OF THE PROTEST

For Americans who remember the protests of the nuclear era, the DAPL protest was ironic. The nation had found in nuclear power a form of energy that, if handled properly, was far cleaner than any resource to date. But the environmentalists had stormed Washington in 1979, chanting demands to shut down nuclear power plants across the country, without any forethought on how to replace the energy. They left the United States no choice but to return to pipelines and fossil fuels to sustain its energy needs. Now, amid the development of pipelines, the environmentalists were still unsatisfied, waving their arms in protest at the injustice of the use of pipelines. Their protests were eerily similar to the 1979 protests, complete with Jane Fonda at the forefront again.

---

64. Bill Dentzer, "That Infamous Moscow Dinner where Michael Flynn and Jill Stein Sat with Putin? Utah's Rocky Anderson Was There, Too," *The Salt Lake Tribune*, published December 21, 2017, updated December 24, 2017, https://www.sltrib.com/news/politics/2017/12/21/that-infamous-moscow-dinner-where-michael-flynn-and-jill-stein-sat-with-putin-utahs-rocky-anderson-was-there-too/.

65. Jon Queally, "With Arrest Warrants Issued, Jill Stein Says Campaign 'Proud' of Pipeline Protest," *Common Dreams*, September 8, 2016, https://www.commondreams.org/news/2016/09/08/arrest-warrants-issued-jill-stein-says-campaign-proud-pipeline-protest.

It was a "damned if you do, damned if you don't" situation.

There were other ironies. The environmentalists claimed to be protecting American Indians from the unfair disruption of pipelines to their livelihoods, but their protests severely disrupted the lives of the residents of Cannon Ball. As the crowd grew at the DAPL construction site, larger numbers of people spilled out of the site and spread onto nearby roadways. A procession of people blocked traffic by traveling two miles on foot on Highway 1806, forcing residents to drive more than forty miles out of their way. Robert Fool Bear claims that the protestors were nothing more than a nuisance and potential menace for the community.

Another unfortunate issue was the mounting tension between protestors and law enforcement. Law enforcement officers in North Dakota were pushed, and one man was hit in the head with a stone. American flags, turned upside down, were waved by several protestors, and signs were made with the words "NO DAPL" written in large black letters. Construction materials such as gates, fencing, and fence posts were torn down, and the pipeline construction activity was halted again.

On August 16, 2016, six days after the first confrontation, a court granted the pipeliners a temporary restraining order against the protestors. The order stated, "Lawful assembly and peaceful protest is the hallmark of our democracy; however, threats of physical harm or violence and criminal activity are unacceptable."

Journalist Jihan Hafiz mistakenly assumed that reporting in North Dakota would be "a walk in the park" compared to her coverage of the Middle East, but it soon became clear that the DAPL protest was dangerous. She was horrified by the response of local law enforcement officials, which included many arrests as well as the use of tear gas, non-lethal bean bag rounds, guard dogs, and powerful water hoses. With temperatures dipping into the mid-twenties, protestors decried these tactics as inhumane.

But Morton County Sheriff Kyle Kirchmeier defended the tactics of law enforcement officials, describing the demonstrations as an "ongoing riot." He showed photographs of protestors starting fires, hurling rocks, sticks, and chunks of firewood at police officers, and attempting to dismantle law-enforcement barricades. Some officers were pelted with bags of urine and feces, and men charged horses at them.[66] He said, "We wanted to make sure that it remained peaceful between the protestors, the workers who have the legal right to be there, and the law enforcement officers. We have nothing to do with the pipeline. We don't put in the pipeline."

Wearing a helmet, shield, and body armor, sheriff's deputy John Moll said, "They're constantly spewing, 'We're peaceful, we're peaceful, we're peaceful,' as they're throwing stuff at you. If you're going to be violent, just say it. Own it. But don't spit your propaganda at me and then try to blame me because I'm doing my job protecting my community."[67]

There were many different factions among the protestors, the pipeline company, and law enforcement. Most identified in whole or in part with the Keep it in the Ground movement, which by that point far outnumbered the tribe that began the protest. As reporters arrived from New York, they faced strict restrictions from each group that influenced the stories that made it to the news. Reporters were denied taking photographs of the Red Warrior camps, where a tribe member admitted to housing youthful members advocating more extreme measures. They couldn't take photographs that didn't portray the camp well, including one scene in which protestors headed to action with makeshift shields, bandanas, and goggles.[68]

66. Sullivan, "Voices from Standing Rock."

67. Sullivan, "Voices from Standing Rock."

68. Renée Jean, "Journalists run obstacle course to tell Dakota Access story," *Williston Herald,* November 15, 2016, https://www.willistonherald.com/news/journalists-run-obstacle-course-to-tell-dakota-access-story/article_f36f61a0-aac6-11e6-bc8f-631edb943957.html.

Reporters were warned not to ask too many tough or uncomfortable questions, and they had to be careful where and of whom they asked such questions. If they were overheard breaching the restrictions, someone might call security. For the first time in their careers, some reporters were challenged to give their "take" on things before being allowed to report on an incident at the protest. They were expected to be protest-friendly.

Reporters noticed factions among themselves, too. When one reporter pointed to a utility line in the distance as the proposed location of DAPL, explaining that the Corps of Engineers had instructed Energy Transfer to construct the pipeline along the same utility easement as the least impactful route, another reporter rolled her eyes and dismissed the information as company propaganda.

In all, the U.S. Department of Justice filed charges against six Native Americans, and North Dakota prosecutors pursued more than eight hundred state cases against people at Standing Rock. The charges included civil disorder, use of fire to commit a felony, criminal trespass, and engaging in a riot.[69] Sheriff Kirchmeier reiterated that the authorities were neither pro-pipeline nor pro-protest but were pro-law.

Sheriff Kirchmeier was prepared—to the tune of $100,000 each week of the protest. That was the cost he estimated was paid by taxpayers for authorities to provide monitoring and enforcement of the DAPL situation. In frustration, Fool Bear angrily appealed to Standing Rock Chairman Dave Archambault to speak up and tell the protestors to go home.[70]

Many of the protestors were extremist environmentalists from out

69. Sam Levin, "'He's a Political Prisoner': Standing Rock Activists Face Years in Jail," The Guardian, June 22, 2018, https://www.theguardian.com/us-news/2018/jun/22/standing-rock-jailed-activists-water-protectors.

70. Jessica Ravitz, "Not all the Standing Rock Sioux are protesting the pipeline," CNN, November 3, 2016, https://www.cnn.com/2016/10/29/us/dakota-pipeline-standing-rock-sioux/index.html.

of state who hijacked the protest, "just adding fuel to the fire," said Cory Bryson. In reality, Bryson said, the pipeliners were not as removed and insensitive as protestors made them out to be. Cory himself went to school with American Indians who were "like brothers" to him. He had compassion and sympathetic concern for his American Indian neighbors, but he believed DAPL could be completed safely and sensitively.[71]

Deputy Moll also noticed the distinction between the American Indians and radical environmentalists. He said he respected the Standing Rock Sioux neighbors, but he had a harsher view of the hard-core protesters from outside North Dakota who "terrified" his community.[72]

Unfortunately, even as the crowds of protestors eventually dwindled and safety concerns slowly abated, the disruptions to the local community remained. Residents were left to deal with many dogs and puppies wandering the area, having been abandoned by their owners. Several of the dogs suffered from frostbite and other health problems including mange. The shelter spent up to $300 to restore the health of each animal. But Tiffany Hardy of Furry Friends Rocking Rescue told *Wildlife Planet* that rescuing the dogs was a challenge because of an even larger problem: the overwhelming piles of garbage left behind.[73]

There was so much trash that, in a sad twist, many residents were concerned that contaminants leaching into the ground would pollute the groundwater. North Dakota officials determined that the waste and debris would indeed pose a hazard if it flowed into the Cannonball River with the melting ice and snow. They hired an outside contractor to tackle the enormous job, which cost $1 million. The cleanup crews worked overtime removing garbage and using bulldozers to push back

---

71. Sullivan, "Voices from Standing Rock."

72. Sullivan, "Voices from Standing Rock."

73. John Sexton, "Dakota Access Pipeline Protesters Left Puppies Behind at Frozen Camp," Hot Air, February 27, 2017, https://hotair.com/archives/2017/02/27/dakota-access-pipeline-protesters-left-puppies-behind-at-frozen-camp.

abandoned cars, propane tanks, and trailers. By March of 2017, forty-eight million pounds of trash had been removed from the protest camp.

Responding to criticism of the trash left behind, the activists argued that the piles paled in comparison to the threat of a pipeline running beneath Lake Oahe. But the dismissive wave of their impact on the environment prompted anger and charges of hypocrisy, and rural residents felt unheard.

Meanwhile, Archambault insisted on the validity of the DAPL protest. "Our purpose is to protect the water," he said. "And no matter what we do, nobody cares. They're going to force this down our throats again."[74]

However, many people have questioned the motives of activists who claim to be "water protectors." Amid criminal activities, violence, negligence to animals, and hazardous piles of garbage that cost taxpayers millions of dollars, are activists *really* concerned about protecting the water?

ACTIVISTS AND ECONOMIC TERRORISM

The truth is that activists are not so concerned about pipelines and water.

That's why it doesn't matter that DAPL doesn't actually cross Indian lands or that an existing pipeline has been operating safely under Lake Oahe for thirty-five years without threatening the water supply. It's why the issue of forty-eight million pounds of trash was brushed away as unimportant.

It's why Sarah Krakoff, a professor of Native American law at the University of Colorado Law School, remained vague when she insisted

74. Jonah Engel Bromwich, "16 Arrested at North Dakota Pipeline Protest," *New York Times,* November 21, 2016, https://www.nytimes.com/2016/11/21/us/dakota-access-pipeline-protesters-police.html.

that the reason for the protests was the construction of oil pipelines "under vital water resources." She knows that *every* source of water is considered "vital" to someone. According to her logic, there is *no* good place for a pipeline. In other words, the millions of miles of existing U.S. pipelines simply shouldn't exist at all.

This exposes the true agenda of environmental activists: to cease the production of fossil fuels altogether, regardless of the safety or merit of a pipeline and the troubling economic consequences to our nation. "Economic terrorism" is a term used to describe their tactics.

This is the real reason that environmental activists have disingenuously latched on to the Native American "Water Protector" campaign. It is not because they actually believe the DAPL pipeline threatens the water. Even the *Washington Post* does not believe DAPL would create a new environmental problem for the Standing Rock Sioux Reservation: it spelled out how activists latched on because shutting down a pipeline disrupts the transportation of oil.[75] The logic of activists is that if the pipeline energy supply chain is disrupted, the oil won't get to market and, therefore, won't contribute to global warming.

They are opposed to *any* type of fossil fuel project. That's why activists have been busy protesting Keystone XL, DAPL, and other projects, such as Line 3, a pipeline carrying oil from Canada into the United States. *The Stanford Review* said that to pretend the pipeline protests are about anything other than stopping oil—such as activists claiming it's about land rights—is "hypocritical" and "deceptive."[76]

Land rights isn't the only claim. Many of the protests surround-

75. Nives Dolšak, Aseem Prakash, and Maggie Allen, "The big fight over the Dakota Access Pipeline, explained," *The Washington Post*, September 20, 2016, https://www.washingtonpost.com/news/monkey-cage/wp/2016/09/20/this-is-why-environmentalists-are-targeting-energy-pipelines-like-the-north-dakota-project/?utm_term=.070801b08134.

76. Harriet Elliot and John Luttig, "The Hypocrisy of the North Dakota Pipeline Protests," *The Stanford Review*, October 30, 2016, https://stanfordreview.org/the-hypocrisy-of-the-north-dakota-pipeline-protests.

ing pipeline protests come from out-of-state people and groups who arrive with all sorts of radical agendas, including anti-oil, anti-fracking, and anti-police.[77] Their activities are funded by organizations such as the Climate Energy Fund, including younger generations of some of America's richest families like the Kennedys and Gettys who say it's time to shift from gradual to disruptive activism.[78] They supply grants, resource support, and networking capabilities so activists can build the movement without concern for cash.[79]

Their approaches vary on how to build the movement, with some radical environmentalists going so far as to prevent the construction of natural gas pipelines in favor of Russian imports. The *Washington Examiner* reported that New England is importing LNG from Russia even though nearly everyone else in the United States uses domestic natural gas. Not only is Russia benefitting financially, but the natural gas travels thousands of miles across the Atlantic Ocean in large vessels that emit carbon from low-grade fuels. All this to avoid domestic gas that would travel a few hundred miles in a secure pipeline. Even the normally left-wing editorial board of the *Boston Globe* decried the ridiculous decision.

Some environmentalists point to their agendas when they vandalize contractor equipment. They say their causes justify their breaking into trailers, blockading critical infrastructure, and damaging environmental safeguards. In 2017, two women vandalized the DAPL pipeline, moving from valve to valve using cutting torches to pierce the steel. They turned to arson and burned valve sites, electric units, and heavy

77. Wittpenn, "'It turned into a war': Pipeline workers thrown into the middle of protests."

78. John Schwartz, "Meet the Millionaires Helping to Pay for Climate Protests," *New York Times*, September 27, 2019, https://www.nytimes.com/2019/09/27/climate/climate-change-protests-funding.html.

79. Joe McCarthy, "Meet the Team Turbocharging the Global Climate Movement," Global Citizen, February 15, 2022, https://www.globalcitizen.org/en/content/climate-emergency-fund/#:~:text=Formed%20in%202019%20by%20three,and%20secure%20decisive%20grassroots%20victories.

equipment throughout Iowa. One incident alone was estimated at $2.5 million in damages. In 2019, more than thirty climate-change protestors dangled low enough from a bridge in Houston to shut down the largest energy-export port for one day, costing the community millions of dollars in lost commerce. They believe their "peaceful" actions are necessary to remedy "government injustices."[80, 81]

Their strategies are escalating into terrorist activities, like the deliberate sabotage of railways that can cause explosions, evacuations, groundwater poisoning, and deaths. In 2020, someone disabled the air brake system of a train and separated the link between two rail cars, causing the train to derail, catch fire, and spill twenty-nine thousand gallons of crude oil in Custer, Washington. More than 120 people were evacuated. In 2021, two women were arrested for installing a rail shunt that would cause oncoming trains to engage their emergency brakes, possibly leading to derailments and explosions. At least forty shunts have been found on railway tracks in Washington State alone.[82]

This may be the biggest display of Americans determined to see their own country lose. Pipelines are not harming America; protests are. For all of the benefits of domestic natural gas, the protests of natural gas pipelines are the most misguided.[83]

States are beginning to fight back. In 2022, Texas approved legisla-

---

80. William Morris, "Appeals Court Upholds 8-year Sentence of Des Moines Activist in Dakota Access Pipeline Sabotage," Des Moines Register, June 6, 2022, https://www.desmoinesregister.com/story/news/crime-and-courts/2022/06/06/dakota-access-pipeline-dapl-protestor-sentence-jessica-reznicek/7535555001/.

81. Erwin Seba, "Greenpeace Members Face Federal, State Charges in Houston Protest," Reuters, September 13, 2019, https://www.reuters.com/article/us-houstonshipchannel-closure-idINKCN1VY1EX.

82. Hilary Beaumont, "The Activists Sabotaging Railways in Solidarity with Indigenous People," The Guardian, July 29, 2021, https://www.theguardian.com/environment/2021/jul/29/activists-sabotaging-railways-indigenous-people.

83. Chris Tomlinson, "More Pipelines Needed to Meet Environmental Goals," April 25, 2018, *Houston Chronicle,* https://www.houstonchronicle.com/business/columnists/tomlinson/article/More-pipelines-needed-to-meet-environmental-goals-12861687.php.

tion imposing harsh criminal penalties for protests near critical infrastructure. The legislation punishes actual damage, the intent to damage, or interference with operating pipelines, ports, feedlots, trucking terminals, dams, petrochemical plants, and other facilities. Texas joins thirty-five states that have considered or enacted legislation restricting the right to protest, making it a felony punishable by fines and prison time.[84] In 2021, one activist was labeled a domestic terrorist, and her sentence was doubled to eight years in prison. She had repeatedly snuck through security fences and vandalized DAPL sites, setting equipment on fire and using chemicals to burn holes in pipelines across Iowa.[85]

The saboteurs claim their acts are in solidarity with Indigenous people, a means to protect sacred land, water, animals, and the next generation. But Native American-owned companies contracting on pipeline projects say it's a false narrative by mostly white protestors who are disrupting work, damaging property, threatening employees, and creating tension within tribal communities. The truth is that most American Indians are supportive of pipelines and appreciate gasoline and plastic products derived from fossil fuels.

Even with the hypocrisy and dishonest agendas, protests like those against DAPL are reshaping the national perception of any environmental project that crosses Native American land.[86] The protestors welcome every supporter—no matter how improbable—as long as the agenda against fossil fuels is advanced. For the first time, the

---

84. Mose Buchele, "New Texas Pipeline Protest Law Is About More Than Pipelines," NPR, Austin, Texas: KUT, September 4, 2019, https://www.kut.org/energy-environment/2019-09-04/new-texas-pipeline-protest-law-is-about-more-than-pipelines.

85. Lucien Bruggeman, Devin Dwyer, and Stephanie Ebbs, "Climate Activist's Fight Against 'Terrorism' Sentence Could Impact the Future of Protests," ABC News, April 28, 2022, https://abcnews.go.com/US/climate-activists-fight-terrorism-sentence-impact-future-protests/story?id=84345514.

86. Louise Liu "Thousands of Protesters Are Gathering in North Dakota—and it Could Lead to 'Nationwide Reform'," Business Insider, September 16, 2016, https://www.businessinsider.com/photos-north-dakota-pipeline-protest-2016-9.

conversation about the pipeline industry has invited a hodgepodge of Native American tribes, environmental activists, ranchers, farmers, and Democratic Party donors. More than sixty-five Hollywood actors, including Leonardo DiCaprio, Robert Downey Jr., Scarlett Johansson, and Mark Ruffalo, sent a letter urging City National Bank to withdraw its support from a pipeline project.[87]

Their tactics and agenda seem to be working. In 2021, Watcom County in Washington state became the first U.S. jurisdiction to ban fossil fuel infrastructure. The unanimous vote prohibits new refineries and restricts existing facilities from expanding.[88]

Professor Sarah Krakoff reflected on why this conversation has been so explosive and far-reaching, generating so much more attention than other protests. She speculated in a *Harvard Civil Liberties Law Review* blog that perhaps the debate over an oil pipeline resonated with the broader movement against fossil fuels and climate change. She also mused that Standing Rock tribal members and supporters were savvy on social media, though she admitted that the possible causes didn't fully explain all the attention. She wondered if there was something else at work but concluded that an explanation mattered less than focusing on next steps.[89]

The professor was wrong. The explanation for the wild support of DAPL *did* matter. And it was later discovered that there *was* something else.

---

87. Janelle Ash, "Mark Ruffalo, Leonardo DiCaprio, Ben Stiller and More Stars Sign Letter Protesting Canada Gas Pipeline," Fox News, March 18, 2022, https://www.foxnews.com/entertainment/mark-ruffalo-leonardo-dicaprio-ben-stiller-letter-protest-canada-gas-pipeline.

88. Oliver Milman, "Washington State County is First in US to Ban New Fossil Fuel Infrastructure," The Guardian, July 28, 2021, https://www.theguardian.com/us-news/2021/jul/28/washington-state-whatcom-county-ban-fossil-fuel-infrastructure#:~:text=In%20a%20vote%20on%20Tuesday,other%20fossil%20fuel%2Drelated%20infrastructure.

89. Michael Haley, "Professor Sarah Krakoff: Standing With Tribes Beyond Standing Rock," *Harvard Civil Rights – Civil Liberties Law Review,* April 21, 2017, http://harvardcrcl.org/sarah-krakoff-standing-with-tribes-beyond-standing-rock.

What she may not have known—what many protestors didn't know—is that some environmental groups were funded by dark money.

DARK MONEY

Everyday activists may not be aware of the connection between environmental groups and dark money. Dark money refers to spending—by both liberals and conservatives—that is meant to influence political outcomes without disclosing the money's source. The influence of dark money is tied to a 2010 Supreme Court ruling referred to as "Citizens United," which gave rise to politically active nonprofits. Today, the dark money phenomenon has expanded beyond politics to cover a range of social issues, such as abortion, social justice, and environmental concerns.

It's the reason the Leonardo DiCaprio Foundation is under the microscope. DiCaprio, whose outspoken support of environmental causes included joining the campaign against DAPL, may be connected to dark money. In 2022, emails showed that his foundation awarded grants to Resources Legacy Fund, a group suspected of donating dark money to fund climate nuisance lawsuits. The watchdog group Government Accountability & Oversight claims DiCaprio and other donors used pass-throughs to hide their involvement in the assault against oil and gas.[90]

Kimberly Reed, the director of the documentary political thriller *Dark Money*, says the influence of untraceable corporate money is one of the greatest threats to democracy right now. Anonymous money spent on issues nobody wants to own is the lifeblood of the environmental movement. According to Reed, donors who don't want their

90. Thomas Catenacci, "Leonardo DiCaprio Funneled Grants Through Dark Money Group to Fund Climate Nuisance Lawsuits, Emails Show," Fox News, August 15, 2022, https://www.foxnews.com/politics/leonardo-dicaprio-funneled-grants-dark-money-group-fund-climate-nuisance-lawsuits-emails-show.

presence known are doing something to potentially undermine our national security, and their networks are becoming more secret and sophisticated over time. The lack of transparency and accountability in funding is deepening the political divide in the United States.[91]

The concern is supported by findings by Big Green, Inc., a database developed by the Institute for Energy Research that tracks environmental grants stemming from fourteen foundations and directed to nearly two thousand grassroots activist groups. The findings show that geopolitics plays a role in environmental advocacy, and the concern for our national security is legitimate.

Big Green, Inc. reports that the underdog narrative by environmental organizations is false: they aren't struggling to make an impact. They outraise the funding of conservative and free-market groups, which affords them a major role in shaping public opinion. Environmental funding has been directed toward policymakers, journalists, academic institutions, elected officials, government organizations, and international institutions. The funding of environmental groups' policy initiatives—which are economically destructive—has been linked to foreign actors trying to influence U.S. energy policy as well as to individuals contributing dark money and benefitting financially from the adoption of environmental policies.[92]

Former Secretary of State Hillary Clinton, a self-proclaimed "big environmentalist," confirmed as much when she said she was up against "phony" anti-pipeline groups funded by dark money. So-called nongovernmental organizations, or NGOs, working endlessly against shale gas—and the security and independence it provides our nation—may be connected to foreign governments threatened by U.S. natural gas

91. Zach Stern, "Dark Money: An Interview with Kimberly Reed," Brown Political Review, May 20, 2022, https://brownpoliticalreview.org/2022/05/dark-money-an-interview-with-kimberly-reed/.

92. "Big Green, Inc. The Money Fueling the Environmental Left," Institute for Energy Research, April 2019, https://www.instituteforenergyresearch.org/wp-content/uploads/2019/04/BigGreenInc.pdf.

production.[93] What is good for American production is bad for their production.

One environmental group that has raised red flags for its convoluted funding arrangements is a philanthropic organization called Sea Change Foundation. Its primary function is bundling millions of dollars for U.S. environmental groups. According to disclosure documents, Sea Change has been funded by its billionaire founder and sole board member, Nathaniel Simons, and by Klein Ltd., a Bermuda-based company that contributed $23 million around 2011 in the form of grants.[94] While the cash may have been intended for clean energy, some were suspicious of Klein Ltd.[95] According to the Environmental Policy Alliance, Klein Ltd. was based out of an offshore law firm with deep connections to foreign governments, which has caused serious uneasiness about the potential for undermining the United States.[96] Because Klein Ltd. was operating under Bermuda law, the company was not required to disclose its donors' identities or countries of origin. The source of its large contribution was essentially untraceable.

Simons eventually denied the allegations that Sea Change is a conduit for dark money.[97] But some people smell something dirty—and it's not only from the diesel fumes from his fifty-four-foot yacht with a 550-gallon gas tank in which Simons commutes to work. Why did the

93. Merrill Matthews, "Investigate Russia's Covert Funding of US Anti-Fossil Fuel Groups," The Hill, March 1, 2022, https://thehill.com/opinion/energy-environment/596304-investigate-russias-covert-funding-of-us-anti-fossil-fuel-groups/.

94. Kevin Mooney, "The Russian Collusion Story the Media Ignores," *The American Spectator,* March 8, 2018, https://spectator.org/the-russian-collusion-story-the-media-ignores/.

95. Alex Lemieux, "Russian Money Funding Pipeline Protests in Southwest Virginia," *The Republican Standard*, July 25, 2018, https://therepublicanstandard.com/russian-money-funding-pipeline-protests-in-southwest-virgina.

96. "From Russia With Love? Examining Links Between US Environmental Funder and the Kremlin," Big Green Radicals, https://www.biggreenradicals.com/wp-content/uploads/2015/01/Klein_Report.pdf.

97. Tate Williams, "Top Climate Change Donors Pull Back the Curtain on Their Past and Future Giving," Inside Philanthropy, July 20, 2018, https://www.insidephilanthropy.com/home/2018/7/20/top-climate-change-donors-pull-back-the-curtain-on-their-past-and-future-giving.

Simons family nonprofit choose a law firm with deep foreign connections, and why is it based in Bermuda?

The alleged connection between dark money and U.S. environmental groups went largely unnoticed by the media. That's why Republican representatives Lamar Smith and Randy Weber wrote a letter in 2017 to U.S. Treasury Secretary Steven Mnuchin demanding an investigation. They said, "The purpose of this circuitous exchange of foreign funds is to shield the source of the money."[98]

Environmental groups aren't likely to lead the way to improving transparency and accountability. In *Cracking Big Green*, investigative journalist Ron Arnold said the total revenue for environmental groups in the United States exceeds $6.5 billion each year. In their desire to advance their own causes and ambitions, these groups are accepting money without asking too many questions, despite the implications for the country. Dreissen said the behavior is typical of greens and other leftists demanding ethics, responsibility, transparency, and accountability from everyone except for themselves.

Environmentalists are disguising both their funding and their true motives for pipeline protests. *The Stanford Review* said, "It is dishonest to say the protesters engaged in good-faith political discourse. Environmentalists are using pipeline bans to stifle oil production in the most blunt way possible."[99]

It's a damning assessment of environmentalist groups, but even more damning is the evidence that has emerged about Russia. Putin is allegedly leveraging soft power—including dark money, environmental

98. Austin Yack, "Russia's Financial Support for Anti-Fracking Groups Is No Coincidence," *National Review,* July 21, 2017, https://www.nationalreview.com/2017/07/anti-fracking-groups-russia-secret-funding-protects-kremlin-interests.

99. Harry Elliot and John Luttig, "The Hypocrisy of the North Dakota Pipeline Protests," *The Stanford Review*, October 31, 2016, https://stanfordreview.org/the-hypocrisy-of-the-north-dakota-pipeline-protests/.

groups, and propaganda—to influence Washington and achieve his goals, possibly shaping the energy agenda. In 2018, the U.S. House of Representatives published a report proving that Russia had been using state-backed and social media to campaign against American energy. Russians were actively undermining our oil, gas, and pipelines—all of which are critical for our national security.

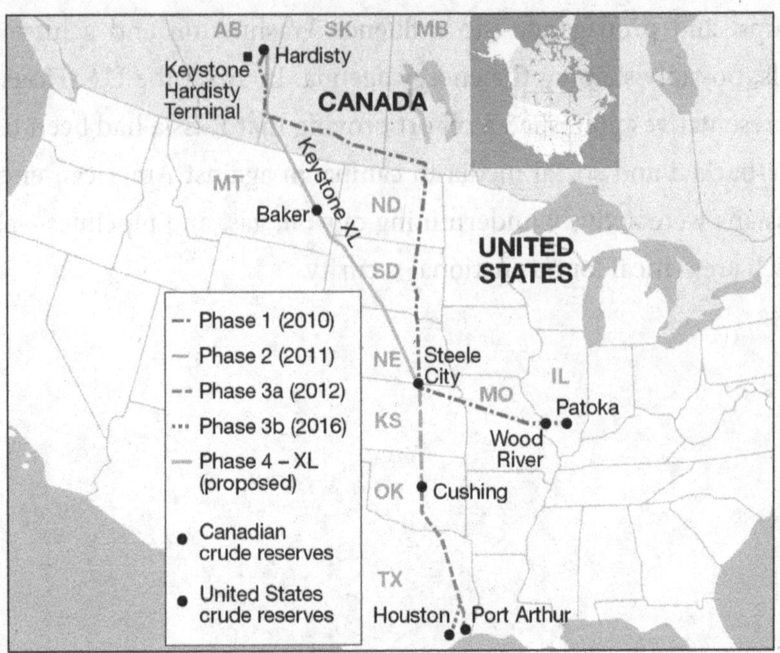

Operational and proposed route of the Keystone Pipeline System. Courtesy of cmglee, Meclee, Flappiefh, Lokal_Profil et al., CC BY-SA 4.0, via Wikimedia Commons.

Protest against Keystone XL Pipeline outside of the Harry S. Truman Building, Washington, DC, August 12, 2013. Photo by Rick Reinhard. Courtesy of NoKXL, CC BY 2.0, via Wikimedia Commons.

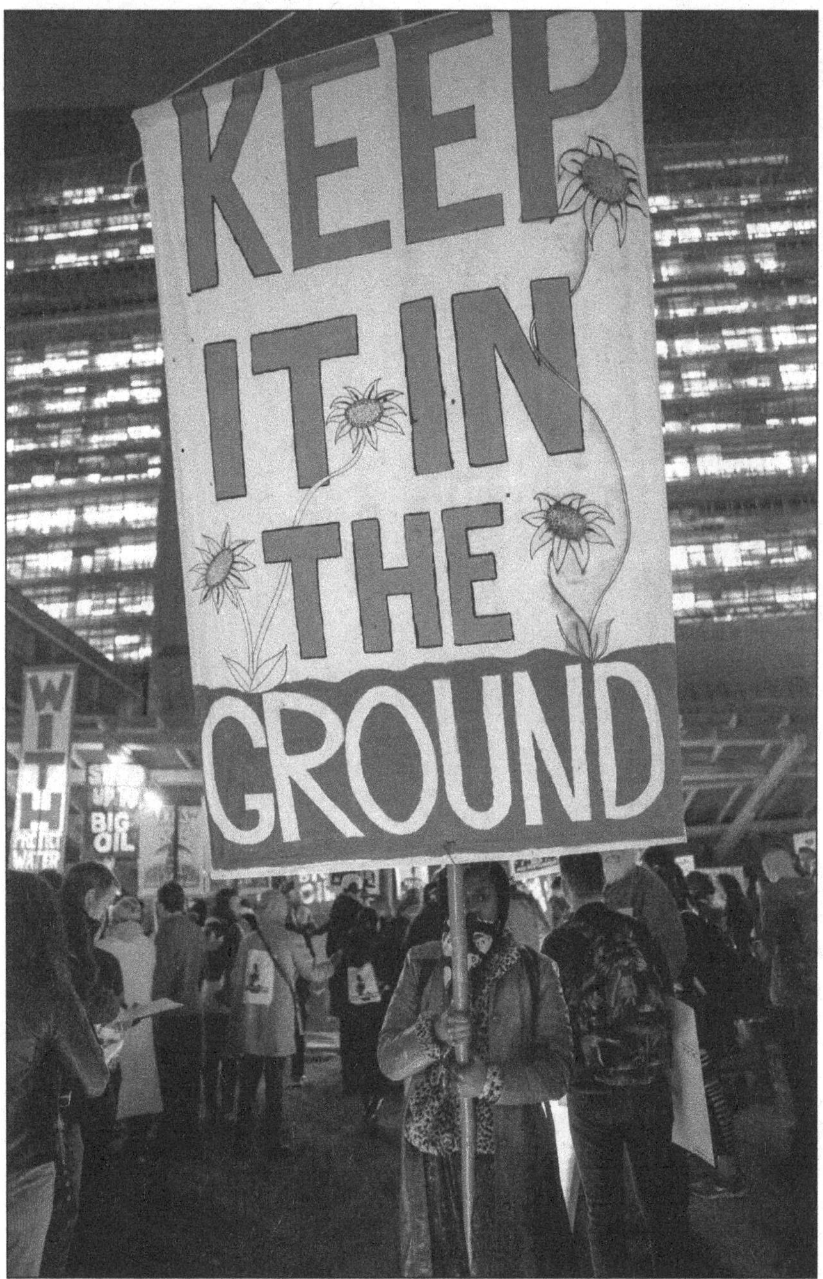

Placard "Keep it in the ground". Protesters against the Dakota Access Pipeline and Keystone XL Pipeline demonstrate outside the San Francisco Federal Building. Courtesy of Pax Ahimsa Gethen, CC BY-SA 4.0, via Wikimedia Commons.

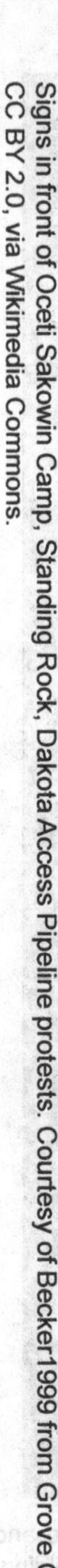

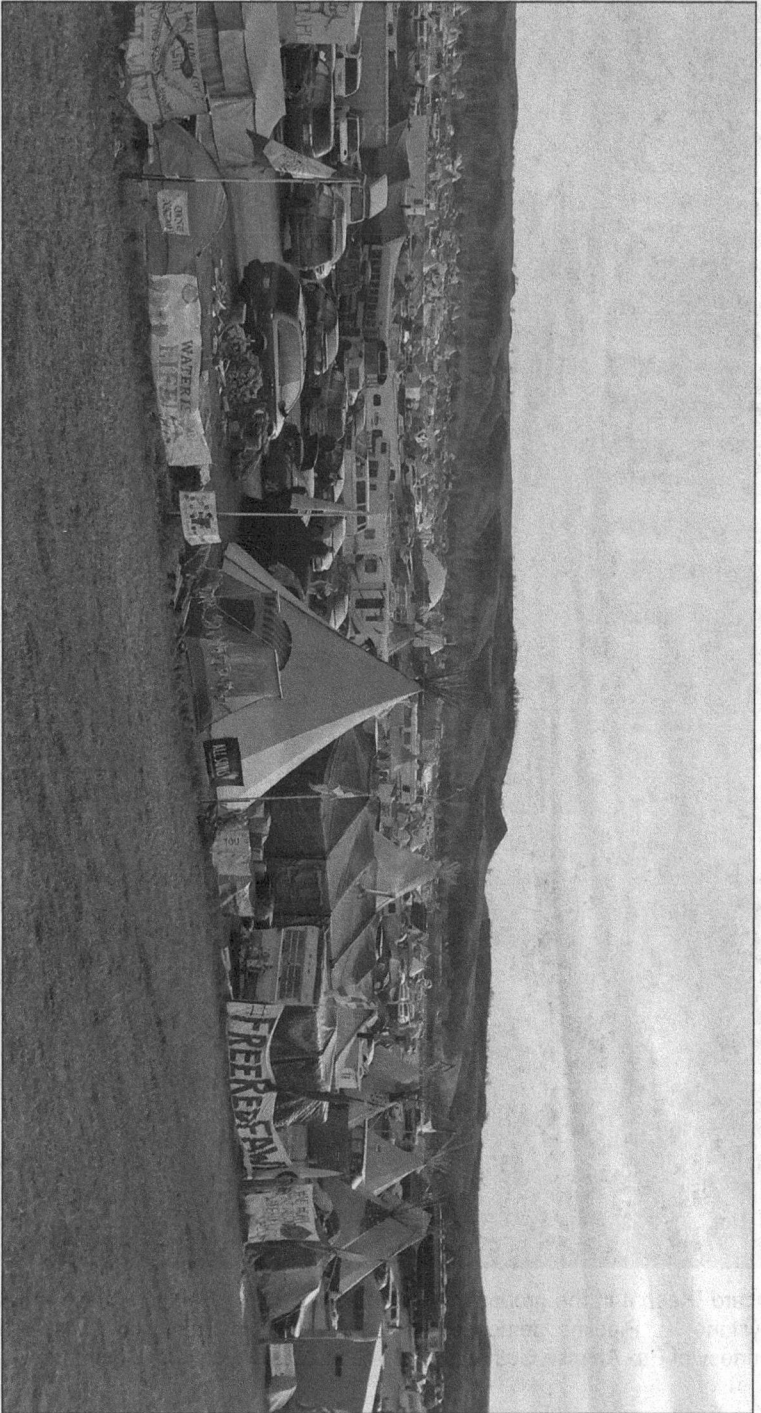

Signs in front of Oceti Sakowin Camp, Standing Rock, Dakota Access Pipeline protests. Courtesy of Becker1999 from Grove City, OH, CC BY 2.0, via Wikimedia Commons.

Protest march in Minneapolis, Minnesota on January 20, 2017. Courtesy of Fibonacci Blue from Minnesota, USA, CC BY 2.0, via Wikimedia Commons.

Medic tent at Oceti Sakowin camp, Standing Rock, Dakota Access Pipeline protests. Courtesy of Becker1999 from Grove City, OH, CC BY 2.0, via Wikimedia Commons.

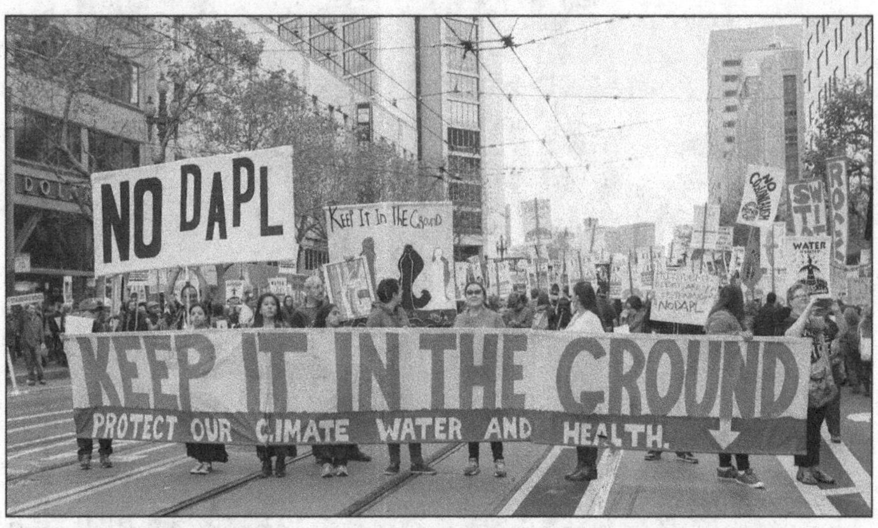

People protesting the Dakota Access Pipeline hold up banners reading "One planet – One people – No pipeline!" and "Water is life." Courtesy of Pax Ahimsa Gethen, CC BY-SA 4.0, via Wikimedia Commons.

CHAPTER 5

RUSSIA'S MASTER MANIPULATION

INFLUENCING THE AMERICAN ENERGY CONVERSATION

"When it comes to controlling human beings, there is no better instrument than lies. Because you see, humans live by beliefs. And beliefs can be manipulated. The power to manipulate beliefs is the only thing that counts."

– Michael Ende

The months leading to the 2016 presidential election were tumultuous for our nation. The big news story at the time was the false allegation that Donald Trump had conspired with Russia to defeat Hillary Clinton and clench the U.S. presidency.

In January of 2023, Jeff Gerth, a Pulitzer Prize-winning investigative reporter writing in the *Columbia Journalism Review*, chronicled an exhaustive post-mortem analysis of the people and sources at the center of the media-led story. Gerth concluded that "journalism's primary missions, informing the public and holding powerful interests accountable, have been undermined by the erosion of journalistic norms and the media's own lack of transparency about its work."[100]

One violated standard was "the need to report facts that run counter to the prevailing narrative." In January 2018, for example, *The New York Times* ignored a publicly available document showing that, after ten months of inquiry into possible Trump-Russia ties, the FBI's lead investigator didn't think there was sufficient evidence. Respected members of the media had eagerly hopped aboard an anti-Trump runaway train that undermined a presidency before it began.[101]

But beneath the ferocious attack on the Trump administration was a bigger issue. The media was so obsessed and blinded by the Trump-Russia election allegations that it overlooked a genuine threat to America—not one advanced by the media with insufficient diligence.

Russia is threatened by American energy.

This startling admission was made by Fiona Hill in the 2019 impeachment hearings of Donald Trump. A former National Security Council official and respected Russian analyst, Hill testified that when she sat next to Putin at a 2011 conference, "he made precisely the

100. Jeff Gerth, "The Press Versus the President, Part Four," *Columbia Journalism Review*, January 30, 2023, https://www.cjr.org/special_report/trumped-up-press-versus-president-part-4.php.

101. Gerth, "The Press Versus the President, Part Four."

point…making it very clear that he saw American fracking as a great threat to Russian interests. We were all struck by how much he stressed this issue."[102]

The media mostly ignored the disclosure. The threat to Russia because of American energy resurgence (due to hydraulic fracturing) was buried under a mountain of manufactured stories of election fraud. The prevailing media narrative about fossil fuels and hydraulic fracturing was that they are bad and therefore unworthy of support and serious media attention.

Pulitzer Prize-winning author Daniel Yergin substantiated Hill's statement. Yergin recalled that Putin "erupted" at him during the St. Petersburg International Economic Forum in 2013 at the mere mention of the words "shale gas." Yergin said, "He launched a broadside, warning against possible shale gas development in Eastern Europe, denouncing shale gas as a grave danger, an environmental threat, a despoiler of land and water."[103]

And Americans, tired of false accusations and media failures, are now less likely to take seriously more allegations of Russian interference in America.

But the Russian interference is real. There were signs of trouble brewing in Russia four years before the 2022 war in Ukraine.

In 2018, no one would have guessed that anything was amiss regarding a bland, unassuming office building in St. Petersburg, Russia. But its inner workings were exposed on February 16th of that year when a United States district court charged Russian entities with "information

102. Philip Klein, "Fiona Hill Says that She Heard Putin Describe American Fracking as a 'Great Threat' to Russia," Washington Examiner, November 21, 2019, https://www.washingtonexaminer.com/opinion/fiona-hill-says-that-she-heard-putin-describe-american-fracking-as-a-great-threat-to-russia.

103. Breck Dumas and Andrew Murray, "Daniel Yergin Spelled Out the Importance of the U.S. Shale Revolution—Before Russia's Attack on Ukraine," Fox Business, March 25, 2022, https://www.foxbusiness.com/politics/daniel-yergin-stresses-importance-energy-independence.

warfare." A Russian company was using the building to secretly run a sophisticated and coordinated campaign that sowed discord among Americans.[104]

The U.S. House of Representatives uncovered the truth in a subsequent report.[105] Russians had worked through its state-backed media and fake personas on social media platforms to confuse the American psyche and influence Americans. In addition to polarizing the energy conversation, they spread propaganda to divide our country on issues such as race, religion, immigration policy, and same-sex marriage. Among the "firehose of falsehoods" was the direct attack on our energy policy and pipelines.[106, 107, 108]

It was a shocking discovery. But a closer look at Russia reveals far-reaching layers of lies and deception. It wasn't the first time the country covertly campaigned in this way against the American people. And it has everything to do with Russia's war in Ukraine and some of the environmental protests around our country today.

DIRTY LENIN

The truth about Russia goes back—way back—to the Russian Revolution. In 1917, the communist Bolsheviks, led by Vladimir Lenin,

---

104. U.S. Congress. Senate. Committee on Foreign Relations. Putin's Asymmetric Assault on Democracy in Russia and Europe: Implications for U.S. National Security. 115th Cong., 2nd sess., 2018. Committee Print 115-21. https://www.govinfo.gov/app/details/CPRT-115SPRT28110/CPRT-115SPRT28110.

105. U.S. Congress, House of Representatives, Committee on Science, Space, and Technology, Majority Staff, "Russian Attempts to Influence U.S. Domestic Energy Markets by Exploiting Social Media," 2018, H. Rep. https://www.hsdl.org/?view&did=808676.

106. United States of America v. Internet Research Agency LLC et al., 1:18-cr-00032-DLF (D.C. 2018), https://www.justice.gov/file/1035477/download.

107. Christopher Paul and Miriam Matthews, "The Russian "Firehose of Falsehood" Propaganda Model," RAND Corporation, 2016. https://www.rand.org/pubs/perspectives/PE198.html.

108. Dan Eberhart, "Impeachment Testimony Describes Putin's Propaganda War On American Fracking," *Forbes*, December 2, 2019, https://www.forbes.com/sites/daneberhart/2019/12/02/kremlin-meddling-shows-value-of-natural-gas-supplies-fracking/?sh=37ba14cb462a.

erupted in frustration over economic problems, the country's involvement in World War I, and the autocratic government. Five years later, four republics merged to form the Soviet Union. From its earliest years, the leadership of the Soviet Union was a stark contrast to the leadership of the United States.[109]

America's first president, George Washington, was credited with saying, "I cannot tell a lie." Although there is debate on whether he really did say these words, the legend is rooted in Washington's reputation for honesty and integrity. To this day, there remains a basic expectation in the United States that leaders should be truthful, a standard ingrained in generations of American schoolchildren.

But the standard was very different in Russia. Honest leadership was not expected by the population because it was not implemented by Vladimir Lenin. Lenin once said, "To speak the truth is a petit-bourgeois habit. To lie, on the contrary, is often justified by the lie's aim."[110]

And Lenin had an ambitious aim: he advocated a society in which all property is publicly and centrally owned. It was an ideology he developed as a disciple of social revolutionary Karl Marx. Marx and Lenin believed that the root of all societal problems was capitalism and its inevitable social classes. In other words, they believed in the very antithesis of the democratic political system and capitalism of the United States.

In the early 1920s, Lenin sought to establish the world's first communist state. But a communist revolution in Russia wasn't enough. He was a fanatic who wanted communism all over the world, the fulfill-

109. "Bolsheviks revolt in Russia," History, A&E Television Networks, last modified November 3, 2021, https://www.history.com/this-day-in-history/bolsheviks-revolt-in-russia.

110. William Safire, "On Language," *The New York Times Magazine,* April 12, 1987, https://www.nytimes.com/1987/04/12/magazine/on-language.html.

ment of Marx's exhortation, "Workers of the world, unite!"[111] He was driven by ideology as well as fear. Lenin worried that his revolution was doomed to collapse under economic failure unless other countries became communist as well. And he was willing to do whatever it took to make that happen.

To bring about worldwide communism, Lenin recruited a special corps of propagandists to form an organization called Communist International. It was a cover and a tool of the Russian Communist Party's international activities.[112] Communist International, also known as the Comintern, successfully took hold in Russia, motivating the opinions of Russian loyalists.

The "foot soldiers" of the Comintern were tasked with pushing the Leninist revolution into every country. They subverted democratic processes, provoked strikes, installed secret armies, and spread government propaganda.[113] Lenin realized that the West could be secretly manipulated to echo the Kremlin's philosophy, so he instructed his new corps of foreign communists not to be "doctrinaire" but "flexible" and to exploit the opportunities afforded by the "rotten" freedoms of the capitalist world. Thus, the communists opportunistically worked through countries, parties, and groups sharing common purposes, including parliaments, trade unions, political blocs, and socialist parties.

To entice supporters from the West, Lenin used money looted from churches or confiscated from the capitalist class. He shipped cash to dozens of groups in other countries so they could start revolutionary movements and establish political parties. In the United States, money

111. Stephane Courtois and Jean-Louis Panne, *The Black Book of Communism: Crimes, Terror, Repression*, (Cambridge Mass: Harvard Univeristy Press, 1999).

112. Volkogonov Dmitriĭ Antonovich and Harold Shukman, Lenin: Life and Legacy, (London: Harper Collins, 2008).

113. Monica Showalter, "To Propagandize The West, Lenin Recruited A Corps Of "Useful Idiots," Investor's Business Daily, December 4, 2013, https://www.investors.com/politics/commentary/lenin-used-useful-idiots-to-spread-propaganda-to-the-west.

was distributed to various parties through several individuals, including American journalist John Reed. The amounts ranged from 209,000 rubles to 1,011,000 rubles, which amounts to approximately $6.3 million to $30.7 million today. While these communist sympathizers stuffed their pockets, the people of the Soviet Union were suffering one of the worst famines in history. More than six million Soviets starved to death between 1921 and 1923.

Of course, the ill-gotten money didn't come without strings. As Lenin's vision for the Comintern gelled, some twenty-one conditions were laid down for socialists who wished to be associated with the organization. Each condition was to be followed to the letter with unquestioning obedience by members. Among the conditions were Mafia-like vows of loyalty, a willingness to carry out propaganda to prepare for civil war, and a promise to do *anything* on Moscow's orders. A good communist was expected to use both legal and illegal means to serve his country. Lenin demanded central organization with sweeping powers, iron discipline, uncontested authority, and unanimous confidence of its members.

It didn't take long for such a conspiratorial organization to start gathering dossiers on its own members to keep out infiltrators. The internal dossiers proved useful to Lenin's intelligence service and secret police force, the GPU, and suspected traitors were "purged" by international roving secret police hit teams. In time, the Comintern became dominated by police agencies.

The communist organization continued despite the long decline of Lenin's health and his subsequent death in 1924. It carried on until 1940 when the Comintern was supposedly dissolved by the new Russian leader, Joseph Stalin. By then, the West was finally catching on to Russia's plans for a worldwide revolution, but the dissolution of the Comintern amounted to only a name change. The organization continued to funnel cash, agitation, and propaganda to foreign communist parties at least through 1991.

With the Soviet Union's collapse that year, it finally seemed that the communist plot to take over the world ended. The country had been plagued by problems throughout the 1980s. Because roughly half of Russia's revenue came from the oil and gas economy, the Russian government lost billions after the collapse of oil prices in the 1980s. The decline in oil prices hastened the end of the superpower's rein. The country was wrecked by Vladimir Lenin's biggest fears: political unrest and economic disaster.

A CULTURE OF LIES

Lenin may be gone, but his culture of lies was firmly planted in the psyche of the Russians. Deception became normal for people, and the habit of lying persists today. As a national pastime, Russians regularly pervert their storytelling with small, white lies.

They even have a name for their unique brand of lying: *vranyo*. *Vranyo* is an exercise in tall-tale imagination for the joy of it, a light-hearted form that suppresses unpleasant truths with no intention of taking advantage of the listener.[114]

"A Russian friend explained *vranyo* in this way," wrote David Shipler in *Russia: Broken Idols, Solemn Dreams*. "You know I'm lying, and I know that you know, and you know that I know that you know, but I go ahead with a straight face, and you nod seriously and take notes."[115]

More serious than *vranyo* is *lozh*, a straightforward lie intended to *deceive*. Some Russians say that ordinary countrymen may not distinguish between the two terms. Although both terms describe a lie, *lozh*

114. Raymond F. Smith, *Negotiating with the Soviets,* (Bloomsburg: Indiana University Press, 1989), 41.

115.David Shipler, *Russia: Broken Idols, Solemn Dreams,* (New York: Penguin Books, 1989).

captures the calculated way Moscow denied plans to invade Ukraine—just days before Russia invaded Ukraine's major cities, indiscriminately killing thousands of civilians.

In Soviet times, Lenin established two acceptable reasons for *lozh*.

The first is to protect the country. To preserve its standing as a superpower, the Soviet system consistently lied to the people to manipulate, maintain control, and create fear and submission. The government refused to admit weakness, so flaws or errors were instantly denied and covered up with embellishments. People who posed with Stalin were erased from photographs when they were later deemed enemies of the state. History was shamelessly deleted and rewritten, and absolute truths were constantly replaced by new truths.[116]

The second acceptable reason for lying is to protect the family. During Soviet times, the people simply didn't have the luxury of holding on to their ethics. While the Party boasted of prosperity and beauty, the people were rotting in the decay and misery of fear, starvation, and war. As they watched their children slowly die, they lied just to stay alive.[117] Those who did not were swiftly carried off to the Gulag—a system of labor camps where millions died—along with their families. If a parent or spouse was arrested and declared an enemy of the state, other family members changed their names and lied to obtain false documents. It was their only chance at finding a job or food. Any attempt at honesty was practically suicidal.[118]

Perhaps Russia's culture of falsehood and self-deception is the

---

116. Marilyn Murray, "Why Lying Has Become a National Pastime," *The Moscow Times,* October 22, 2012, https://www.google.com/amp/s/themoscowtimes.com/articles/why-lying-has-become-a-national-pastime-18754%3famp.

117. Samuel Rachlin, "Propaganda and the Russian Art of Lying" (presentation), *The International Forum on Challenges and Responsibilities in Contemporary Journalism, LRT,* March 10, 2015, https://www.lrt.lt/en/news-in-english/29/96536/propaganda-and-the-russian-art-of-lying.

118. Dima Vorobiev, "Is Cheating and Lying Acceptable in Russian Culture?" *Quora,* September 11, 2018, https://www.quora.com/Is-cheating-and-lying-acceptable-in-Russian-culture.

reason Soviet citizens did not admit they needed help after the fall of the Soviet Union in 1991. Many genuinely believed their leaders who claimed that Russia was superior among all countries, and in the confusing aftermath of surrendering their national identity as a superpower, Russians resorted to the familiar pattern of serial lying.[119] According to Jack Barsky, a former Russian agent who operated inside the United States in the 1970s and 1980s, this is a fundamental difference between Americans and Russians.[120] Whereas Americans are more ashamed by lying, Barsky said Russians don't care.

The culture of lies may also be the reason that Russians weren't bothered when their president admitted to the involvement of Russian forces in the 2014 revolution of Crimea, even after he had previously denied any role. Russians found nothing strange about lying to protect the country.[121]

With the horrifying experiences that the Russian people have endured under leaders like Lenin and Stalin, it's no wonder that lies are woven into Russian culture. The Russian people are not necessarily to blame for propaganda working to warp the attitudes of—and about—Americans. The political leadership in Moscow is driving an insidious Russian propaganda machine.[122] The Russian government was—and always has been—threatened by America and the West and its economic strength, particularly U.S. energy.

Moscow's propaganda was in the new guise of media, both social

119. Marilyn Murray, "Why Lying Has Become a National Pastime," *The Moscow Times,* October 22, 2012, https://www.google.com/amp/s/themoscowtimes.com/articles/why-lying-has-become-a-national-pastime-18754%3famp.

120. Justin Rohrlich, "Ex-Russian Spies Say the US is Losing because it Can't Control Social Media," Quarz, December 17, 2018, https://qz.com/1498526/ex-russian-spies-say-social-media-is-why-the-us-is-losing/amp.

121. Vorobiev, "Is Cheating and Lying Acceptable in Russian Culture?"

122. Paul Starobin, "Looking West from Red Square," *City Journal*, (Summer 2018), https://www.city-journal.org/html/what-russians-think-of-america-16040.html.

media and Russia's state-backed news channel, but it had been cultivated since the days of Lenin as an artful form of lying. And its power is now wielded by another Vladimir—Vladimir Putin, named after his predecessor, Vladimir Lenin—who emerged in 1999 from the ashes of the failed Soviet Union.

PUTIN'S PERSPECTIVE

A former member of the Communist Party and colonel in the security agency of the USSR, Vladimir Putin rose to the presidency almost one hundred years after the Bolshevik Revolution led by Lenin. He had hardly taken over as president in May 2000 when he closed down independent media organizations and gained full control of the media. From the beginning, his singular focus has been restoring the legacy of Russia. He offers the people a new form of Russian nationalism.[123]

His perspective was forged in a difficult childhood, particularly in the siege of his native Leningrad—now St. Petersburg—by German forces in World War II. Although Putin wasn't born for another eight years, he and his family were defined by that "deadliest blockade of a city in human history" that killed millions of Russians, including his one-year-old brother and nearly his mother. While his predecessors Mikhail Gorbachev and Boris Yeltsin talked about the future, Putin fixated on correcting the perceived wrongs of the past and restoring his country's former glory.

He obsesses over the ways he feels Russia has lost its glory and resents the involvement of America. In 2003-2004, his attitude toward the United States hardened from cooperative to confrontational after the revolutions in Georgia and Ukraine. In 2011, he was furious when

123. Samuel Rachlin, "Propaganda and the Russian Art of Lying," *The International Forum on Challenges and Responsibilities in Contemporary Journalism,* presented March 10, 2015, https://www.lrt.lt/en/news-in-english/29/96536/propaganda-and-the-russian-art-of-lying.

Al-Qadhdhāfī was overthrown by Libyan forces after he acquiesced to U.S. pressure. In 2012 and 2014, he blamed America for street protests and the ousting of a Moscow-backed leader from Ukraine. The final straw has been America's support of the Ukrainian shift away from Russia since before 2014.[124]

The United States has downplayed Russia as a threat. In 2012, then-President Barack Obama mocked former Governor Mitt Romney for naming Russia as the biggest geopolitical threat against our nation.[125] But nearly three decades ago, an earlier U.S. president with foreign policy expertise predicted the moves we're seeing Putin make today. Former President Nixon wrote a final *New York Times* op-ed in 1994 that warned us about Russia.[126] He recognized the fragility of its democracy after the fall of the Soviet Union and its vulnerability to an old-school expansionist like Putin. Nixon underscored the connection between the stability of Ukraine and the national security of the United States.

The Russian president, once naively described by George W. Bush as straightforward and trustworthy, has grown increasingly isolated and rigid in his stance against the West. In a 2022 speech, Putin skipped pleasantries and declared the end of a "unipolar era" of singular, global thinking dominated by the United States and our democratic allies. He accused the West of treating neighbors like second-class citizens and blaming its troubles on his "special operation" in Ukraine.[127]

124. Vladimir Putin, "Article by Vladimir Putin 'On the Historical Unity of Russians and Ukrainians,'" President of Russia, Kremlin.ru, last modified July 12, 2021, http://en.kremlin.ru/events/president/news/66181.

125. Natalie Musumeci and John Haltiwanger, "Obama—Who Scoffed at Threat Posed by Russia During 2012 Campaign—Now Says 'Danger Was Always There' with Putin," Business Insider, April 12, 2022 ,https://www.businessinsider.com/obama-says-danger-always-there-with-putin-2022-4.

126. Monica Crowley, "Why Nixon's Prediction About Putin and Ukraine Matters" Opinion, *Newsweek*, March 10, 2022, https://www.newsweek.com/why-nixons-prediction-about-putin-ukraine-matters-opinion-1686536.

127. Ivana Kottasová, Sugam Pokharel, and Radina Gigova, "Putin Lambasts the West and Declares the End of 'The Era of the Unipolar World'" CNN, June 18, 2022, https://www.cnn.com/2022/06/17/europe/russia-president-vladimir-putin-speech-spief-intl/index.html.

Putin privately refers to Americans in disgust as "Yankees" and appeals to his people using old Russian lies. For Putin, lying is part of the job. Many Russians not only accept Putin and his lies, but they embrace him. Despite recent condemnation from around the world for his Ukrainian invasion, Putin appeals to Russian thinking. He draws from the shared trauma of Leningrad and dislike of the West to justify aggression as patriotic and heroic. He's popular because he's feared, and in Russian culture, fear equals respect. Russians want a strong, even brutal, leader who will protect their country, and that is what motivated Putin to invade Ukraine in February 2022 with the intent to destroy its independence.

In a 2022 speech, Putin listed out his grievances against the West—namely the expansion of NATO and the perceived manipulation of Ukrainian identity—that justified a "special military operation."[128] He seized the opportunity to dominate Ukraine as part of Russia's big-picture strategy. He wants his country to reemerge as a world power after the humiliating fall of the Soviet Union in 1991.

Ukraine matters to Russia's strategy for many reasons. Russia has always considered Ukraine part of its Motherland, despite its independence since 1991. Putin sees Ukraine as the symbolic center of his concept for a New Russia, his expansionist dream to restore Russia's glory. Also, the country allows critical trade access to the Mediterranean Sea. The invasion aims to capture the region before it can solidify its relationship with NATO.

At its core, the invasion is about power and influence. Ukraine serves as a buffer between the clashing ideology and aims of Russia and the West. Russia may have been forced to accept Ukrainian's borders to temporarily appease the independent state when it first turned to

128. Jeffrey Mankoff, "Russia's War in Ukraine: Identity, History, and Conflict," Center for Strategic and International Studies, last modified April 22, 2022, https://www.csis.org/analysis/russias-war-ukraine-identity-history-and-conflict.

NATO, but now Putin is ready to crush the democracy and prosperity of Ukraine. The Kremlin is convinced that it threatens Russia's ability to become a global leader.

But as the United States watches the assault in horror, many of us are missing the covert assault that Russia is waging on our nation's energy. Although we may have won the Cold War in 1991, American influence over international order is weakening. Russia is battling Western democracy—and accelerating its attack through a calculated war on truth.

"USEFUL IDIOTS" AND THE WAR ON TRUTH

In his war against Ukraine, Putin is using more than troops to breach cities. He is using propaganda and psychological warfare.

It is evidenced by a Ukrainian man who raged to reporters about the deaths of his mother and stepfather after a rocket hit their home. He insisted his family was killed by Ukrainian artillery even though no Russian targets were in his city of Lysychansk and the projectiles had come from a neighboring city seized by Russian forces. He and his neighbors believe the pro-Russian disinformation channels picked up by their generators, and he wants "Uncle Putin" to get revenge. He believes his fellow Ukrainians are to blame. It's an example of Russia's disinformation campaign against Ukraine.[129]

And there's evidence of Putin's psychological warfare in the United States since 2016. Russia barraged Americans with a sophisticated social media campaign that attacked fossil fuels, pipelines, and energy policy.

Of course, Putin denied any plot to interfere with America. He quickly drew distinctions between himself and Lenin, his scheming

---

129. Thomas Gibbons-Neff and Natalia Yermak, "Russians Breached This City, Not With Troops, but Progaganda," *New York Times*, June 17, 2022.

predecessor. At a forum in 2016, he said that he liked communist and socialist ideas very much and that his commitment to the Party was unwavering, but he attributed the USSR's fall to some misguided moves by Lenin.[130]

However, there was one thing Putin wasn't saying: he has more in common with Lenin than communist values. He has communist methods. Putin brought with his presidency a legacy, handed down from the Comintern, of valuable methods of propaganda dissemination honed by Lenin, the father of Russian propaganda. He brought *vranyo* and *lozh*, using them to serve whatever purpose he desires.

That's why Russia modernized one of the oldest, time-honored tricks in its playbook: propaganda. Using Soviet-style techniques of *vranyo* that had been refined to perfection, Putin spread misinformation and conspiracy theories as a weapon in the war against the truth. His tilted narrative depicted his country as entirely blameless. He painted the West as decadent, amoral, rife with strife and corruption. He was banking on the deep belief that a Russian would be willing to sacrifice himself for an idea while a Westerner was lulled by comfort and success.

But this time Russia had a new trick: social media. Putin took full advantage of techniques unavailable and inconceivable during the Cold War. A "firehose of falsehoods" was spewed at Americans using a combination of Russia Today, social media, the Internet, and the evolving landscape of opinion journalism. The approach was designed to entertain, confuse, and overwhelm. According to a Rand report, it was a "high volume and multi-channel" approach, and it's more persuasive because messages are received in greater volume and from more sources.

Because of the basic cultural expectation for truthfulness in the

130. Damien Sharkov, "Russia's Putin: I've always liked Communist and Socialist ideas," *Newsweek*, January 25, 2016, https://www.newsweek.com/russias-putin-says-he-always-liked-communist-socialist-ideas-419289.

United States, Americans fell for the misinformation hook, line, and sinker. Putin's objective was to strengthen Russia by making America weaker. He was helping Americans dismantle our own country.

There's an old saying that goes, "The capitalists will sell us the rope with which to hang them." Some attribute it to Lenin; some say it was Marx. While the original source is unknown, one thing is certain: the United States unwittingly supplied social media as the rope with which Russia could hang our country.

The disinformation campaign was Putin's payback for the West meddling in Russian affairs in the 1990s, when his country was weak and Putin was shocked by the fall of the Soviet Union. The campaign was also a counter response to the isolation that the United States imposed on Moscow in 2014, which was when Russia illegally annexed Crimea and invaded eastern Ukraine. Afterward, Russia was expelled from the exclusive G-8 club of world leaders and found itself on the outside of diplomatic relationships.[131,132]

Fueled by these old grudges, Putin bolstered his standing at home by disrupting and discrediting America and disuniting the West. And he used "useful idiots," an insulting term supposedly coined by Lenin.[133] The term was mentioned in 1987 by Zbigniew Brzezinski, the former national security advisor under President Jimmy Carter, to describe Westerners who responded favorably to a speech by Mikhail Gorbachev, the leader of the Soviet Union at the time.

A useful idiot is the type of naïve person who, in Lenin's view, is essential to attaining communist goals. The *Financial Post* explained that "by leveraging the sincerely held views and beliefs of unwitting

131. Kim Trail, "Why Russia and the West can't get along," ABC News, December 19, 2017, https://www.google.com/amp/amp.abc.net.au/article/9254632.

132. Sean Illing, "How the Cold War can explain our current standoff with Russia," *Vox,* March 1, 2018, https://www.vox.com/world/2018/3/1/17045888/putin-russia-cold-war-trump.

133. United States of America v. Internet Research Agency LLC et al., 1:18-cr-00032-DLF (D.C. 2018), https://www.justice.gov/file/1035477/download.

agents, the Kremlin is able to exploit polarized issues in American democracy to influence action in furtherance of its agenda."[134] The Russian approach is to get people to act in Russian interests without realizing it.

There were allegations that Russia targeted a particularly useful idiot: U.S. environmental groups. There's no denying that the Kremlin's interests align with the interests of professional eco-activists motivated by money or ideology. When the shale gas revolution began, some environmentalists initially welcomed it. By 2011, waning U.S. production was revived, and we became the biggest natural gas producer in the world. But today, environmental efforts to shut down U.S. energy—reflected in fossil-fuel delays, red tape, and skyrocketing gas prices—all benefit Russia.

Allegations aside, Russia's misinformation campaign was revealed in a 2018 House report. Putin had used propaganda and "useful idiots" to indirectly shape public opinion on American energy.

A MISINFORMATION CAMPAIGN AGAINST PIPELINES AND OIL & GAS

Russia began its campaign against American democracy and energy in 2014. Its first task was to create the Internet Research Agency, an organization for "information warfare against the United States of America." The purpose was to sow great division among the U.S. population and more than two dozen countries. The State Department alleges that Russia has since covertly spent more than $300 million to influence policy.[135]

134. Claudia Cattaneo, "Russian meddling in Canadian oil pipelines uses old Soviet 'useful idiots' ploy," *Financial Post*, March 2, 2018, https://business.financialpost.com/commodities/energy/russian-meddling-another-worry-for-canadian-energy-exports.

135. "Russia Has Spent $300 Million to Covertly 'Manipulate Democracies from the Inside,' U.S. Says in Diplomatic Cable" Associated Press, MarketWatch, September 19, 2022, https://www.marketwatch.com/story/russia-has-spent-300-million-to-covertly-manipulate-democracies-from-the-inside-u-s-says-01663102499.

Senior staff were put in place in spring 2014, one month after President Obama signed an executive order implementing Ukraine-related sanctions. The organization was headed by a management group with a multi-million-dollar budget funded by Yevgeny Prigozhin—sometimes referred to as Putin's chef—who serves as Putin's go-to oligarch for special, unsavory projects. Hundreds of employees were organized into several departments in its office hub in St. Petersburg, where the organization obscured its activities through several Russian entities.[136]

It was like the Comintern all over again, except this time Russians used RT and exploited Google, YouTube, Facebook, Instagram, and Twitter. They used all the platforms on which Americans depended for news, entertainment, friendships, and political discourse, designing social media pages and groups that would attract American audiences. They falsely claimed to be controlled by American activists to address divisive political and social issues in the United States.

In 2018, the U.S. House Science, Space, and Technology Committee provided evidence of how the Russian media campaign contributed to our domestic energy and environmental policy. The Kremlin had unleashed propaganda against the oil and gas and the pipeline industry, and the Congressional report details extensive attempts to disseminate deceptive news on energy policy.[137]

The intelligence report called RT "the Kremlin's principal international propaganda outlet."[138] In 2015 alone, RT combatted America's

136. "Foreign Interference in a U.S. Election Designations; Cyber-Related Designations; Ukraine-/Russia-Related Designations; North Korea Designations Update" Office Of Foreign Assets Control - Sanctions Programs and Information, U.S. Department of the Treasure, last modified September 30, 2019, https://home.treasury.gov/policy-issues/financial-sanctions/recent-actions/20190930.

137. Claudia Cattaneo, "Russian meddling in Canadian oil pipelines uses old Soviet 'useful idiots' ploy," *Financial Post,* March 2, 2018, https://business.financialpost.com/commodities/energy/russian-meddling-another-worry-for-canadian-energy-exports.

138. Drew Johnson, "Intelligence: Putin Is Funding the Anti-Fracking Campaign," *Newsweek*, January 29, 2017, https://www.newsweek.com/intelligence-putin-funding-anti-fracking-campaign-547873.

growing hydraulic fracturing industry by bombarding viewers with sixty-two different anti-fracking television stories and news reports. Additionally, a largely discredited anti-fracking documentary regularly aired on RT around the world.

Over the next three years, thousands more Russian-backed posts or tweets regarding U.S. energy policy circulated across social media, about three posts on each platform daily. The campaign contributed to hostility toward pipelines, including DAPL and Keystone XL. Useful American idiots suspicious of the energy industry took the bait, unwittingly threatening an industry that is part of the very backbone of the United States, thus harming the health of the American economy. The Russians provided just enough truth in their firehose of falsehoods to encourage protests to snowball into an international affair.

A closer examination of the campaign reveals Russia's approach. Posts against DAPL incited fear of oil spills and highlighted the "brutalization" of Native Americans. One post, for example, showed a young girl peering out over an unspoiled prairie and read: "Love Water, Not Oil. Protect Our Mother. Stand with Standing Rock." Another post depicted law enforcement officers clashing with protestors and said, "We're about to celebrate Thanksgiving and tell schoolchildren we made peace with Native Americans while DAPL protestors are being tear-gassed."

Tweets against Keystone XL made claims like "the Keystone Pipeline would transport some of the dirtiest fuel on this planet," or "Keystone pipeline springs leak in South Dakota." The campaign contributed to President Obama's decision to halt Keystone XL and President Biden's decision to revoke its permit again in 2021.

Along the way, Russian operatives were careful to avoid inadvertently uniting Americans by posting contentious viewpoints from across the political and ideological spectrum. Depending on the geographical region of the audience, some posts expressed concern about climate change while other posts mocked the possibility. One Russian account, for example, used a phony Texan identity to advocate for drilling and oil positions. It said, "I don't care what ecologists say. Texas is the top oil-producing state, an' I'm proud of it! Let's douse the Yankees with it and then just throw a burning match."

The Kremlin's information war against the West worked its way across the country, influencing public opinion in both Russia and America. In the Motherland, Putin's propaganda against the West centered on a steady message: he impressed on his people that Americans were trying to destroy their way of life. By the time of the Ukrainian invasion, action by the Russian president was not seen as aggressive but necessary to stand up for themselves.

Meanwhile, in America, the campaign turned public opinion against fossil fuel projects like the Sabal Trail Pipeline and led to resolutions to cut the financing of others, including the Colonial Pipeline, the Bayou Bridge Pipeline, and Enbridge Inc.'s Line 5. The United States became a divided nation as Russia leveraged our own people and resources against each other. Their reason for disrupting the energy market was obvious.

RUSSIA'S ENERGY STRATEGY

Russia has been trying to thwart the American energy market because it's threatened. America's growing shale oil and natural gas supplies compete with Russia's natural gas in Europe. This competition is partly why Putin is increasingly belligerent toward the West—and why the Russians are trying so hard to covertly stop or hinder pipeline projects in the West.

Putin remembers what happened to Gorbachev, the eighth and final leader of the Soviet Union. Following a "golden season" of wealth related to oil production in the 1970s, the 1986 collapse of oil undermined the stability of Gorbachev's government. It spread discontent, hastening his loss of power.

Putin is determined not to fall to the same fate. And Putin is keenly aware of Russia's excessive dependence on its exports of oil and natural gas to Europe. Just as Gorbachev's regime had, the fortune of Putin's regime depends on production and sales of oil and gas. Russia is the third-biggest oil producer in the world, behind Saudi Arabia and the United States. Half of its revenue comes from the oil and gas economy.

The strength of American pipelines could loosen Putin's iron grip on his country.[139] Russia wants to suppress—even encourage the complete abandonment of—anything that would strengthen the U.S. energy market, including fossil fuels and related technology. Russia's economic aim is to protect its market share and maintain Europe's dependence on Russian oil and gas products. Putin resents the United States for the fact that his country is no longer a superpower, and he's determined to change that through oil and natural gas revenue and public influence.

Putin's strategy is to influence public sentiment in the West about fossil fuels. That's why some suspect the Russians of flooding activists with fake news and money. The environmental policies designed to appease activism are undermining the stability of the West, such as regulatory reforms that will discourage energy investments. By not developing their own resources, Western countries are left to accommodate competitors prepared to do whatever it takes to protect and grow their *own* interests.

In addition to using social media and cash, Moscow is also dividing the West with a divisive pipeline known as Nord Stream 2, which was

139. Leonardo Maugeri, "Why Low Oil Prices Could Make Russia's Putin Even More Combative," *Belfer Center for Science and International Affairs John F. Kennedy School of Government*, November 19, 2014, https://www.belfercenter.org/publication/why-low-oil-prices-could-make-russias-putin-even-more-combative.

mysteriously damaged in an explosion in September 2022. The mega project would double the capacity of Russian gas entering Europe and provide a direct link between Russia and Germany, further undermining Ukraine's economy. This geopolitical power play gives Russia leverage to punish wayward neighbors and blackmail European powers. Europe has grown reliant on Russian natural gas to keep the lights on. Even as the West placed sanctions on Russian oil in the first months of war, six European buyers couldn't resist cheap supplies and accounted for nearly half of Russia's revenue from fossil-fuel exports.[140]

Germany is especially vulnerable because it imports about half of its gas from Russia. Its bet on green energy and its reliance on Putin's benevolence is bordering on economic disaster: Russia began tightening gas flows to Germany in August 2022 as political punishment, blaming it on a so-called malfunction. As reserves rapidly deplete, the fallout could irreparably damage the energy market and shock the global financial system.[141] Germany has no choice but to shelve its climate-change goals and switch to survival mode so it can fill natural-gas storage facilities and survive the next winter. The country is resorting to the dirtiest forms of energy it largely phased out of Europe a decade ago.[142] Germany is also considering repurposing parts of the Nord Stream 2 pipeline for U.S. liquified natural gas.

Putin is fighting back against the threat of America supplying oil and natural gas to Europe. In 2022, he signed a new navy doctrine

140. Zahra Tayeb, "These 6 European Countries Paid Russia $40 billion for Fuel in the Three Months of the War, Despite Impending Bans and Sanctions on Imports," Yahoo! Finance, June 19, 2022, https://finance.yahoo.com/news/6-european-countries-paid-russia-080000439.html.

141. Tristan Bove, "'The Whole Market is in Danger of Collapsing': Germany Warns of a 'Lehman Moment' if Russia Cuts Off Natural Gas to Europe," Yahoo! Finance, June 23, 2022, https://finance.yahoo.com/news/whole-market-danger-collapsing-germany-214337451.html.

142. Patricia Weiss and Christoph Steitz, "As Russia Cuts Gas, German Industry Grapples with Painful Choices" Yahoo! Finance, last modified June 22, 2022, https://finance.yahoo.com/news/russia-cuts-gas-german-industry-050233842.html.

targeting our country as Russia's biggest global enemy. He warned of plans to equip Russian warships with hypersonic weapons in efforts to resist our country's power.[143] He's also demanding payment for its gas in rubles and threatening to cut gas deliveries to "unfriendly" countries that refuse. Amid rising inflation, the shock waves reaching the West are a nod to Vladimir Lenin's observation that the best way to destroy a capitalist system is to undermine the currency.[144]

As the threat of U.S. energy persists, so does the Kremlin's incentive to influence energy operations in Europe and the United States. And as they have demonstrated, Russians have used and will continue to use all tools at its disposal—a truth expressed by Dmitry Medvedev, former president of Russia and one of Putin's allies who said he'll "do anything" to eliminate enemies of Moscow. Russia will stop at nothing to dominate energy around the world.[145]

RUSSIA-CHINA TIES

In its quest to dominate the West, Russia has a compatriot in China. When Putin and the president of China, Xi Jinping, met in 2022, they discussed a "comprehensive strategic partnership" and a desire to reshape the international order. They also talked about using information as the primary strategy to accomplish their goals.[146]

143. Anders Hagstrom, "Vladimir Putin Targets US in New Russian Navy Doctrine, Warns of Using Hypersonic Weapons," Fox News, July 31, 2021, https://www.foxnews.com/world/vladimir-putin-targets-us-new-russian-navy-doctrine-warns-using-hypersonic-weapons.

144. Colin Lodewick, "A 100-year-old Quote from a Legendary Economist Explains Why Americans are so Angry about Inflation. Lenin Agreed," Yahoo! Finance, June 11, 2022, https://finance.yahoo.com/news/100-old-quote-legendary-economist-120000017.html.

145. John Haltiwanger, "Russia's Former President, a Putin Ally, Says He'll 'Do Anything' to Make Moscow's Enemies 'Disappear,'" Yahoo! News, June 7, 2022, https://www.yahoo.com/news/russias-former-president-putin-ally-182026860.html.

146. David Bandurski, "China and Russia Are Joining Forces to Spread Disinformation," Brookings, March 11, 2022, https://www.brookings.edu/techstream/china-and-russia-are-joining-forces-to-spread-disinformation/.

The two leaders share a disdain for the West and an ambition for an authoritarian global vision. And China has a history of leveraging information and technology against us: a declassified report on China's activities reveals that Chinese-backed hackers used email fraud to target and breach nearly two dozen pipeline companies.[147] The F.B.I. and the Department of Homeland Security said China's purpose was likely to prepare to take control of the pipelines.[148]

The F.B.I. says that its top counterintelligence priority is confronting China's threat to the economic well-being and democratic values of the United States—a threat that is evident in the fate of Chinese agents. More than twelve Chinese agents who have volunteered to spy for the C.I.A. have been killed or imprisoned in the last ten years.[149]

As the two like-minded countries grow closer, China is amplifying Russia's disinformation on its state-run media. Its people are hearing untruths about the hypocrisy and dysfunction of the West. U.S. intelligence officials warned in an advisory that the two countries would amplify untruths before midterms to undermine the integrity of America, especially the issues and people they see as threats to Beijing's interests.[150]

Meanwhile, Russia has become China's biggest oil and gas supplier. As the world's top importer, China used several of its supertankers to

147. Christian Vasquez and Blake Sobczak, "China Hacking Threat Prompts Rare U.S. Pipeline Warning," E&E News, July 21, 2021, https://www.eenews.net/articles/china-hacking-threat-prompts-rare-u-s-pipeline-warning/.

148. Nicole Perlroth and David E. Sanger, "China Breached Dozens of Pipeline Companies in Past Decade, U.S. Says," New York Times, published July 20, 2021, updated July 26, 2022, https://www.nytimes.com/2021/07/20/us/politics/china-hacking-pipelines.html.

149. James Bamford, "How China Planted an FBI Mole Who Was Discovered Only After Gutting the CIA's Vast Spy Network," Business Insider, January 17, 2023, https://www.businessinsider.com/james-bamford-chinese-mole-fbi-cia-spy-network-gutted-2023-1.

150. Eric Tucker and Nomaan Merchant, "US Warns about Foreign Efforts to Sway American Voters," Yahoo! News, October 3, 3022, https://www.yahoo.com/news/us-warns-foreign-efforts-sway-205807927.html.

ship Russian crude to China despite Western sanctions.[151] And China is moving forward with Russian pipeline projects, tying the two countries closer together in energy and economics.[152] A Russia-China pipeline is expected to break ground in 2024. The project benefits both countries: China is eager to loosen its dependence on the natural gas of geopolitical rivals; Russia is ready to strengthen its oil flows as Europe reduces its reliance on Moscow.[153]

Additionally, China owns the majority of the solar panel supply chain, globally dominating renewable energy infrastructure and materials globally. The country made the majority of solar panels as early as 2010, but its average market share has jumped from 55 percent to 84 percent in the last twelve years. Now China owns at least 75 percent of each key step of worldwide manufacturing and processing.[154]

The country's stranglehold extends to other renewables. In 2021, China built more offshore wind turbines than all other countries combined over five years. And it's the leading producer and processor of rare-earth minerals essential for turbine generators. It's a precarious situation for Europe and North America, which demand more than one-third of the global supply of solar panels but average only 3 percent of each stage of manufacturing solar panels.[155]

---

151. Nidhi Verma and Chen Aizhu, "Russian Oil Shipped to Asia in Chinese Supertankers amid Ship Shortage," Reuters, January 13, 2023, https://www.reuters.com/business/energy/russian-oil-shipped-asia-chinese-supertankers-amid-ship-shortage-2023-01-13/.

152. Chen Aizhu, "China May Oil Imports from Russia Soar to a Record, Surpass Top Supplier Saudi," Reuters, June 20, 2022, https://www.reuters.com/markets/commodities/chinas-may-oil-imports-russia-soar-55-record-surpass-saudi-supply-2022-06-20/.

153. Brian Evans, "A Russia-China Gas Pipeline Will Begin Construction in 2024 While the EU Signs a Supply Deal with Azerbaijan, Reports Say," Business Insider, July 18, 2022, https://www.businessinsider.in/stock-market/news/a-russia-china-gas-pipeline-will-begin-construction-in-2024-while-the-eu-signs-a-supply-deal-with-azerbaijan-reports-say/articleshow/92963514.cms.

154. Niccolo Conte, "Visualizing China's Dominance in the Solar Panel Supply Chain," Visual Capitalist, August 30, 2022, https://www.visualcapitalist.com/visualizing-chinas-dominance-in-the-solar-panel-supply-chain/.

155. Conte "Visualizing China's Dominance in the Solar Panel Supply Chain."

For Russia and China, the energy campaign has everything to do with their future. If we're going to outlast the energy strategies of our competitors, the United States needs to look at our playbook from the past.

LESSONS FROM OUR HISTORY

Long before the Ukrainian invasion, Fiona Hill and Daniel Yergin saw the truth: Putin's reaction to hydraulic fracturing and shale was about his ability to leverage gas supply for his geopolitical objectives. America's shale revolution is important for U.S. national security and for European allies, which poses a challenge for Russia. U.S. shale gas eliminated the need for importing LNG to the United States. Our country has now redirected domestic natural gas supplies to Europe and reinforced our ability to compete with Russian gas.

That's why Russia is determined to undermine U.S. LNG. American LNG exports to Europe would undermine the grand plan for Russian dominance of the European energy industry, a plan carefully laid for nearly twenty-five years under Putin's rule. Shale could ruin everything. Putin may have been too late to stop the U.S. shale revolution, but Putin won't make the same mistake in Europe. He began a massive propaganda campaign against hydraulic fracturing to stop English shale development before it got started—even though England sits on top of one of the largest shale basins in Europe.[156] And it worked: the U.K. doesn't allow hydraulic fracturing.

The reason energy matters so much to Russia is because, for a country so large, it's a small fish in the global economy. Russia's economy is only about the size of Spain or the state of Texas, but half of its GDP

156. Matt Ridley, "The Plot Against Fracking," The Critic, December 2019, https://thecritic.co.uk/issues/december-2019/the-plot-against-fracking/.

depends on the sale of fossil fuels to Europe. Economist Jason Furman described the country as "a big gas station," which is partially true. It's more like a super convenience store on a busy corner that supplements its sale of fossil fuels with sales of alcohol, tobacco, and sundry food items across the economic trade routes of Europe. It's all part of Russia's plan to dominate surrounding regions. According to Yale historian Timothy Snyder, the impact of the war on Ukraine's global food supply and the resulting food insecurity is part of Putin's "hunger politics," similar to that of his predecessor, Lenin. Snyder said the Russian president aims to starve some countries as the next stage in his war in Europe.[157]

Although technically a democracy, no serious observer would call Russia that today. Its leaders operate it like a mafia family business, with Putin as their godfather. He doesn't hesitate to intimidate, poison, or kill political rivals. As bodies pile up of Putin critics who died violently or suspiciously, his motto could be, "Workers unite…or else." He's indifferent to the suffering of his own people, as one Russian observed in a phone call to his wife. During his call, which was reportedly intercepted by Ukrainian intelligence, the soldier said forces opened fire on a Russian town to provoke anti-Ukrainian sentiment.

Make no mistake: Putin is at war with democracy and the West. It is a different type of war, a soft war, but a war nonetheless. His tactics are sometimes hard to identify and pin down, but a mosaic of evidence serves as a smoking gun in Putin's war against America.

He viciously attacks democratic competitors like his nemesis, anti-corruption activist Alexei Navalny, who was poisoned and later imprisoned in solitary confinement. At least five prominent Russian businessmen died by "suicide" in 2022, including a Russian energy

---

157. Kelsey Vlamis, "Putin Is 'Preparing to Starve Much of the Developing World' in order to Win Russia's War in Ukraine, Yale Historian Says," Business Insider, June 11, 2022, https://www.businessinsider.com/putin-preparing-to-starve-developing-world-ukraine-war-yale-historian-2022-6.

boss whose body washed ashore after falling overboard from a boat.[158] His death is one in a recent string of mysterious deaths, such as that of the chairman of Russian oil and gas giant Lukoil who criticized Putin's invasion of Ukraine. A statement said the chairman died after a "severe illness," but it didn't mention that he fell six stories from a hospital window.[159] Coincidentally, four others died in similar ways in recent years, all falling from balconies or down stairs.[160,161] While their deaths are unexplained, it seems anything above the first floor could be hazardous to a Russian critic's health.

Putin harbors a deep resentment toward anyone who gets in the way of his goals, including America for its role in the decline of the former Soviet Union as a respected and feared world power. His resentment only deepens as his country remains vulnerable to commodity price declines and the reemergence of the United States as the world's largest producer of oil and gas. He curses technological breakthroughs by the U.S. oil and gas industry like hydraulic fracturing and LNG. Both inventions mean competition for Europe, Putin's largest customer.

Oil and gas developments like pipelines, hydraulic fracturing, and LNG *are* existential threats—but not to the environment like Putin claims. They are existential threats to Putin himself. They threaten his

158. Mia Jankowicz, "Putin Ally Falls into the Sea, Adding to List of Mysterious Deaths Suffered by Russian Energy Bosses," Business Insider, September 13, 2022, https://www.businessinsider.in/international/news/another-russian-energy-boss-has-died-in-mysterious-circumstances-after-putin-ally-falls-off-boat-into-sea/articleshow/94178643.cms.

159. Rhoda Kwan, "Head of Russian Oil Giant that Criticized Ukraine War Dies After Reportedly Falling from Hospital Window," NBC News, September 1, 2022, https://www.nbcnews.com/news/world/russian-lukoil-exec-dies-falling-hospital-window-reports-say-rcna45823.

160. Mia Jankowicz, "A Kremlin Ally Died Falling Down the Stairs, Report Says—The Latest in a Series of Unexplained Deaths Among Prominent Russians," Business Insider, September 22, 2022, https://www.businessinsider.com/another-russian-official-dies-reportedly-after-falling-down-stairs-2022-9.

161. Rhoda Kwan, "Head of Russian Oil Giant that Criticized Ukraine War Dies After Reportedly Falling from Hospital Window," NBC News, September 1, 2022, https://www.nbcnews.com/news/world/russian-lukoil-exec-dies-falling-hospital-window-reports-say-rcna45823.

presidency and his carefully constructed dream to return Russia to its former glory and position in the world.

That's what makes an energy plan like the Green New Deal dangerous (see Exhibit A in the Appendix). It is shaped to appease activism and ignore our national strengths. It leaves the United States vulnerable. And it's exactly what Russia wants in its war against U.S. energy.

The threat of the U.S. oil and gas industry to Russia cannot be overstated. Nor can Putin's determination to weaken NATO and destroy America, starting with our energy industry. With Ukraine's 2014 shift toward the West and away from Russia, Putin is determined to maintain his grip on the European market. His cryptic warnings about the "painful" fallout of moving away from Russian oil should not be taken lightly. He is prepared to use every dirty trick to eliminate competition and increase Europe's dependence on Russian natural gas, regardless of human cost.[162]

That's why oil, gas, and pipelines are critical in protecting Western democracy from enemies. Our past should inspire us—the government, energy firms, and Americans—to collaborate on solutions that advance our country while preserving our environment.

Our history should give us the courage to reexamine the prevailing narrative about American energy to find the best path forward for our nation.

162. Nathan Hodge, "Restoration of Empire is the Endgame for Russia's Vladimir Putin," CNN, June 11, 2022, https://www.cnn.com/2022/06/10/europe/russia-putin-empire-restoration-endgame-intl-cmd/index.html.

Vladimir Lenin. Courtesy of Pavel Semyonovich Zhukov (1870-1942), Public domain, via Wikimedia Commons.

The Internet Research Agency building, dubbed the Russian troll factory, is seen at Savushkina Street in St. Petersburg, Russia. The building is now for rent. Courtesy of Charles Maynes, Public domain, via Wikimedia Commons.

Russian activist Maria Butina, who was convicted in 2018 of acting as an unregistered foreign agent of Russia within the United States. Courtsey of Rodrigo Fernández, CC BY-SA 4.0, via Wikimedia Commons.

Daniel Yergin, Chairman, IHS CERA, USA and Oil & Gas Community Leader 2012; Global Agenda Council on Energy Security is captured during the session 'Global Energy Outlook' at the Annual Meeting 2012 of the World Economic Forum at the Davos Congress Centre in Davos, Switzerland, January 28, 2012. Courtesy of World Economic Forum, CC BY-SA 2.0, via Wikimedia Commons.

United States House of Representatives
Committee on Science, Space, and Technology

Majority Staff Report

Russian Attempts to Influence U.S. Domestic Energy Markets by Exploiting Social Media

March 1, 2018

2018 U.S. House Science, Space, and Technology Committee staff report uncovering Russia's extensive efforts to influence U.S. energy markets through divisive and inflammatory posts on social media platforms. The report details Russia's motives in interfering with U.S. energy markets and influencing domestic energy policy, and its manipulation of Americans via social media propaganda. The report includes examples of Russian-propagated social media posts. From *Homeland Security Library*, https://www.hsdl.org/?view&did=808676

Example of a Russian social media post aimed at influencing U.S. energy policy. Courtesy of U.S. Congress, House of Representatives, Committee on Science, Space, and Technology, Majority Staff, Russian Attempts to Influence U.S. Domestic Energy Markets by Exploiting Social Media, 2018, H. Rep. https://www.hsdl.org/?view&did=808676.

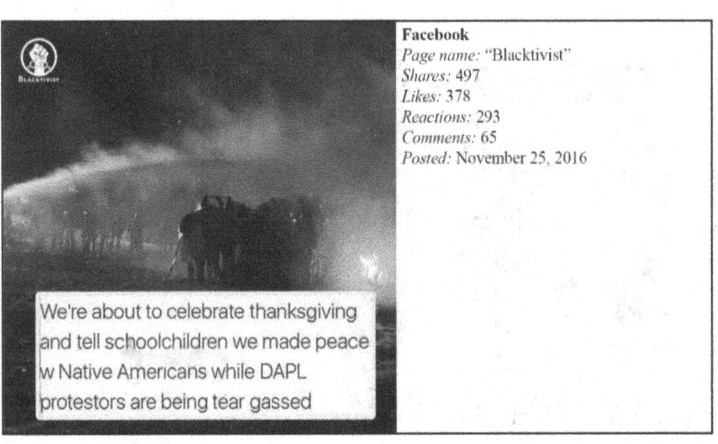

We're about to celebrate thanksgiving and tell schoolchildren we made peace w Native Americans while DAPL protestors are being tear gassed
Facebook
Page name: "Blacktivist"
Shares: 497
Likes: 378
Reactions: 293
Comments: 65
Posted: November 25, 2016

Example of a Russian social media post aimed at influencing U.S. energy policy. Courtesy of U.S. Congress, House of Representatives, Committee on Science, Space, and Technology, Majority Staff, Russian Attempts to Influence U.S. Domestic Energy Markets by Exploiting Social Media, 2018, H. Rep. https://www.hsdl.org/?view&did=808676.

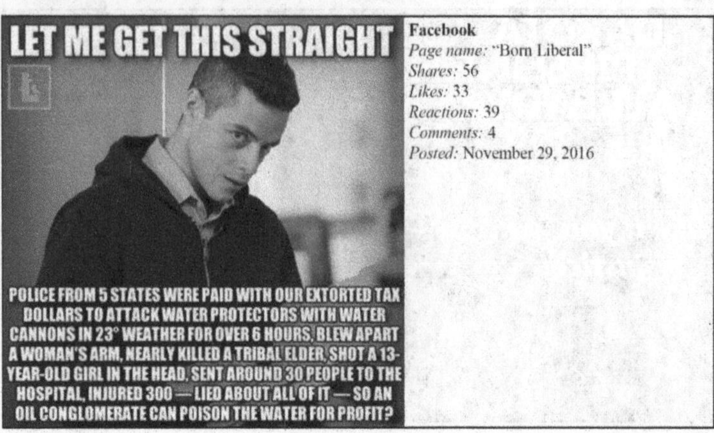

Example of a Russian social media post aimed at influencing U.S. energy policy. Courtesy of U.S. Congress, House of Representatives, Committee on Science, Space, and Technology, Majority Staff, Russian Attempts to Influence U.S. Domestic Energy Markets by Exploiting Social Media, 2018, H. Rep. https://www.hsdl.org/?view&did=808676.

Example of a Russian social media post aimed at influencing U.S. energy policy. Courtesy of U.S. Congress, House of Representatives, Committee on Science, Space, and Technology, Majority Staff, Russian Attempts to Influence U.S. Domestic Energy Markets by Exploiting Social Media, 2018, H. Rep. https://www.hsdl.org/?view&did=808676.

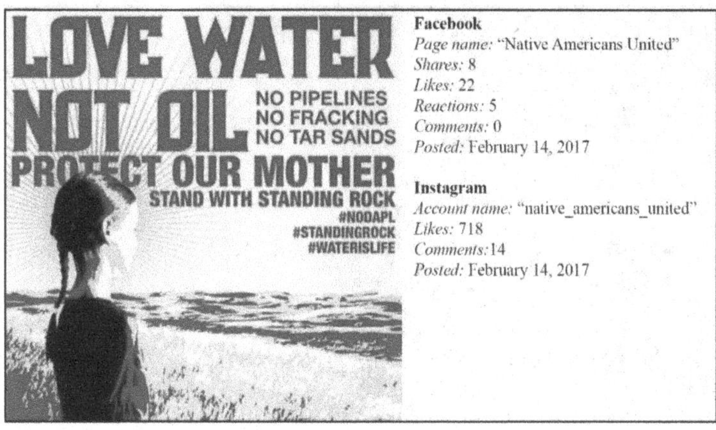

Example of a Russian social media post aimed at influencing U.S. energy policy. Courtesy of U.S. Congress, House of Representatives, Committee on Science, Space, and Technology, Majority Staff, Russian Attempts to Influence U.S. Domestic Energy Markets by Exploiting Social Media, 2018, H. Rep. https://www.hsdl.org/?view&did=808676.

NO
PIPELINE
Facebook
Page name: "Native Americans United"
Shares: 5
Likes: 13
Reactions: 6
Comments: 0
Posted: February 1, 2017
Instagram
Account name: "native_americans_united"
Likes: 473
Comments: 7
Posted: February 2, 2017

Example of a Russian social media post aimed at influencing U.S. energy policy. Courtesy of U.S. Congress, House of Representatives, Committee on Science, Space, and Technology, Majority Staff, Russian Attempts to Influence U.S. Domestic Energy Markets by Exploiting Social Media, 2018, H. Rep. https://www.hsdl.org/?view&did=808676.

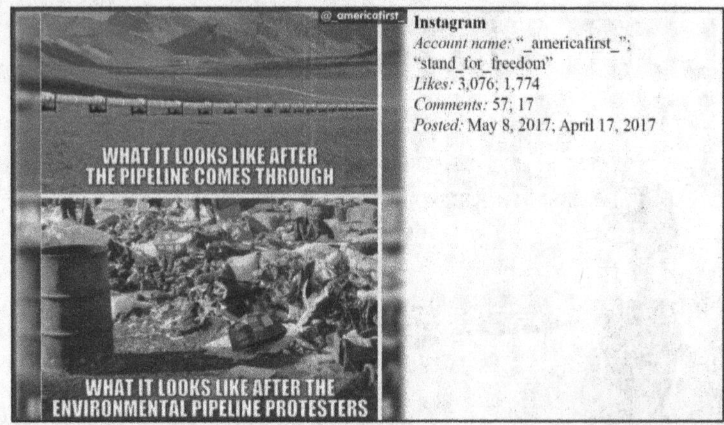

Example of a Russian social media post aimed at influencing U.S. energy policy. Courtesy of U.S. Congress, House of Representatives, Committee on Science, Space, and Technology, Majority Staff, Russian Attempts to Influence U.S. Domestic Energy Markets by Exploiting Social Media, 2018, H. Rep. https://www.hsdl.org/?view&did=808676.

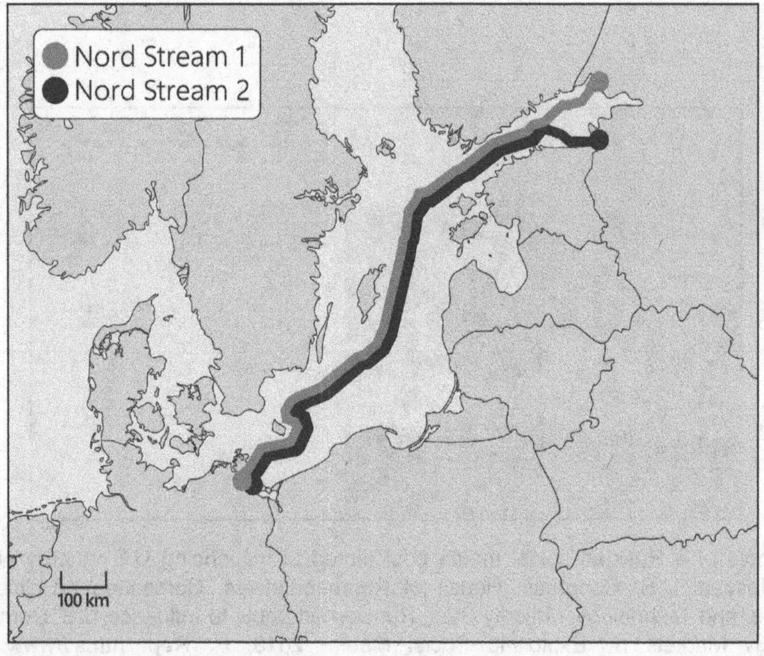

Locations of Nord Stream Pipelines 1 and 2. Courtesy of FactsWithoutBias1, CC BY-SA 4.0, via Wikimedia Commons.

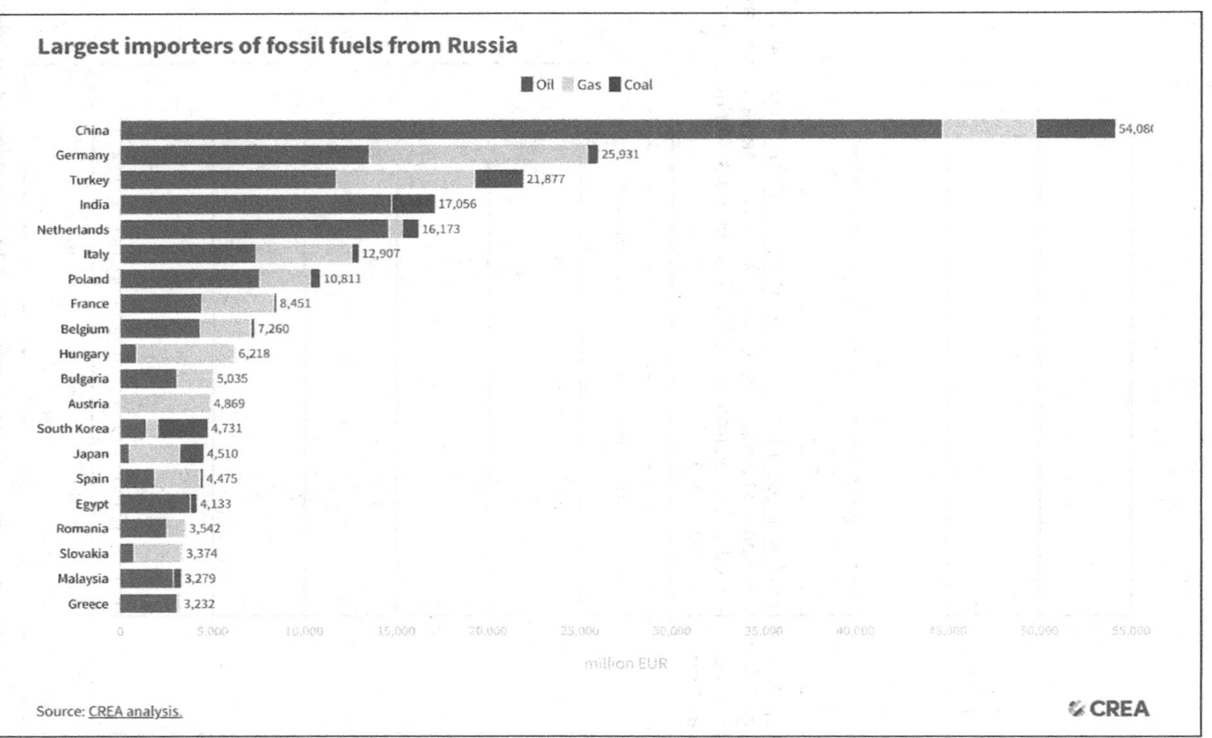

Largest importers of fossil fuels from Russia. Courtesy of the Centre for Research on Energy and Clean Air (CREA).

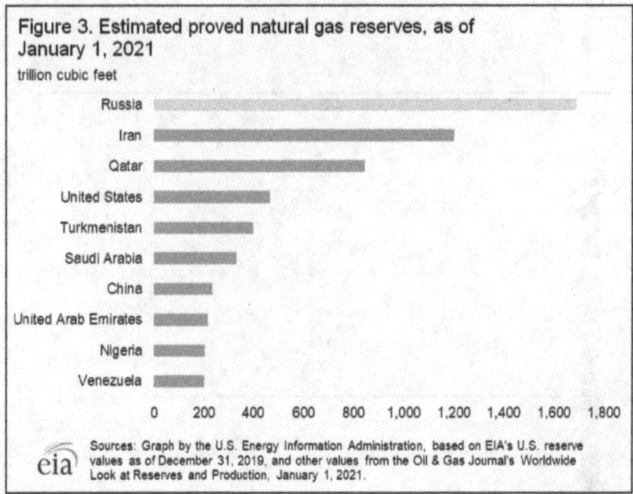

Estimated proved natural gas reserves, as of January 1, 2021. Courtesy of the U.S. Energy Information Administration, based on EIA's U.S. reserve values as of December 31, 2019, and other values from the Oil & Gas Journal's Worldwide Look at Reserves and Production, January 1, 2021.

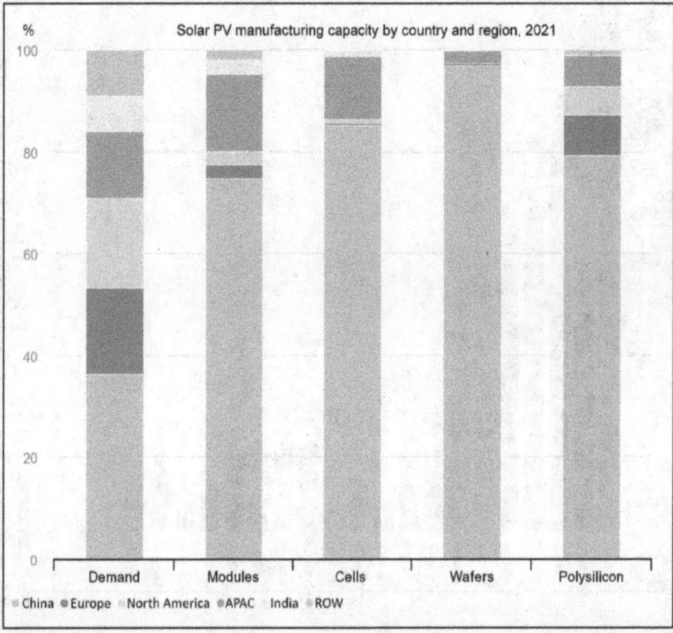

Solar PV manufacturing capacity by country/region, showing demand as well as manufacturing capacity of various components, n.b. APAC stands for *Asia-Pacific, excluding India*; ROW stands for *rest of the world*. Courtesy of IEA, Solar PV manufacturing capacity by country and region, 2021, IEA, Paris https://www.iea.org/data-and-statistics/charts/solar-pv-manufacturing-capacity-by-country-and-region-2021, IEA. Licence: CC BY 4.0.

CHAPTER 6

RENEWABLE ENERGY SOLUTIONS

RENEWABLES AREN'T AS CLEAN, GREEN, OR SAFE AS PEOPLE THINK

"God has cared for these trees, saved them from drought, disease, avalanches, and a thousand tempests and floods. But he cannot save them from fools."

– John Muir, founder of the Sierra Club[163]

163. John Muir, *John Muir: His Life and Letters and Other Writings,* Terry Gifford (1996), The Mountaineers Books, p.373.

RENEWABLES REQUIRE LAND — LOTS OF LAND

Renewable sources of energy are touted as the shiny new answer to replace fossil fuels. While environmentalists protest oil and gas pipelines, Americans are increasingly infatuated by electric cars, mobile phones, and solar power.

That's why President Joe Biden doubled down on his promises at his international climate summit in 2022. He laid out his environmental goals for the United States, including cutting greenhouse gas emissions in half by 2030 and achieving net-zero carbon by 2050.

What President Biden didn't lay out was the amount of land required to reach his goals. He didn't say that his goals may require much more land than is currently dedicated to energy. While researchers debate on how much, one thing is certain: the U.S. will need to reassess land use.

After President Biden's summit, *Bloomberg News* estimated what it'll take to achieve Biden's net-zero vision by 2050. Data was analyzed from the U.S. Departments of Energy, Interior, and Agriculture and the Nuclear Regulatory Commission. *Bloomberg* also looked at five scenarios by Princeton University's Net-Zero America project, focusing on the two scenarios requiring the least and most amounts of land. Both scenarios make clear the investments, challenges, and benefits.[164]

The Current Scenario

The U.S. economy currently needs about eighty-one million acres of land, according to *Bloomberg News,* to fuel its electric grid, home-heating, manufacturing, and transportation, the last of which consumes

164. Content throughout this section was derived from Dave Merrill, "The U.S. Will Need a Lot of Land for a Zero-Carbon Economy," published April 29, 2021, updated June 3, 2021, Bloomberg, https://www.bloomberg.com/graphics/2021-energy-land-use-economy/ and Eric Larson et al., "Net-Zero America: Potential Pathways, Infrastructure, and Impacts," Princeton University, Princeton, NJ, 29 October 2021, https://netzeroamerica.princeton.edu/the-report.

two-thirds of our energy resources. Altogether, our energy footprint is about the size of Iowa and Missouri combined, or 4 percent of the contiguous United States.

The Most Land-Intensive Scenario: More Than 30,000 Acres Per Day

The most land-intensive plan of Princeton's scenarios eliminates all fossil fuels and nuclear plants by 2050. In their place, wind and solar energy would provide 98 percent of the electricity to power vehicles, homes, and industrial processes. A backup combination of batteries, hydropower, and combustion turbines burning synthetic fuels and hydrogen would be used to boost the grid when demand peaks.

Bloomberg News estimates that this scenario quadruples the size of the U.S. energy footprint. We would need to acquire, clear, pave, or repurpose an additional 267 million acres of land, the majority of which would be used to build wind farms, a land mass equal to the states of Arkansas, Iowa, Kansas, Missouri, Nebraska, and Oklahoma. That's because wind farms, solar installations, and other forms of clean power take up more space on a per-watt basis than their fossil-fuel sources. *Bloomberg News* compared the footprints of a natural-gas power plant and a wind farm generating the same amounts of power, noting that the power plant would fit onto a single city block while the wind farm would require turbines spread over thirteen square miles. We don't have that kind of land to squander when we consider that the global population is likely to increase by 2.3 billion people in forty years.[165]

To live up to the Green New Deal, we better get busy. A plan that relies on wind and solar energy by 2050 means we'd have to clear land and install windmills and solar panels at a rate of 30,563 acres *per day*, working six days a week for the next twenty-eight years. Ramping up

165. Robert Bryce, "Get Dense," *City Journal*, Winter 2012, https://www.city-journal.org/html/get-dense-13448.html.

production of solar and wind farms in our country also requires large volumes of water and the paving of vast areas of land with steel and silicon for clean manufacturing, such as battery facilities, solar panel factories, and wind turbine factories.

The Least Land-Intensive Scenario

To achieve a carbon-free economy by 2050 using the least amount of land, Princeton says that the current pace of wind and solar development would remain constant—no more than 1.4 times the record rate of installation seen in the U.S. to date—but our reliance on wind and solar energy would need to drop from 98 percent to 44 percent. The majority of our power would come from emission-free nuclear plants and natural gas plants outfitted with systems to capture the carbon dioxide before it escapes into the atmosphere. That's because natural gas and nuclear energy are very compact power sources. *Bloomberg News* noted the difference in footprints between nuclear and wind energy: a one-gigawatt reactor operating on 1,000 acres has the same energy capacity as a wind farm spanning 100,000 acres.

Even with compact power sources, this scenario presents serious land challenges. Carbon capture and nuclear power would grow at unprecedented rates. We'd need to build a network of carbon-capture pipelines and storage facilities to support new, emission-free natural-gas-fired power plants, which *Bloomberg News* estimated would require land easements totaling 500,000 acres, about half the size of Rhode Island, and $100 billion in investments over the next decade. We'd also need to build 250 one-gigawatt nuclear plants, or several thousand smaller modular reactors, and few people want to live near nuclear power plants.

The Common Denominator

The biggest land challenge in either scenario may be building transmission lines. They're must-haves for large-scale deployment of "clean" energy because the most productive regions for capturing wind and solar energy are far from where most Americans live. Without transmission lines, new wind and solar projects won't operate.[166]

The existing system of transmission lines is far from ready. Princeton estimates that transmission capacity would need to more than triple in the highest-renewable scenario. But if progress to date is any indication, then building at that pace poses a problem. Of the five transmission line projects initiated by former President Barack Obama's Rapid Response Team for Transmission—whose purpose is to speed the permitting of line projects—only one is under construction. Three still face permitting delays, and one was canceled. They're a major bottleneck to deploying renewable resources.[167]

Transmission lines face intense local opposition. In Maine, the second-highest turnout of voters shot down a $1 billion hydropower project that required 145 miles of transmission line. Even environmental groups questioned the ecological impact and the claims of clean energy. Former State Senator Tom Saviello described it as "giving up a lot for getting nothing."[168]

There's no easy pathway to replace fossil fuels by 2050. The irony of an environmentalist group like the Sierra Club is that it advocates for renewables that take up the most land—the very land that the founder of the club, John Muir, aimed to preserve. Muir dedicated his life to pro-

166. Catherine Clifford, "Fierce Local Battles Over Power Lines Are a Bottleneck for Clean Energy," CNBC, June 26, 2022, https://www.cnbc.com/2022/06/26/why-the-us-has-a-massive-power-line-problem.html.

167. Clifford, "Fierce Local Battles Over Power Lines Are a Bottleneck for Clean Energy."

168. Robin Levinson-King, "Maine Energy: How One Hydropower Project Sparked a $100m 'Hoohah'," BBC News, July 12, 2022, https://www.bbc.com/news/world-us-canada-62072844.

tecting sections of forests where cutting would be forbidden.[169] But the wind and solar solutions his group wants—along with President Biden's net-zero deadline—demand a lot more land than our current energy footprint. The solutions come with other environmental casualties, including the biofuels "solution" that's destroying American forests.

BIOFUELS

An emerging biofuel solution is to replace coal with wood. That's because wood is advertised as a renewable source of energy, like solar and wind: if forests can regrow, proponents say the carbon dioxide released by cutting and burning trees will be absorbed by the new trees. It's presented as a net-zero transaction producing a zero-emissions fuel, and governments are climbing on board to meet their renewable energy targets, including the United States. As the largest exporter, we're cranking out millions of tons of lightweight wood pellets that are the length of a fingernail and the width of a straw. "Woody" biofuels are a rapidly growing industry valued in 2020 at $50 billion globally.[170]

On paper, it all looks good, but wood is neither renewable nor a solution. It's a fallacy comprising economic and political injustices and massive, carbon-intense deforestation of critical habitats.

That's why five hundred scientists sent a letter to world leaders in 2021 warning that cutting trees for bioenergy is worse for the climate. Woodburning smokestacks—like one on the mouth of North Carolina's Cape Fear River—are emitting more greenhouse gasses than coal. The biomass industry is undermining the fight against GHG emissions and

169. William O. Douglas, "John Muir's Public Service," Sierra Club, https://vault.sierraclub.org/john_muir_exhibit/life/john_muirs_public_service_by_william_o_douglas.aspx.

170. Content throughout this section was derived from Sarah Gibbons, "Europe Burns a Controversial 'Renewable' Energy Source: Trees from the U.S.," *National Geographic*, November 11, 2021, https://www.nationalgeographic.com/environment/article/europe-burns-controversial-renewable-energy-trees-from-us.

accomplishing the opposite of America's environmental goals, causing some policy and advocacy groups to call it "the green myth." Worse, the chopped and burned trees aren't even for U.S. energy; they're replacing coal in Europe.

Americans should be outraged at the absurdity of clear-cutting our forests to accommodate phobic European demands for so-called "green energy." The large-scale burning of forest biomass undermines global efforts at addressing GHG emissions.[171] If current logging rates continue, British Columbia's endangered inland rainforest is susceptible to ecological collapse within only one decade, having already lost 95 percent of its "core habitat."[172] Yet wood pellet production continues to grow: the global pellet trade reached twenty-nine million tons in 2021, 50 percent higher than in 2017.[173] The multi-billion-dollar industry is expected to double again in the next five years.[174]

Scientists say several problems with wood complicate its net-zero image. Fundamentally, trees take a long time to grow; it takes decades—if not centuries—for forest regrowth to repay the debt of harvesting, transporting, and burning trees for large-scale energy production. Planting a tree for each tree burned is not an even equation: young trees don't absorb carbon as fast as mature trees, and soil carbon losses delay a forest's return to status up to twenty more years. And unlike mining coal, harvesting trees immediately stops them from removing carbon from the atmo-

171. "Satellite Images Show Link Between Wood Pellet Demand and Increased Hardwood Forest Harvesting," Southern Environmental Law Center, March 2022, https://www.southernenvironment.org/wp-content/uploads/2022/03/Biomass-White-Page.pdf.

172. Brian J. Barth, "Burning Up: The Controversial Biofuel Threatening BC's Last Inland Rainforests," The Walrus, published March 28, 2022, updated June 30, 2022, https://thewalrus.ca/wood-pellets/.

173. Håkan Ekström, "Global Wood Pellet Trade Reached Record-High 29 Million Tons in 2021," Forest2Market, April 26, 2022, https://www.forest2market.com/blog/global-wood-pellet-trade-reached-record-high-29-million-tons-in-2021.

174. Robert Hunziker, "Wood-Pellet Manufacturing Destroys Our Rainforests," City Watch, April 4, 2022, https://www.citywatchla.com/index.php/climate/24228-wood-pellet-manufacturing-destroys-our-rainforests.

sphere. Studies on forest harvesting in specific sourcing areas confirm that destruction exceeds growth, resulting in a net loss of forested areas.

Also, wood burns less efficiently and releases more carbon than coal for the same amount of energy produced. One kilowatt-hour of electricity generated emits one and a half times the carbon dioxide of coal and three times that of natural gas. In their 2021 letter, the five hundred scientists explained to world leaders that trees are more valuable alive than dead: supplying just 2 percent more global energy from biomass would mean doubling total global wood harvests.[175]

But countries are getting away with calling wood a net-zero "renewable" source because of flawed accounting in international agreements. A complicated global system for counting emissions has created a loophole that doesn't require countries to count emissions from wood-fired power plants. Not only does the loophole fail to limit biomass burning, but policymakers say it incentivizes it. A coal-burning power plant that switches to burning wood pellets would appear to have drastically dropped its emissions. The real costs of tree harvest and transport are ignored.[176]

Complicated accounting allows the biomass industry to remain economically viable. The expensive process is propped up by renewable energy credits, billions in taxpayer subsidies, and high consumer costs. The industry would not be profitable if companies paid the full cost.[177]

Analyses are deceiving, too. The majority don't account for the most-common production for woody biomass—harvesting full trees into pellets—and incorrectly assume that pellets are made from timber

175. Michael Grunwald, "The 'Green Energy' That Might Be Ruining the Planet," Politico, March 26, 2021, https://www.politico.com/news/magazine/2021/03/26/biomass-carbon-climate-politics-477620.

176. Meaghan Lee Callaghan, "Let's Say It Again: Wood Pellets Are Not a Sustainable Fuel Source," Audubon, February 27, 2017, https://www.audubon.org/news/lets-say-it-again-wood-pellets-are-not-sustainable-fuel-source.

177. Sharon Guynup, "COP26: Surging Wood Pellet Industry Threatens Climate, Say Experts," Mongabay, November 9, 2021, https://news.mongabay.com/2021/11/surging-wood-pellet-industry-threatens-climate-say-experts/.

scraps and waste. Also, the industry focuses on national or regional trends in forest growth, which skew conclusions about the environmental footprint and impacts. A closer look at specific sourcing areas reveals that people directly suffer from wood-pellet production: communities within a seventy-mile radius experience higher rates of tree loss, increased flooding risk, and lower air and water quality.[178]

Countries are allowing themselves to be seduced by the image of the "renewable solution" rather than facing its realities. EU's top climate chief says that Europe should rely on biomass to meet clean energy goals. Throughout the southeastern United States, twenty-three wood-processing facilities are exporting pellets to Europe, and eight more facilities are proposed.

But not all countries are jumping on the wood-pellet bandwagon. Three countries are proving that strong protection of carbon-absorbing forests is necessary in controlling emissions. Bhutan, Suriname, and Panama are the only countries in the world that are carbon-negative, which means they are removing more carbon dioxide from the atmosphere than what they are emitting.

They share core values and beliefs, primarily that conservation is a priority. Rather than cut down forests for farms and industry, Bhutan's king in the 1970s advocated for sustainable forest management.[179] Today, 72 percent of Bhutan is covered by forests and trees. Meanwhile, Suriname is known for its pristine rainforests, and Panama is a pioneer in taking excellent care of its forests.[180]

---

178. Alexandra Wisner et al., "Clear Cut: Wood Pellet Production, the Destruction of Forests, and the Case for Environmental Justice," Rachel Carson Council, 2019, https://www.sec.gov/rules/petitions/2019/ptn4-741-exb.pdf.

179. Laurie Goering, "Forget Net-Zero: Meet the Small-Nation, Carbon-Negative Club," Reuters, November 3, 2021, https://www.reuters.com/business/cop/forget-net-zero-meet-small-nation-carbon-negative-club-2021-11-03/.

180. "Carbon-Negative – These Countries Lead the Way," Woodly, November 12, 2021, https://woodly.com/carbon_neutrality/carbon-negative-these-countries-lead-the-way/.

It's a far cry from countries like Scotland, where nearly fourteen million trees have been cut down to make space for wind turbines. With an aim to generate 100 percent of electricity from renewable resources, the Scottish government is compromising its forests for green energy.[181]

Bhutan, Suriname, and Panama tell a different story. These three political and environmental dark horses show that becoming carbon-negative is possible without making our land barren.[182] There is a way, and it takes compassionate leadership, creative use of resources, and collective sacrifice.

Louisiana is following suit. My native state is prioritizing the preservation and replacement of existing forests. In 2021, Governor John Bel Edwards signed a law that banned the harvesting of the bald cypress tree on over one million acres of state land. The iconic tree was named the official state tree in 1963. With its peculiar "knees" and flared trunk, the bald cypress uniquely identifies the culture and landscape of southern Louisiana.

Cypress trees are in the same family of trees as the giant redwood in California. They're slow growing and can survive for two thousand years or more. The "ancient" trees are massive. The largest one in Louisiana on Cat Island near St. Francisville measures fifty-three feet in circumference. Hugging it requires at least nine people.

Cypress trees were highly prized in the 1800s and early 1900s due to cypressine oil, a natural preservative buried in the heartwood of the tree. It made the wood resistant to rot and insects, perfect for building boats and homes. In addition to construction materials, cypress wood was also ideal for roof shingles, posts and pilings, water

181. David Bol, "14m Trees Have Been Cut Down in Scotland to Make Way for Wind Farms," The Herald (Scotland), February 28, 2020, https://www.heraldscotland.com/news/18270734.14m-trees-cut-scotland-make-way-wind-farms/.

182. "How Bhutan Became a Carbon-Negative Country," GVI, June 9, 2022, https://www.gviusa.com/blog/bhutan-carbon-negative-country-world/.

tanks, caskets, and walkways. Although sometimes lumped into the category of hardwood, cypress is a relatively soft wood and easy to work with, which makes it desirable for skilled artisans and woodworking professionals.

Due to the wood's desirability and size, industrial harvesting of the large, virgin cypress forests began around 1880 and continued for about forty years. Companies overharvested hundreds of thousands of acres throughout Louisiana and other areas of the southeastern United States and shipped much of this lumber to Europe, which had overharvested its own forests years before. By the 1920s, the precious natural resource of Louisiana was largely depleted due to the highly efficient, cut-out-and-get-out policies of the time. Left behind were "ghost forests," vast swaths of desolate, stagnated swamps called "stumpscapes" that still exist today. These stumpscapes can be witnessed while traveling down the Interstate 10 corridor and Interstate 55 near Manchac, Louisiana, just north of New Orleans. Almost without exception, the grand trees that remain are hollow shells, spared the lumberman's axe because they weren't worth the effort to fell.

Environmentalists rightly acted. Thanks to today's preservation efforts, the indiscriminate clearing of cypress trees on state land in Louisiana by industrial timber barons is part of our history, but not our future.

May we remember the lessons learned from the destruction of Louisiana cypress trees so that we prevent our current forests from suffering the same fate at the hands of the wood-pellet industry. The "clean" wood solution appeases short-term requirements but causes long-term environmental damage.

Renewables have their place in the energy solution, but they have limitations. As it turns out, there are issues with renewable energy across the globe.

DIRTY LITTLE SECRETS

Most of us like the idea of a clean future, but few of us understand what it'll take to get there. Many appreciate the benefits of new technology, but rarely do we ask how they're made.

Some organizations have begun asking and understanding. In 2016, Amnesty International investigated companies using electric technology. The human rights organization discovered that renewables are not as clean, green, or safe as people think. Renewable energy solutions have a dark side.

In the firestorm that followed Amnesty International's 2016 investigation, the National Resources Defense Council revealed that not all energy sources marketed as "renewable" are beneficial to the environment. One problem is cobalt.[183]

Cobalt, the most expensive battery metal, provides the stability and density that allows lithium-ion batteries to operate safely and for longer periods. Without it, our lives could not function as they do now. However, the ingredient introduces a significant problem for people, children in particular.

The problem is born deep in mines in the Democratic Republic of the Congo (DRC), where cobalt is found. The rare-earth metal comes at a steep price—so much so that cobalt is considered the "blood diamond of batteries."[184, 185] It is mined at government sites that are harsh, dangerous, and environmentally hazardous. Cobalt is extracted by underpaid

---

183. John Merline, "Green New Deal: Is 100% Renewable Energy Even Possible, Or Good For The Environment?" *Investor's Business Daily,* February 3, 2019, https://www.investors.com/politics/commentary/renewable-energy-possible-good-environment/.

184. Angela Chen, "Elon Musk Wants Cobalt Out of His Batteries—Here's Why That's a Challenge," *The Verge,* June 21, 2018, https://www.theverge.com/2018/6/21/17488626/elon-musk-cobalt-electric-vehicle-battery-science.

185. Ellen Airhart, "Alternatives to Cobalt, the Blood Diamond of Batteries," Wired, June 7, 2018, https://www.wired.com/story/alternatives-to-cobalt-the-blood-diamond-of-batteries/.

workers, including an unknown number of illegal child laborers.[186]

Fortune Magazine told the story of a fifteen-year-old cobalt digger who walks two hours from his village to an artisanal mine every day, using his hands to dig small quantities of cobalt from a hole for eight hours. Other Congolese children act as human mules for the diggers. These child laborers don't go to school; many earn just two dollars per day to support their families and survive. Despite the riches of the cobalt industry, which accounts for 80 percent of the African country's earnings, the average worker receives only $700 annually, has no running water or electricity at home, and can expect to live to only sixty years old.[187]

Although the DRC is the fourth-poorest country in the world, its southeastern province sits on a concentrated mineral vein known as the "Copperbelt," which produces two-thirds of the global supply of cobalt.[188] Whereas oil is found in many countries and under every ocean, cobalt is heavily concentrated in one sliver of a country plagued with conflict, poverty, and dysfunction. Transparency International, a global anti-corruption agency, ranks the DRC as number 161 of 180 countries, among the worst 11 percent in terms of corruption.[189] The mismanagement of their natural resources has caused the land of the Congolese people to epitomize a "resource curse."

Meanwhile, the rest of the world remains oblivious. These facto-

---

186. Lizzie Wade, "Tesla's Electric Cars Aren't as Green as You Might Think," Wired, March 31, 2016, https://www.wired.com/2016/03/teslas-electric-cars-might-not-green-think/.

187. Most of the information in this section is derived from: Vivienne Walt and Sebastian Meyer, "Blood, Sweat, and Batteries," *Fortune,* August 23, 2018, https://www.google.com/amp/amp.timeinc.net/fortune/longform/blood-sweat-and-batteries.

188. *World Population Review,* "Poorest Countries in the World 2019," http://worldpopulationreview.com/countries/poorest-countries-in-the-world/.

189. Peter Tertzakian, "Lithium may be the new oil, but a double whammy looms for the battery market," *Financial Post,* July 25, 2017, https://www.google.com/amp/s/business.financialpost.com/commodities/energy/lithium-may-be-the-new-oil-but-theres-a-double-whammy-looming-for-the-new-energy-source/amp.

ries and mines continue to operate, thanks to U.S. demand for cheap production.[190] The global appetite is soaring for just a quarter-ounce of cobalt. California carmaker Tesla capitalized on the environmental momentum when it unveiled its Model 3, the most hyped vehicle of the decade. Within a week, more than three hundred thousand reservations poured in from buyers around the globe for the first mass-market electric vehicle. Within three years, it became the all-time best-selling plug-in electric car in the United States. The slick, fun design was a dreamy alternative to gas-guzzling transportation, which comprises 25 percent of global energy use. The Model 3 was called "the frontman of a generation, the face of a movement,"[191] and *Bloomberg* declared it "the reigning replacement for the internal combustion engine."[192]

But in electric cars, the demand for minerals is great. Each car battery needs about seventeen to twenty-two pounds of lithium, and there's already not enough lithium globally to meet demand.[193] Each battery needs about eighteen pounds of cobalt, for which demand could triple by 2025 and then double again by 2035. Car companies are planning to build more giant battery factories within a decade to keep up.

In America, one company is attempting to gain domestic control of minerals. MP Materials, one of the few U.S. rare-earth mining companies, began building out its domestic refining capabilities after

190. "Elon Musk: Our Lithium Ion Batteries Should Be Called Nickel-Graphite," *Benchmark Mineral Intelligence*, June 5, 2016, https://www.benchmarkminerals.com/elon-musk-our-lithium-ion-batteries-should-be-called-nickel-graphite.

191. Andrew Hard, "Tesla Model S news roundup: All you need to know about the world-class EV," Digital Trends, January 3, 2018, https://www.digitaltrends.com/cars/tesla-model-s-release-date-price-specs-news.

192. David Stringer and Kevin Buckland, "Before the Electric Car Takes Over, Someone Needs to Reinvent the Battery," *Bloomberg*, January 6, 2019, https://www.bloomberg.com/news/articles/2019-01-06/before-the-electric-car-takes-over-someone-needs-to-reinvent-the-battery?srnd=premium.

193. Akiko Fujita, "'We Don't Have Enough' Lithium Globally to Meet EV Targets, Mining CEO Says," Yahoo! Finance, September 5, 2022, https://finance.yahoo.com/news/lithium-supply-ev-targets-miner-181513161.html.

China doubled tariffs on minerals in the 2019 trade war with the United States. If successful, MP Materials would mitigate national security concerns as well as the over-reliance on China, the world's largest processor and producer of the seventeen specialized minerals that are used to build weapons, electronics, and parts for wind turbines and solar panels. America will become critically dependent on China if we do not develop domestic mineral mines.[194, 195]

But shifting control of mineral production to the United States still leaves the problem of consuming too much land. Robert Bryce, a Texas-based writer, film producer, and host of the *Power Hungry Podcast*, says that the call by environmentalists for the smallest possible footprint in the natural world is complicated. He agrees that the proposed policies, as nature friendly as they sound, squander land.[196]

Ironically, many environmentalists who protest fossil fuels aren't happy with renewable alternatives, either. The Sierra Club, Natural Resources Defense Council, and Defenders of Wildlife filed suit to stop a 4,600-acre Calico solar plant northeast of Los Angeles, calling it one of the most ecologically damaging renewable energy projects in the state. Environmentalists also succeeded in blocking GreenHunter Energy's five hundred-megawatt wind project for a remote part of Montana near the Canadian border. A U.S. Chamber of Commerce report, *Project No Project,* cited 140 renewable projects that have been delayed or shut down after fierce opposition from environmental groups.[197]

---

194. Ernest Scheyder, "California rare earths miner races to refine amid U.S.-China trade row," Reuters, August 23, 2019, https://www.reuters.com/article/us-usa-rareearths-mpmaterials/california-rare-earths-miner-races-to-refine-amid-u-s-china-trade-row-idUSKCN1VD2D3.

195. "If You Think the U.S. Can Go 100% Renewables, You're Fantasizing," Natural Gas Now, February 8, 2019, https://naturalgasnow.org/if-you-think-the-u-s-can-go-100-renewables-youre-fantasizing/.

196. Robert Bryce, "Get Dense," *City Journal,* Winter 2012, https://www.city-journal.org/html/get-dense-13448.html.

197. Merline, "Green New Deal: Is 100% Renewable Energy Even Possible, Or Good For The Environment?"

ALL THAT GLITTERS IS NOT GOLD

Another problem is graphite. Known primarily as the glittery ingredient in pencils, graphite benefits our society in many ways, but the lack of regulation around its extraction does not.

In a remote Chinese village, newcomers are greeted with a wide, proud billboard that says, "City of Graphite." It is in the Heilongjiang Province, the world's single largest source of graphite. But according to the *Washington Post,* the villagers refer to graphite with disgust, explaining that it makes everything *mái tai,* a local term meaning "dirty." The lustrous gray dust from the graphite factories has an "otherworldly, almost fairy-tale quality" at night. The air "sparkles" when any hint of light hits the particles. By daylight, the fantasy dissipates into a sobering sight as the pollution settles on everything like a blanket, stifling the corn crops.[198]

A field used by small farmers is now so polluted that "not even the weeds can grow." Clean laundry hung outside to dry is begrimed with the dust. At the dinner table, the residue from graphite leaves a sandy grit on the food, causing an unpleasant taste that never seems to go away. The particles now fill the air, aggravating lung disease, reducing lung function, and causing an array of breathing difficulties. According to the U.S. Environmental Protection Agency, the dust is linked to heart attacks in people with heart disease.

Because of lax environmental controls in China, the old-fashioned industrial pollution is churning in the well water and local waterways, too. Nearby poplar trees that once thrived have died, and villagers now retrieve their drinking water from over a mile away. Sixty percent of groundwater supplies in China is now classified as "bad or very bad,"

198. Most of the information in this section is derived from: Peter Whoriskey, "In Your Phone, In Their Air," *Washington Post,* October 2, 2016, https://www.washingtonpost.com/graphics/business/batteries/graphite-mining-pollution-in-china.

according to a nonprofit group called China Water Risk.

The pollution problem is worsening as the industry is booming—and not because of its use in pencils. The demand for graphite is growing because it is used in lithium-ion batteries, the small but powerful rechargeable storage solution. Lithium-ion batteries are promoted by renewable energy experts as the "new oil," a "clean" way to power smartphones, tablets, laptops, and electric cars.[199]

Many believe the "new oil" is the answer to fossil fuels and pipelines. Without environmental controls, however, the pollution associated with this answer is undermining the benefits. Dirty air from China is drifting across the Pacific Ocean and raising ozone levels in the western part of the United States. Graphite is part of the energy solution, but we must control the pollution problem by monitoring and regulating its extraction.

Pollution is growing from other renewable resources too—so much so that green energy is a looming environmental threat. Supporters equate renewables with no waste, but the reality is all energy technologies produce new kinds and volumes of waste that must be managed responsibly.[200] Green technologies, however, lack a strategy for end-of-life management. In a 2020 brief, the EPA identified the recycling of renewables as a critical aspect of our future. But inadequate planning and systems introduce serious risks to our health, environment, and economic opportunities.[201]

Wind turbine blades, for example, are cheaper to dump in a landfill at a cost of less than one dollar than to recycle them at a cost of twelve to

199. Tyler Durden, "Energy Transition Goals At Risk as EU May Label Lithium as Toxic," Zero Hedge, June 19, 2022, https://www.zerohedge.com/energy/energy-transition-goals-risk-eu-may-label-lithium-toxic.

200. "Renewable technologies can't escape the issue of waste management," ANS Nuclear Cafe, Nuclear Newswire, February 3, 2021, https://www.ans.org/news/article-2599/renewable-technologies-cant-escape-the-issue-of-waste-management/.

201. "EPA Releases Briefing Paper on Renewable Energy Waste Management," EPA, January 6, 2016, https://www.epa.gov/newsreleases/epa-releases-briefing-paper-renewable-energy-waste-management.

twenty-five dollars.[202] The reason is their components: fiberglass, steel, wood, and resin are tougher to sort. Because few U.S. recycling facilities are equipped to handle the mammoth blades and the complex materials, they must be shipped hundreds of miles.[203] The Electric Power Research Institute estimates that four million tons of blade waste will be piled into U.S. landfills by 2050.[204]

Solar panel waste is concerning as well. In 2006, California offered subsidies as early incentives to push rooftop solar power. But the 1.3 million solar rooftops installed across the state are nearing the end of their typical lifespans of twenty-five to thirty years, and regulators and manufacturers haven't formed a clear plan for safe disposal. Most consumers don't know that solar panel components contain toxic heavy metals that can contaminate groundwater. It's a problem not just for California but for the nation, as the solar industry is expected to quadruple in size by 2030.[205]

As with wind turbine blades, recycling solar panels is not easy. It requires workers to separate parts, highly specialized equipment, and expensive restrictions on handling the hazardous materials. That's why only one in ten panels are recycled, according to industry expert Sam Vanderhoof: "The industry is supposed to be green, but in reality, it's all about the money."[206]

---

202. Michelle Lewis, "Where Do Solar Panels Go When They Die?" Electrek, August 24, 2020, https://electrek.co/2020/08/24/where-do-solar-panels-go-when-they-die/.

203. Shahla Farzan, "How to Recycle a 150-Foot Wind Turbine Blade? Haul it to Louisiana, MO," St. Louis Public Radio, May 27, 2022, https://news.stlpublicradio.org/health-science-environment/2022-05-27/how-to-recycle-a-150-foot-wind-turbine-blade-haul-it-to-louisiana-mo.

204. Katie Hill, "What To Do With a 'Tidal Wave' of Texas Wind Turbine Blades," Texas Observer, January 28, 2021, https://www.texasobserver.org/what-to-do-with-a-tidal-wave-of-texas-wind-turbine-blades/.

205. Joe Silverstein, "LA Times Report Warns About 'Environmental Danger' in Solar Transition," Fox News, July 14, 2022, https://www.foxnews.com/media/la-times-op-ed-warns-about-environmental-danger-solar-transition.

206. Rachel Kisela, "California Went Big on Rooftop Solar. Now that's a Problem for Landfills," *Los Angeles Times*, published July 14, 2022, updated July 15, 2022, https://www.latimes.com/business/story/2022-07-14/california-rooftop-solar-pv-panels-recycling-danger.

The solar waste issue is even more pressing for governments of poor and developing nations. They're less equipped to deal with an influx of toxic solar waste and at higher risk of suffering the consequences. According to a 2015 United Nations Environment Program report, 60-90 percent of waste is illegally traded and dumped in poor nations.[207]

It's pretty easy to predict the next big environmental crisis within the next twenty years: properly disposing of "renewable" waste from solar, wind and battery components being installed and manufactured today. A sizeable percentage of this waste will end up at the bottom of our oceans, rivers, lakes and streams, when a new generation of legitimate "water protectors" will be in dire need.

In addition to pollution, there are other dire reasons for which we should be cautious about quickly embracing alternate-energy solutions.

UNRELIABILITY

An inconvenient fact about renewable energy solutions is their inherent unreliability. The sun doesn't always shine, and the wind doesn't always blow. Solar and wind power are vulnerable to locations, times of day, seasonal variations, climates, and weather conditions. Whereas states like California and Montana can rest in the fact that wind speeds match the seasonal electricity demands of their residents, other states with wind variations can experience power outages, a troubling hurdle in a modern country that demands electricity all the time.[208]

The problem is illustrated by Germany's energy transition program,

207. Michael Shellenberger, "If Solar Panels Are So Clean, Why Do They Produce So Much Toxic Waste?" *Forbes*, May 23, 2018, https://www.forbes.com/sites/michaelshellenberger/2018/05/23/if-solar-panels-are-so-clean-why-do-they-produce-so-much-toxic-waste/?sh=6481f0a121cc.

208. Arne Alsin, "Q&A: MIT Professor Donald Sadoway On The Future Of Battery Storage And Renewable Energies," *Forbes*, August 24, 2018, https://www.forbes.com/sites/aalsin/2018/08/24/qa-mit-professor-donald-sadoway-on-the-future-of-battery-storage-and-renewable-energies/#1ac56acd2c62.

Energiewende, which eliminated nuclear power and doubled renewables in its energy mix. But the intermittency of its wind and solar power is so pervasive that Germany was forced to add a backup energy source, which is costly and inefficient.[209] Because nuclear power had been eliminated, the country turned to dirty brown coal plants as its second energy source. Today, 40 percent of Germany's energy comes from coal plants, six of which top the list of Europe's most-polluting power plants.

Energiewende traded nuclear for renewables—one carbon-free source for another—then dirtied the deal with coal. Electric vehicles make a similar trade: greenhouse gases are eliminated at the pump, but EVs run on electricity that must first be generated by a fuel source. It's a global trade-off: the IER concluded in 2017 that emissions of carbon dioxide and consumption of coal and natural gas all increased, despite record growth in wind and solar power.[210, 211]

REVERSAL OF FORTUNE

Affordability is another problem. The endless hunger for mobile devices is causing a growing mineral crisis and driving up costs.

Whereas petroleum cars only need oil, batteries for electric cars need many different raw material supply chains, which are immature and involve significant lags in production. That's why the price of cobalt is volatile and the price of lithium has doubled in just a few years—with

209. "If You Think the U.S. Can Go 100% Renewables, You're Fantasizing." Natural Gas Now.

210. Ariel Cohen, "California's New 100% Green Energy Target May Do More Harm Than Good," *Forbes*, September 21, 2018, https://www.forbes.com/sites/arielcohen/2018/09/21/californias-new-100-green-energy-target-may-do-more-harm-than-good/?sh=64d9487d675e.

211. Richard Rhodes, "A Sensible Climate Solution, Borrowed from Sweden," *New York Times*, February 5, 2019, https://www.nytimes.com/2019/02/05/books/review/bright-future-joshua-s-goldstein-staffan-a-qvist.html.

long-term demand likely pushing prices upward.[212,213,214,215]

The writers of the Green New Deal insist that renewable energy pays for itself through the prevention of fossil fuel-related diseases, including asthma, heart attacks, strokes, and cancer. However, the costs are proving to be a financial pothole. While the cost of some renewable parts declines, such as that of wind turbines, the cost of energy simultaneously increases. German economist Leon Hirth predicted this economic paradox a decade ago: because of its fundamentally unreliable nature, wind produces excess energy when society doesn't need it—and not enough when society *does* need it.

The lack of utility-scale storage for the excess energy puts a tremendous strain on the grid. The excess must be either wasted or offloaded to other utilities for a fee, making it difficult for renewable sources to compete with cheap U.S. natural gas.[216] Places like Germany, Denmark, and California are paying neighboring nations or states to take the extra energy off their hands. This fact isn't often reported in the news, which misleads policymakers and the public about the capabilities and economic realities of using wind energy.

The lack of storage leaves alternate energy solutions incapable of sustaining our needs without costly backup systems. Natural gas plants, hydroelectric dams, and batteries are idling on standby to be ready immediately during periods of low wind or solar radiation. If Germany

212. Amit Katwala, "The spiralling environmental cost of our lithium battery addiction," May 8, 2018, Wired, https://www.wired.co.uk/article/lithium-batteries-environment-impact.

213. Priscila Barrera, "Lithium Outlook 2022: Demand to Outpace Supply, Price Upside to Remain," Investing News Network, January 12, 2022, https://investingnews.com/daily/resource-investing/battery-metals-investing/lithium-investing/lithium-outlook/.

214. "How Much Does a Car Battery Cost?" Batteries Plus, https://www.batteriesplus.com/battery-tips/car-battery-cost#:~:text=Car%20batteries%20typically%20last%20anywhere,%24200%20for%20a%20premium%20typ.

215. "What is the Lifespan of an Electric Car Battery?" iSeeCars, Yahoo! News, September 2, 2022, https://autos.yahoo.com/lifespan-electric-car-battery-183002281.html.

216. Ariel Cohen, "California's New 100% Green Energy Target May Do More Harm Than Good."

continues the Energiewende program, complete with backup coal and increased imports, the country will have the most expensive electricity in Europe.

Distribution also drives up costs. Whereas a natural gas plant requires just one transmission line to reach the grid, a utility-scale wind or solar plant can require dozens of longer, less efficient power lines that stretch from remote locations. The longer the transit, the more energy is lost along the way. The cost of the technology relative to energy output is one reason solar is significantly more expensive than other energy sources.

For now, renewables are only feasible because the U.S. government subsidizes wind and solar with tax credits. U.S. states mandate their production, forcing utilities to invest in them or purchase their power regardless of cost, stability, or need. As a result, states with more stringent mandates have double the electricity rates than states with no mandates, and innovation is discouraged because it's difficult for competitors to compete with the low wholesale prices.[217, 218]

The increasing costs plus inefficient results make clean technology difficult to embrace.[219] Despite the promises of the Green New Deal, many Americans worry it's full of "empty promises that leave American taxpayers on the hook."[220]

217. John Merline, "Green New Deal: Is 100% Renewable Energy Even Possible, Or Good For The Environment?"

218. "If You Think the U.S. Can Go 100% Renewables, You're Fantasizing," Natural Gas Now.

219. Arne Alsin, "Q&A: MIT Professor Donald Sadoway On The Future Of Battery Storage And Renewable Energies," *Forbes,* August 24, 2018, https://www.forbes.com/sites/aalsin/2018/08/24/qa-mit-professor-donald-sadoway-on-the-future-of-battery-storage-and-renewable-energies/#1ac56acd2c62.

220. Ari Natter and Billy House, "Ocasio-Cortez Begins to Sketch Out Details of 'Green New Deal,'" *Bloomberg,* February 4, 2019, https://www.yahoo.com/news/ocasio-cortez-begins-sketch-details-201005324.html.

THE FUNDAMENTAL FLAW: ENERGY DENSITY

Even with decades of government subsidies and mandates, just 8 percent of energy in the United States comes from solar and wind energy.[221] No city has been able to achieve 100-percent renewable energy. No plan for 100-percent renewable energy works because it is inherently flawed: it ignores energy density entirely.

Energy density is the amount of energy that can be stored in a given mass of any energy source. The higher, the better. An energy source with high density produces more energy than it takes to create. It's more efficient because it packs more energy into the same amount of volume.[222] It's more bang for your buck. Robert Bryce calls density "the real organizing principle for a green future" that can sustain our nation *and* meet environmental goals."[223]

The problem with a plan for 100-percent renewable energy is that it dismisses high-density sources of energy—such as fossil fuels and nuclear power—as "dead-end industries." It puts all of its money on the least-dense sources of energy, the six renewables: hydropower, biomass, biofuels, geothermal, wind, and solar energy. At the very bottom of the list are wind energy and solar energy, the darlings of renewables.[224, 225]

The fundamental density flaw prevents renewable energy from being a practical solution, certainly not in the decades ahead in which climate solutions must be found. Producing the least-dense resources

221. "What is U.S. electricity generation by energy source?" EIA, https://www.eia.gov/tools/faqs/faq.php?id=427&t=3.

222. J.M.K.C. Donev et al., "Energy Education: Energy density," accessed April 26, 2019, University of Calgary, https://energyeducation.ca/encyclopedia/Energy_density.

223. Bryce, "Get Dense."

224. John Hofmeister, "Refreshing the Energy Outlook Given the Intervention of the Green New Deal" (speech), The Houston Economics Club, March 26, 2019, Federal Reserve Bank of Dallas – Houston branch.

225. John Hofmeister, "Refreshing the Energy Outlook Given the Intervention of the Green New Deal" (speech).

has proven to be inefficient, environmentally unfriendly, and expensive. A plan for 100-percent renewables does not make mathematical sense.

Decarbonization requires two things: replacing existing fossil fuels *and* meeting new demand from carbon-free sources. While the Green New Deal addresses the first goal of replacing fossil fuels, it falls short of meeting new demand. In their book, *A Bright Future,* Joshua Goldstein and Staffan A. Qvist explain that renewable energy cannot scale up fast enough to fulfill energy needs. It is mathematically impossible to take high-density fossil fuels off the market and quickly replace them with low-density renewable fuels without a major disruption.

A WORKING SOLUTION

Renewables, particularly wind and solar energy, are the darlings for good reasons. Renewable energy sources can potentially lift the economies of the poorest nations, as they are suited for rural, remote areas and developing countries that critically need energy. Unlike fossil fuels that are concentrated in a few resource-rich countries, renewable resources exist over wide geographical areas.

However, we're not there yet. Renewable energy is simply not efficient enough to meet the demand, nor will it be any time in the foreseeable future, according to the Institute for Energy Research (IER). An alternative solution should lead us to more affordable, more reliable, more abundant power—not less, as is the case with renewables.

The call to "keep it in the ground!" makes for a tidy tagline but is not a working solution. It isn't even an option, according to the 2017 energy outlook by the Energy Information Administration (EIA). Petroleum, natural gas, and coal make up 80 percent of the energy used in the United States and 75 percent of world energy consumption.[226]

226. "International Energy Outlook 2017," U.S. Energy Information Administration, September 14, 2017, https://www.eia.gov/outlooks/ieo/pdf/0484(2017).pdf.

In the decades ahead, energy needs will rise significantly to keep up with growth in the world's population and economy, coupled with rapid urbanization.

An abrupt abandonment of fossil fuels would threaten our way of life even more than CO_2 levels. Proposing that Americans can thrive on 100-percent renewable energy is not only an irresponsible fantasy; such a plan endangers our country to the point of catastrophe.[227]

We know from experience what happens when we make hasty energy decisions. In our rush to move away from nuclear power in 1979 and return to fossil fuels, we failed to consider the implications of CO_2 emissions. That's how we ended up with the high emissions that are prevalent today.

Renewables *are* a means to address GHG emissions, and there may come a day when they can replace oil and natural gas. But we need to be honest about their shortcomings. Renewables are not the holy grail of energy. We need to use *all* tools in the toolbox to achieve rapid decarbonization while protecting our country.

As we develop renewable energy, we should also take Daniel Yergin's advice to view shale and LNG in a whole new dimension as "a geopolitical strategic asset in foreign policy."[228]

---

227. "If You Think the U.S. Can Go 100% Renewable, You're Fantasizing," Natural Gas Now.

228. Breck Dumas and Andrew Murray, "Daniel Yergin Spelled Out the Importance of the U.S. Shale Revolution—Before Russia's Attack on Ukraine," Fox Business, March 25, 2022, https://www.foxbusiness.com/politics/daniel-yergin-stresses-importance-energy-independence.

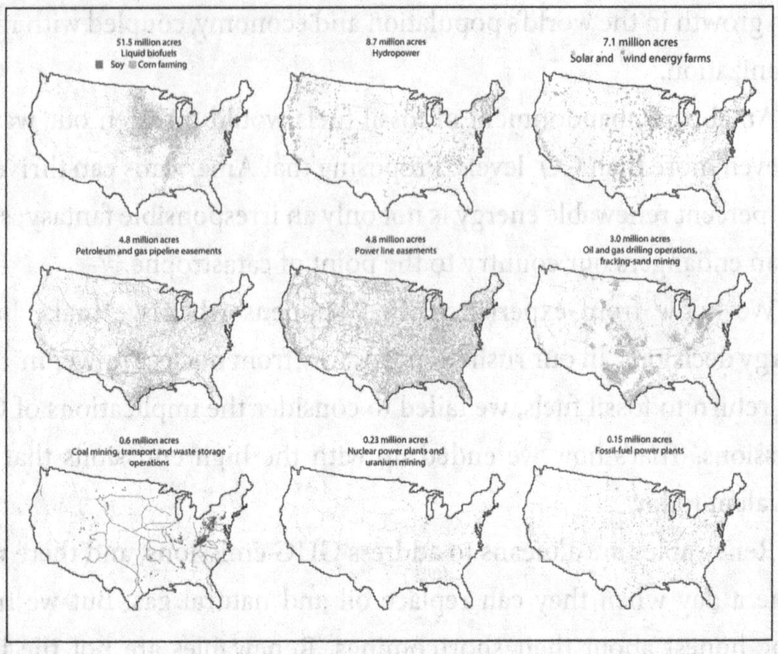

Today, the U.S. Uses 81 Million Acres to Power Its Economy. Note: Liquid biofuels map depicts soy and corn farming. One dot equals 10,000 crop acres. About one-third of the nation's corn and soy crops are used for biofuels.

Source: Current land-use estimates are based on a Bloomberg News analysis of data from several sources, including the U.S. Departments of Energy, Interior and Agriculture and the Nuclear Regulatory Commission. A methodology and complete list of sources is available at the end of the story. Maps are based on data from the U.S. Energy Information Administration, Department of Homeland Security and U.S. Department of Agriculture. Image and Caption courtesy of Dave Merrill, "The U.S. Will Need a Lot of Land for a Zero-Carbon Economy," published April 29, 2021, updated June 3, 2021, Bloomberg, https://www.bloomberg.com/graphics/2021-energy-land-use-economy/.

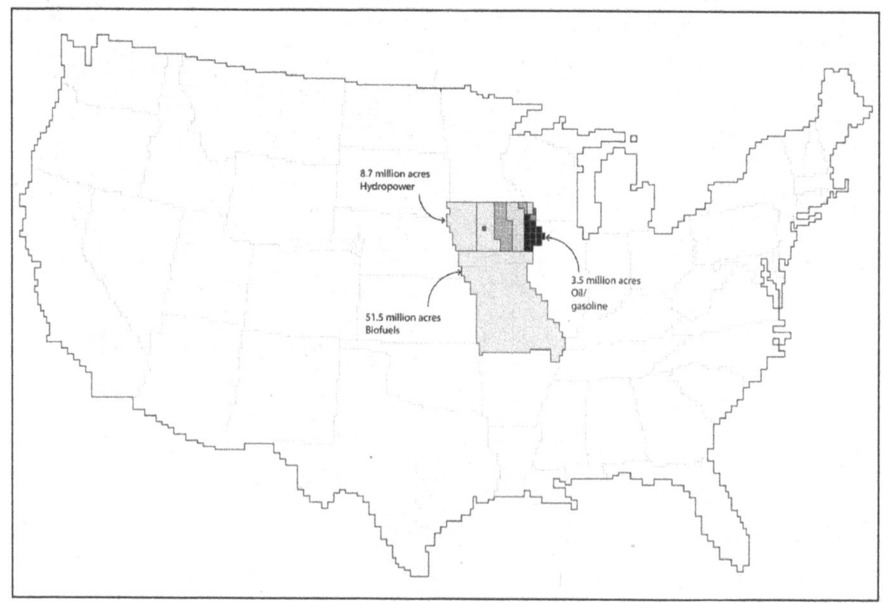

Here's how 81 million acres of energy acres lumped together looks on a U.S. map. Our current energy footprint, according to the Bloomberg News analysis, is about the size of Iowa and Missouri combined, covering roughly 4% of the contiguous U.S. states. Map source: Current land-use estimates are based on a Bloomberg News analysis of data from several sources, including the U.S. Departments of Energy, Interior and Agriculture and the Nuclear Regulatory Commission. A methodology and complete list of sources is available at the end of the story. Image and Caption courtesy of Dave Merrill, "The U.S. Will Need a Lot of Land for a Zero-Carbon Economy," published April 29, 2021, updated June 3, 2021, Bloomberg, https://www.bloomberg.com/graphics/2021-energy-land-use-economy/.

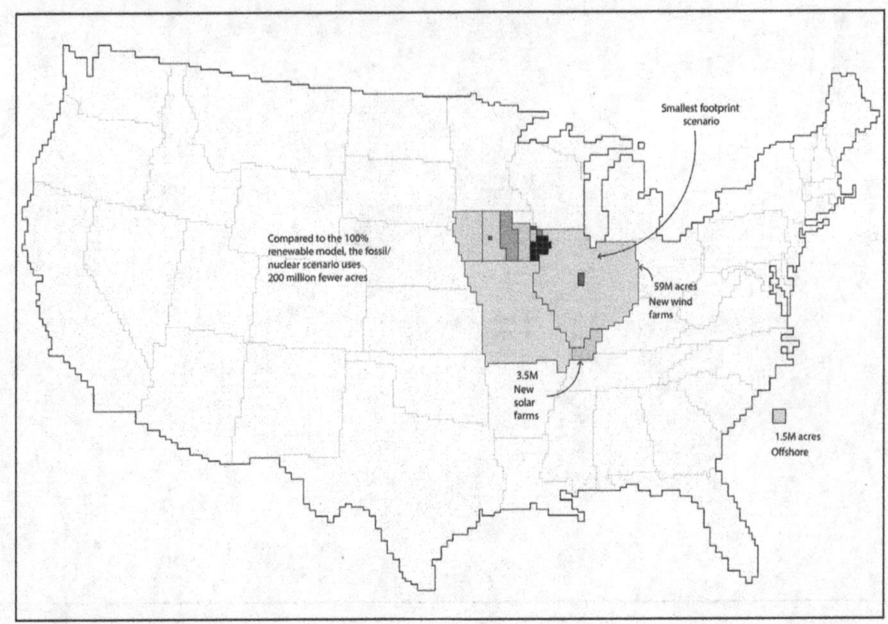

In Princeton's least land-intensive scenario, the current pace of wind and solar development remains constant, but carbon-capture and nuclear power grow at historically unprecedented rates. Under this scenario, the U.S. would need to build 250 nuclear plants with capacity of at least 1 gigawatt, or several thousand smaller modular reactors. Natural gas and nuclear energy are very compact power sources. A conventional 1-gigawatt reactor operating on 1,000 acres produces the same amount of energy as a wind farm spanning 100,000 acres. Map source: 2050 wind and solar footprint: Princeton University's Net-Zero America project, Bloomberg News analysis. Image and Caption courtesy of Dave Merrill, "The U.S. Will Need a Lot of Land for a Zero-Carbon Economy," published April 29, 2021, updated June 3, 2021, Bloomberg, https://www.bloomberg.com/graphics/2021-energy-land-use-economy/.

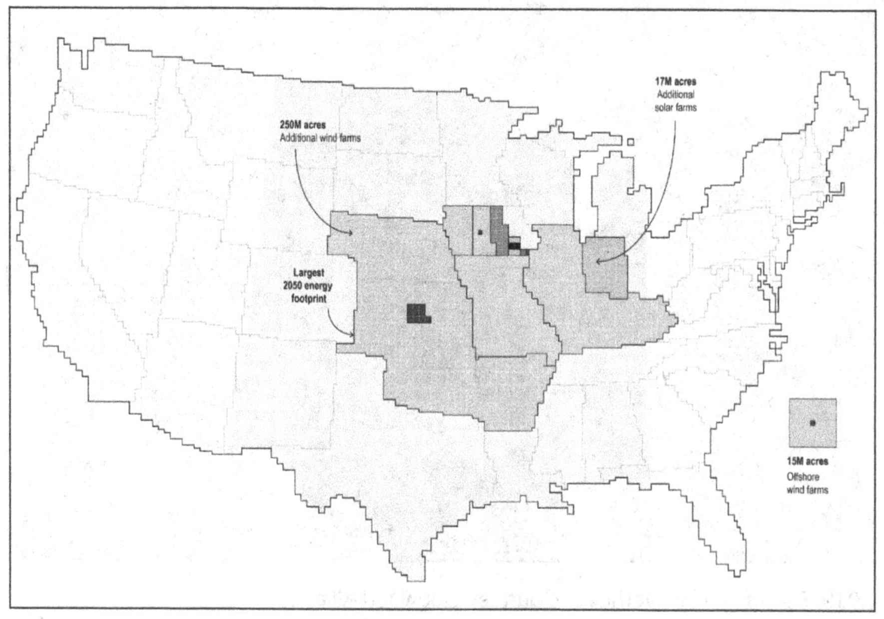

The most land-intensive plan eliminates all fossil fuels and nuclear plants. Wind and solar provide 98% of electric power by 2050. The U.S. energy footprint quadruples in size. Wind farms occupy land areas equivalent to Arkansas, Iowa, Kansas, Missouri, Nebraska and Oklahoma. Map source: Princeton University's Net-Zero America project. Image and Caption courtesy of Dave Merrill, "The U.S. Will Need a Lot of Land for a Zero-Carbon Economy," published April 29, 2021, updated June 3, 2021, Bloomberg, https://www.bloomberg.com/graphics/2021-energy-land-use-economy/.

2019 Enviva facility overhead. Courtesy Dogwood Alliance.

Original caption: The Log Pond, late in the season special attention is given to filling the log pond at the mill to provide for a busy winter's work. From "American Forestry" the magazine of the American Foresty Association, vol. XX_ 1914. Courtesy of Internet Archive Book Images, No restrictions, via Wikimedia Commons.

Original caption: Cutting the top from a Head Spar on which is placed the Main Cable Rigging for a Cableway Skidder. From Logging: The Principles and General Methods of Operation in the United States, Ralph Clement Bryant, Stanhope Press, 1913. Cypress Forest, Louisiana. Courtesy of Internet Archive Book Images, via Wikimedia Commons.

Original caption: Long train at the Deweyville plant of the Sabine Tram Company. Courtesy of C. E. Walden. Book: Harry Yandell, 1869-1937; Courtesy of C. E. Walden From *The Book of Texas*, H. Y. Benedict and John A. Lomax, Doubleday, Page & Company, 1916. Courtesy of C. E. Walden, via Wikimedia Commons.]

A large cypress tree containing 6 logs scaling 14,162 feet of choice "Louisiana Cypress." Courtesy of Louisiana Sea Grant Digital Images Collection, Louisiana Department of Conservation. Tenth Biennial Report of the Department of Conservation of the State of Louisiana, 1930-1931. New Orleans: Department of Conservation, 1932.

Aerial view of Manchac, LA, 2008. This is an aerial view of a former cypress swamp that is now a "stumpscape." You can see the "wagon wheel" type remaining landscape which shows how trees were systematically cut and dragged to the center and then rafted out in the canal dredged to the open water where they were then bundled and sent to market. Courtesy of Donald W. Davis Slide Collection, Louisiana Sea Grant Collection Images, Louisiana Digital Libraries.

Abellon biomass pellet. The pellets are marketed as a carbon-neutral and environmentally friendly fuel for boilers and utilities. Courtesy of Kapilbutani, CC BY-SA 3.0, via Wikimedia Commons.

Clear-cut forests near Eugene, Oregon. Courtesy of Calibas, CC BY-SA 3.0, via Wikimedia Commons.

Piles of trees and wood residuals stacked in preparation for wood pellet production at Enviva's Northampton County facility. Courtesy Dogwood Alliance.

Enviva opened its second company built plant in Northampton County, NC, in 2013. Courtesy Dogwood Alliance.

Enviva wood trucks. Courtesy Dogwood Alliance.

Manufacturing sites like those in the U.S. Southeast transform trees–growing in biodiverse forests–into highly compressed, uniform wood pellets for burning in industrial power plants. Courtesy Dogwood Alliance.

Industrial logging. Courtesy: Dogwood Alliance.

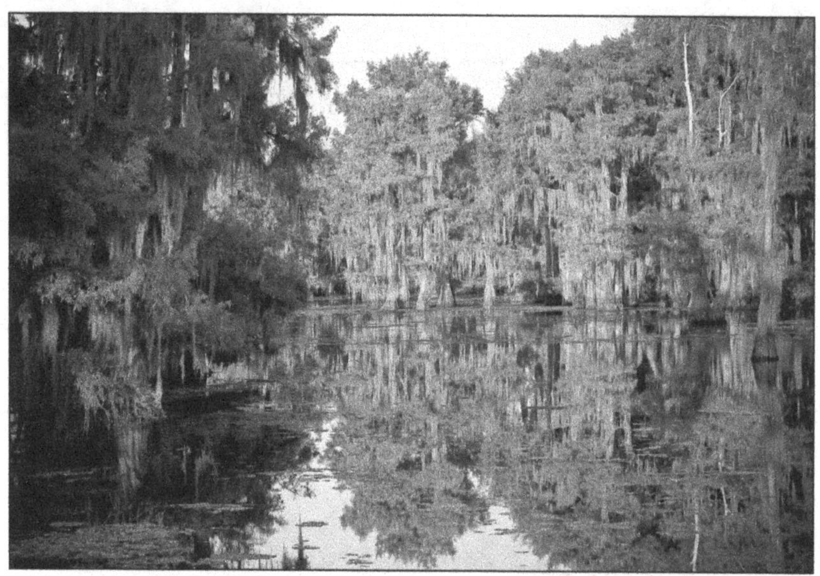

Densely populated cypress trees in Lake Bistineau State Park in Webster Parish, Louisiana. Courtesy of Michael McCarthy, CC BY 2.0 via Wikimedia Commons.

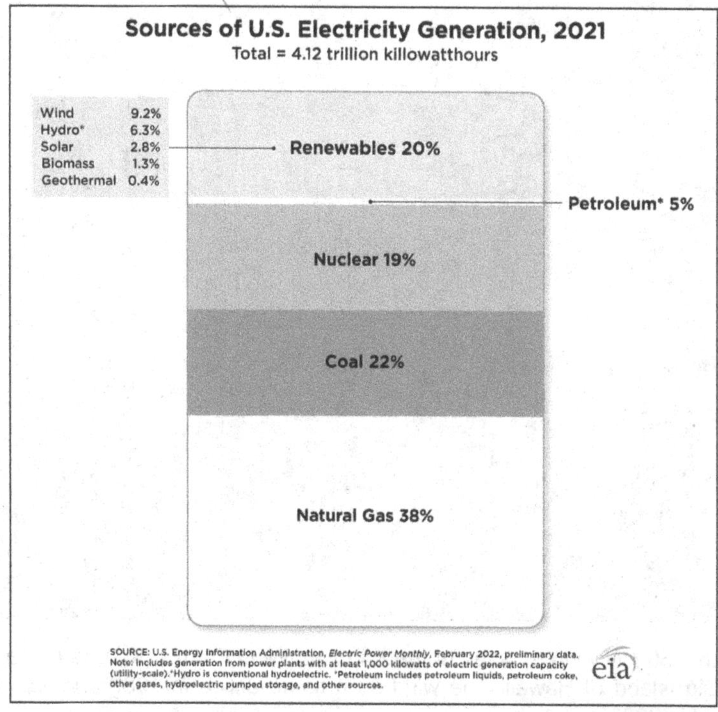

Sources of U.S. electricity generation, 2021. Courtesy of U.S. Energy Information Administration (Feb 2022).

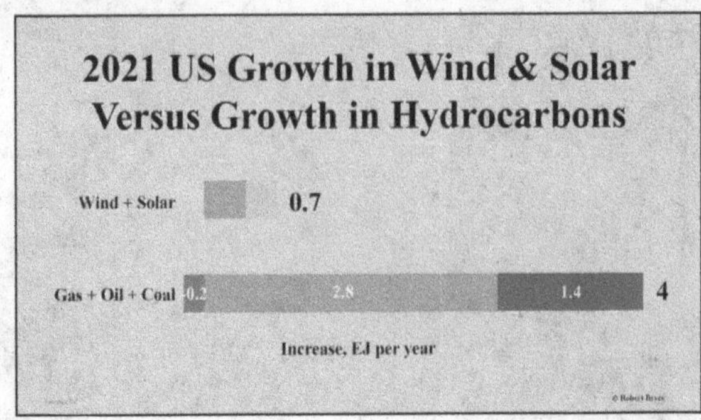

2021 U.S. growth in wind & solar versus growth in hydrocarbons. Courtesy Robert Bryce.

Mitsubishi 250 kW wind turbines of the Kama'oa Wind Farm in Ka Lae (a.k.a. South Point), Big Island of Hawaii. The wind farm came online in 1987 and was decom missioned in 2006.

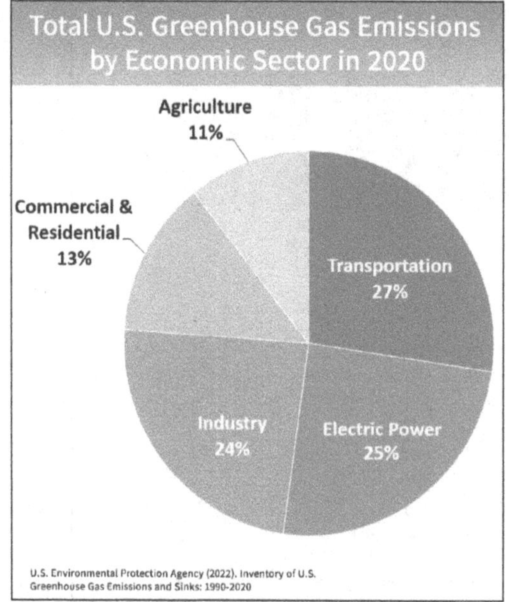

Total U.S. greenhouse gas emissions by economic sector in 2020. Courtesy of U.S. Environmental Protection Agency.

Sources Greenhouse Gas Emissions, https://www.epa.gov/ghgemissions/sources-greenhouse-gas-emissions.

Aerial view of Luwowo Coltan mine in Rubaya, Democratic Republic of Congo. Courtesy of MONUSCO via Wikimedia Commons.

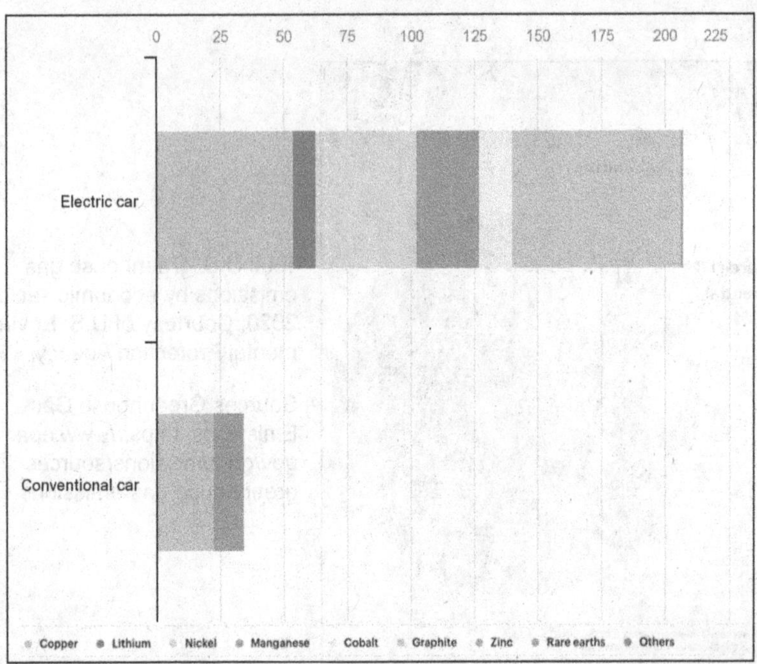

Minerals used in electric cars compared to conventional cars, n.b. steel and aluminum are not included. Courtesy of IEA, Minerals used in electric cars compared to conventional cars, IEA, Paris https://www.iea.org/data-and-statistics/charts/minerals-used-in-electric-cars-compared-to-conventional-cars, IEA. Licence: CC BY 4.0.

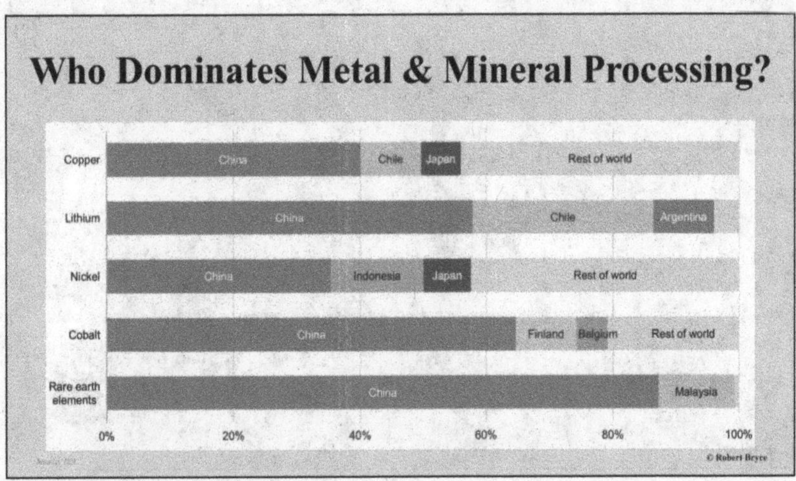

A breakdown of the countries that do the largest shares of metal and mineral processing, clearly showing China's dominance. Courtesy of Robert Bryce. Source material from IEA

PART III

A BALANCED ENERGY PLAN FOR OUR FUTURE

CHAPTER 7

A SENSIBLE APPROACH

HOW TO BALANCE ENERGY OPTIONS

"Your judgment is only as good as your facts."

– Lyndon B. Johnson

ONE OF THE SHARPEST REACTIONS to the war in Ukraine is the U-turn toward liquefied natural gas (LNG).

Just months before the Russian invasion of Ukraine, the leaders of the world's seven biggest economies were charging toward green climate commitments. In the United States, President Biden was determined to accelerate the transition to renewables.

The invasion caused leaders to reconsider energy policy.

Now the G7 leaders are scrambling to invest in LNG and store enough supplies to last the winter. Though President Biden maintains his renewable energy goals, he is moving oil to Europe and urging other countries to pump more.

The crisis in Ukraine has underscored the need for a balanced approach to energy that includes LNG. But it also underscores that it's not enough to backtrack suddenly in response to crises. A balanced plan takes time to explore, produce, and store many energy sources.[229]

That's what makes companies like Cheniere Energy ingenious. In 2016, the LNG company moved on an opportunity at the right time, and it changed everything.

At the time that one of Cheniere's terminals was constructed in Louisiana in 2005, energy experts predicted that the U.S. would run out of natural gas. Cheniere's facility was constructed to import natural gas and help offset the decline in U.S. natural gas production. With the invention of horizontal hydraulic fracturing in the early 2000s, the U.S. was swimming in natural gas, and the original import business model was upended for the company as well as for international competitors.[230]

The solution was converting the *import* facility into an LNG *export*

229. Daniel Yergin, "The Global Search for Energy Security," *The Wall Street Journal,* July 6, 2022, https://www.wsj.com/articles/energy-security-oil-gas-natural-prices-independent-america-russia-ukraine-export-eu-11657140599.

230. Clifford Krauss, "Global Demand Squeezing Natural Gas Supply," *New York Times,* May 29, 2008, https://www.nytimes.com/2008/05/29/business/29gas.html.

facility, allowing Cheniere to turn the tables on international competition. *Forbes* hailed the move as "represent(ing) the kind of innovative adjustment that's always been the hallmark of American capitalism."[231]

The geopolitical impact of the U.S. LNG business was remarkable. Prior to the perfection of hydraulic fracturing, many declared we were in the era of "peak oil," the theoretical point of maximum fossil fuel production. During this era, few environmental complaints were heard regarding the importing of LNG to the United States. After all, Russia couldn't complain: American imports of LNG simply opened up another huge market for Russian natural gas. However, when Cheniere and other import facilities were converted to export terminals, the environmental protests snowballed into international calls against hydraulic fracturing and fossil fuels.

There's a reason for the vehement protest against U.S. LNG. Exciting technological breakthroughs such as hydraulic fracturing allow fossil fuels and pipelines to be more than capable of sustaining our energy needs. They are also restoring our country's energy independence and economic power, providing more benefits than protestors would have America believe.

EXPANDING LNG TO REPLACE COAL

The phenomenon of hydraulic fracturing initiated an unprecedented boom in U.S. energy production, not only for Cheniere Energy but for the nation. U.S. oil production—as well as associated natural gas—turned upward in 2009 and has risen at the fastest rate in U.S. history.[232]

231. Christopher Helman, "How Cheniere Energy Got First In Line To Export America's Natural Gas," *Forbes,* April 17, 2013, https://www.forbes.com/sites/christopherhelman/2013/04/17/first-mover-how-cheniere-energy-is-leading-americas-lng-revolution/#3d43a8262995.

232. Robert Rapier, "How The Fracking Revolution Broke OPEC's Hold On Oil Prices," *Forbes,* July 22, 2018, https://www.forbes.com/sites/rrapier/2018/07/22/how-the-fracking-revolution-broke-opecs-hold-on-oil-prices/#363fb64c48ef.

We are now awash in cheap natural gas, which has been called a "gift" to the country from the late George Mitchell, the pioneering oilman who improved and commercialized horizontal hydraulic fracturing.

"Few businesspeople have done as much to change the world as George Mitchell," said the *Economist*.[233] His gift to the country has fundamentally reshaped the global energy landscape in several ways.[234]

Superpower

One dramatic way LNG has reshaped the U.S. is the competitive advantage the influx brings to our nation. As our products gradually make their way into the global marketplace, America is experiencing a reversal of fortune moving from an energy importer to an energy exporter, enabling the reemergence of the U.S. as an energy superpower. Because of hydraulic fracturing, the U.S. increased its domestic oil production by 6.2 million barrels per day.[235] Before that, many thought the peak of oil production was approaching, but the drilling innovation changed everything. America's strong position in oil allowed our country to win a 2014 energy-price war with Saudi Arabia and surpass the Middle Eastern country as the world's leading producer of oil and liquids.[236] Meanwhile, energy companies across North America are discovering new reservoirs of oil and natural gas.

233. "The father of fracking: Few businesspeople have done as much to change the world as George Mitchell," *The Economist*, August 3, 2013, https://www.economist.com/business/2013/08/03/the-father-of-fracking.

234. Matt Egan, "America is set to surpass Saudi Arabia in a 'remarkable' oil milestone," *CNN Business*, March 21, 2019, https://edition.cnn.com/2019/03/08/business/us-oil-exports-saudi-arabia/index.html.

235. Rapier, "How The Fracking Revolution Broke OPEC's Hold On Oil Prices."

236. Prableen Bajpai "What Countries Are the Top Producers of Oil?," Nasdaq, March 15, 2022, https://www.nasdaq.com/articles/what-countries-are-the-top-producers-of-oil.

Diversification

Another remarkable change is the diversification afforded by LNG. As we lessen our dependence on politically volatile regions, America can help diversify into countries like China and India, which are now buying our exported products. We can also make Europe less dependent on Russian gas. Nearly half of the natural gas imported into Europe is from Russia, which Moscow is leveraging as power over smaller countries. America's abundance of LNG poses a serious threat to the Russian economy and its control of surrounding regions. It can loosen Moscow's grip by reducing its market share and revenues from oil and gas production, which is the backbone of the Russian economy.[237, 238] Russia has always dismissed any rivalry, but the American energy threat has become so serious that Gazprom, a leading supplier of gas exports, acknowledges our threat to their dominant position in Europe.[239]

Cleaner Energy

LNG is much cleaner than coal. The cleaner-burning resource is estimated to emit as little as half the carbon than coal, reducing emission levels at power plants to those in 1990.[240] In fact, in 2017, the United States had the most significant decline in carbon dioxide emissions in the world because of the shift from coal to natural gas. Meanwhile, carbon dioxide emissions increased among the two hundred nations of the

237. Greg Gordon, "Russian trolls' phony messages boost pipeline protests," *The Seattle Times*, May 1, 2018, https://www.seattletimes.com/nation-world/russian-trolls-phony-messages-boost-pipeline-protests.

238. "Russia's use of the 'energy weapon' against Western European countries a strategic threat," Rice University, *EurekAlert, American Association for the Advancement of Science,* July 19, 2017, https://www.eurekalert.org/pub_releases/2017-07/ru-ruo071917.php.

239. Oksana Kobzeva, "Russia acknowledges threat from Trump's energy policy on EU gas market," Reuters, January 13, 2017, https://www.reuters.com/article/us-russia-usa-lng-idUSKBN14X1SU.

240. Brigham McCown, "Why Pipeline Opposition Undermines Environmental Progress And Safety," *Forbes*, January 17, 2019, https://www.forbes.com/sites/brighammccown/2019/01/17/why-pipeline-opposition-undermines-environmental-progress-and-safety/?sh=4fa379a847f2.

Paris Agreement, a pact nations made to voluntarily reduce greenhouse gas emissions.[241]

And while hydraulic fracturing involves large amounts of water, sand, and some chemicals, most drillers handle the process safely and properly. Mitchell believed that hydraulic fracturing warranted protection to ensure that "wild, smaller independent drillers" are punished for doing anything wrong or dangerous.[242]

National Defense

National defense is a significant use of oil and gas products. Our history in World War II tells us that we need it refined into diesel, gasoline, and jet fuel for the military. With America as a world leader, the importance of fossil fuels in fighting wars cannot be overstated. Our pipelines were born in a time when America desperately needed fuel to survive, and we still rely on pipelines and fossil fuels to maintain our security among other nations.

Economic and Environmental Progress

Pipelines are one solution to breaking two million American Indians out of cyclical poverty, as evidenced by T. J. Plenty Chief and MHA Nation.[243] On Standing Rock Sioux Reservation alone, 41 percent of its members live below the poverty line, which contributes to higher rates of crime, suicide, alcoholism, gangs, and sexual abuse.[244] It hasn't helped that previous ways the federal government helped American

241. "In 2017, the U.S. Had the Largest Reduction in Carbon Dioxide Emissions in the World," Institute for Energy Research, August 3, 2018, https://www.instituteforenergyresearch.org/fossil-fuels/gas-and-oil/in-2017-the-u-s-had-the-largest-reduction-in-carbon-dioxide-emissions-in-the-world/.

242. Christopher Helman, "Billionaire Father Of Fracking Says Government Must Step Up Regulation," *Forbes,* July 19, 2012, https://www.forbes.com/sites/christopherhelman/2012/07/19/billionaire-father-of-fracking-says-government-must-step-up-regulation/#6aed6eba8d97.

243. Naomi Riley, "One Way to Help Native Americans: Property Rights," *The Atlantic,* July 30, 2016, https://www.theatlantic.com/politics/archive/2016/07/native-americans-property-rights/492941.

244. Phil McKenna, "2016: How Dakota Pipeline Protest Became a Native American Cry for Justice," *Inside Climate News,* December 27, 2016, https://insideclimatenews.org/news/22122016/standing-rock-dakota-access-pipeline-native-american-protest-environmental-justice.

Indians make money included controversial industries such as tobacco and casino gambling, both of which introduced new problems and continued the cycle of poverty.

To combat unemployment, pipeline unions are creating partnerships with tribes in which young American Indians can cultivate trade skills and establish careers. The goals are employability, self-sufficiency, and economic growth on reservations. The emerging tribal-union partnerships relieve the labor issues of American Indians and the rising labor strain on the pipeline industry. Unions are offering new members a turnkey workforce development solution in the form of free, high-quality training, apprenticeship opportunities, and job placement.[245] The partnerships and their turnkey workforce solutions are providing more than jobs—they're offering life-changing career paths.[246]

Equally life-changing are the innovative ideas that have emerged from oil and gas companies. One radical idea was the lithium-ion battery that fuels electric devices, an invention that originated in a technology lab at international oil and gas company ExxonMobil.[247]

In Mr. Mitchell's wake, technology advancements are increasingly focused on mitigating the environmental effects of fossil fuels. Together with the government, the industry is producing new technologies—including satellites, global positioning systems, mobile rigs, horizontal and directional drilling approaches, and 4D seismic technologies—to discover oil reserves in larger areas while drilling fewer exploratory wells and reducing the size of affected areas.

---

245. Bradley Kramer, "An Industry on the Rise: Pipeline Experts Provide Market Outlook," *North American Oil and Gas Pipelines,* June 4, 2018, https://napipelines.com/industry-rise-pipeline-market-outlook/.

246. Lou Thompson, "Labor Reserves: Tribal-Union Workforce Partnerships Address Pipeline Labor Shortage," *North American Oil and Gas Pipelines,* October 3, 2018, https://napipelines.com/labor-teamsters-pipeline-tribal-workforce-partnerships.

247. ExxonMobil, "Pioneers of Innovation: The Battery that Changed the World," *Energy Factor,* September 22, 2016, https://energyfactor.exxonmobil.com/science-technology/battery-changed-world/.

There is also greater enforcement of safety and environmental laws and regulations. Thanks to the Rigs-to-Reefs program, old offshore rigs are plugged and tipped over to rest on the ocean floor as artificial reefs that attract marine life, increasing fish populations and opportunities for recreational fishing and diving. Within a year, the rigs are covered with barnacles, coral, sponges, clams, and other sea creatures.

LOUISIANA INVESTMENTS IN CARBON CAPTURE AND STORAGE

Louisiana is spearheading a particularly ambitious climate initiative in the Gulf South region called "carbon capture and storage," or CCS. CCS is touted as an efficient, safe way to capture and store carbon dioxide produced by fossil fuel and pipeline projects before the waste enters the atmosphere. While there's debate about its effectiveness—Greenpeace calls it the "Great Carbon Capture Scam"—it's worth serious examination as part of the solution to decarbonize and mitigate GHG emissions.[248]

It's one reason Louisiana is known as the carbon capture capital of the South, forging a model that attracts business investments.[249,250] One such business investment is Shell's donation to Louisiana State University to fund the research, discovery, and solutions in energy-related initiatives, with an aim to transition energy in Louisiana and the

248. Daniel Greenfield, "Biden's New EPA Rule May Double Power Bills," Sultan Knish The Journalism of Daniel Greenfield, April 27, 2023, http://www.danielgreenfield.org/2023/04/bidens-new-epa-rule-may-double-power.html.

249. Adam Daigle, "Carbon Capture Project Will Create Over 1,000 jobs in Louisiana," Governing, April 12, 2022, https://www.governing.com/now/carbon-capture-project-will-create-over-1-000-jobs-in-louisiana.

250. Greg Hilburn, "How Louisiana Became the Carbon Capture Capital of the South with $6 Billion in Projects," *Lafayette Daily Advertiser*, April 17, 2022, https://www.theadvertiser.com/story/news/2022/04/18/how-louisiana-became-carbon-capture-capital-south-john-bel-edwards-bill-cassidy-air-products-cleco/7330762001/.

nation.[251] Another is electric utility firm Cleco's project to capture the CO_2 of the highest-emitting power plant, reducing the plant's carbon emissions by 95 percent, promising thousands of jobs, and potentially reducing the rates of regular retail customers.

Until renewables can sustain our nation, Louisiana's climate action initiatives point to a promising path forward, a practical compromise between meeting increasing energy needs in a reliable way while mitigating the environmental impact. It is supporting an industry wrongly portrayed as the enemy. Whereas protestors call for the complete abandonment of the oil and gas industry, CCS makes fossil fuels a safer resource.

The majority of fossil fuels are converted into transportation fuel for airplanes, cars, and trucks. They're used in the heating and air conditioning of our homes and the construction of asphalt roads and sturdy buildings. They help produce chemicals, medicines, plastics, and synthetic materials that are in nearly everything we use. The inherently high density of fossil fuels supports industries—including iron, steel, cement, chemicals, and heavy freight—where renewables have no acceptable solution.[252] Fossil fuels provide the strength and flexibility necessary for our bridges, buildings, and automobiles.

Ultimately, domestic oil and gas—like the LNG with CCS technology from Louisiana—empower our nation. Americans enjoy increased life expectancy, better health, higher income, more leisure time, and higher education. These aspects of our lives are tightly linked to increased access to fossil fuels.[253]

---

251. Aris Williams "LSU Announces $27 Million Gift from Shell Oil, the Largest Investment in Energy-Related Initiatives," LSU Reveille, published June 23, 2022, updated July 1, 2022, https://www.lsureveille.com/news/lsu-announces-27-million-gift-from-shell-oil-the-largest-investment-in-energy-related-initiatives/article_de7e2014-f35a-11ec-8f02-e7e995829144.html.

252. Allen Brooks, "Shell's 'Sky' Scenario: Pie-in-the-Sky Greenwashing?" Master Resource, May 10, 2018, https://www.masterresource.org/shell/shells-sky-scenario/.

253. Alex Epstein, "What's the Deal with the Green New Deal?" Prager U, July 29, 2019, https://www.prageru.com/video/whats-the-deal-with-the-green-new-deal/.

CONTINUING RESPONSIBLE OIL AND GAS

While we work to balance the reduction of emissions with the protection of our forests, our nation can count on an ever-increasing demand for energy. Pressed on all sides by national security and daily energy needs, the answer is not to demonize fossil fuels, nor is it to stop the flow of oil and gas. It's to continue stewarding our existing resources as safely and efficiently as possible as we grow with renewable energy.

It's a challenge when radical environmental activists are literally trying to burn down the foundation on which our nation was built. Pipelines were once celebrated as innovative breakthroughs in winning World War II, but today, people no longer assume that pipelines are the best way to transport oil and gas over a long distance from where it is produced to where it can be refined and, ultimately, where it will be consumed. Public perception has changed dramatically.

Are pipelines as bad as activists say they are?

Pipelines are only one of four methods of moving oil and gas. The other transportation methods are rail, ship, and truck. While each one plays a unique role, it also has trade-offs in light of economics, safety, cost, and the environment.[254]

Methods of Delivering the Goods

Road transportation is useful in moving smaller quantities of oil and gas over shorter distances and when crossing areas lacking pipeline or rail infrastructure. But the capacity of trucks is extremely limited and the most costly method, four times that of pipelines. Worse, trucks spill more oil and gas than rail and pipeline combined.[255] And because trucks

254. James Conca, "Pick Your Poison for Crude—Pipeline, Truck, Rail, or Boat," *Forbes,* April 26, 2014, https://www.forbes.com/sites/jamesconca/2014/04/26/pick-your-poison-for-crude-pipeline-rail-truck-or-boat/#2fbc38dd17ac.

255. Megan Hansen, "Pipelines, Rail and Truck," Strata, August 1, 2017, https://www.heartland.org/publications-resources/publications/pipelines-rail--trucks.

are closer to the general public, where accidents have greater potential for human fatality and injury, road transportation is at the bottom of the list when it comes to safety.

Another method is by ship, which is flexible, readily available, and one of the least costly methods.[256] However, the large capacities of tank barges carrying huge amounts of oil mean large capacities for environmental destruction. Five out of the ten largest oil spills in U.S. history are from ships, like the *Exxon Valdez* that spilled more than ten million gallons of crude oil near Alaska in 1989, causing the immediate deaths of hundreds of thousands of animals and eventually covering 1,300 miles of coastline and 11,000 square miles of ocean. Additionally, World War II taught us that ships were easy targets for wartime enemies.

Yet another method of delivery is rail transportation, the most-used alternative to pipeline transportation. It can access remote regions, takes less time and energy to construct and approve, can transport more quickly across large distances, and has a safety advantage because it passes through rural areas.[257] But the amount of oil spilled by rail has skyrocketed, and rail can't meet the oil and gas demand due to its constrained capacity and congestion—certainly not in wartime.

The Best Oil and Gas Transporter

Of the four ways to transport oil and gas, pipelines are the most commonly used method, moving the majority of all domestically produced petroleum products. They perform the best by every measure: safety, cost, environment, and economics.

The anti-pipeline movement hinges on the claim that pipelines harm

256. "Pipeline, Ship, and Rail: The Benefits and Needs of Different Oil and Gas Transport Methods," STI Group, February 2, 2016, https://setxind.com/midstream/pipeline-ship-rail-benefits-needs-different-oil-gas-transport-methods.

257. Hansen, "Pipelines, Rail and Trucks."

people and the environment. However, pipelines are safer compared to rail and road transportation. Oil and gas transportation by pipeline is 70 percent safer than rail and 600 percent safer than trucks. Americans are seventy-five times more likely to be killed by lightning than they are in an incident related to an oil or gas pipeline.[258]

Spills and leaks do happen but are rare in relation to the massive quantity of product the pipes, mostly occurring in facilities well-equipped to contain them and recover quickly. When the amount transported is considered, transportation by pipeline is 4.5 times less likely to result in a spill than transport by rail. Since 2013, over 99.999 percent of petroleum product made it end to end in pipelines without incident. The statistically near-perfect safety rate doesn't dismiss leaks but puts them in perspective.[259]

It's worse for the environment *not* to have pipelines. If environmentalists succeeded in shutting down every pipeline carrying low-sulfur light crude oil, it would not slow the demand of oil. With the shutdown of the Keystone XL pipeline, the only thing protesters accomplished was forcing crude out of pipelines and onto rail cars and diesel trucks, redirecting the crude onto more cumbersome, dangerous, and polluting conveyances and negatively impacting the environment in the United States and around the world.

It's also worse for our national security not to have pipelines. When Big and Little Inch pipelines filled a gaping need in World War II, we learned that pipelines ensure American stability and security in ways that ships or trucks cannot provide for our country.

Regarding cost, pipeline projects require more time and much higher upfront costs than other methods. In the long run, they require much less human capital, are more efficient at moving the product over

258. Hansen, "Pipelines, Rail and Trucks."

259. McCown, "Why Pipeline Opposition Undermines Environmental Progress and Safety."

large distances, and are generally cheaper than rail or road. The other modes of transportation require diesel fuel, the price of which significantly impacts the cost of delivery.[260]

Pipelines also support high employment and a thriving economy for producers, refineries, consumers, and workers. Without pipelines to supply the goods, refiners would simply buy high-sulfur heavy crude from foreign producers to meet demand.[261]

When we look at the big picture and weigh all variables, pipelines are the sensible option to transport energy across the United States. They ensure the safety of communities, the security of our nation, the support of our economy, and the transition to cleaner energy for the climate. Pipelines are the veins and arteries supplying our nation with necessary energy while we move away from coal and develop viable renewable solutions. Demanding to leave fossil fuels in the ground is like demanding that humans interrupt their blood flow because of high cholesterol.[262, 263, 264]

We need more states like Louisiana that are willing to pave the way in a sensible approach to climate action. As a leader in the Gulf South region, the state is moving forward with oil and gas production and introducing new carbon capture technology. It is protecting iconic cypress forests from the wood pellet industry and attracting industries, like a graphite plant in Vidalia, Louisiana. With supplies from Africa and a binding agreement with Tesla, the aim of the Vidalia plant is to responsibly process the minerals necessary to expand renewable

---

260. James Conca, "Which Is Safer for Transporting Crude Oil: Rail, Truck, Pipeline or Boat?"

261. "Economic Impact of Investment in Pipeline Infrastructure," Snelson Companies, Inc., https://www.snelsonco.com/economic-impact-investment-pipeline-infrastructure/.

262. McCown, "Why Pipeline Opposition Undermines Environmental Progress and Safety."

263. "Construction Jobs," *Association of Oil Pipelines,* http://www.aopl.org/pipelines-create-jobs/construction-jobs.

264. McCown, "Why Pipeline Opposition Undermines Environmental Progress and Safety."

solutions. With the proper regulation and best-in-class rules of the United States, our graphite manufacturing plants are better managed and controlled than those in China that lack environmental regulation. The Vidalia plant is also one step toward loosening our dependence on China, which controls the global supply chain of rare earth minerals.

In addition to new fossil fuel technologies, another technology that is paving the way with promise is nuclear energy. If you had asked me forty years ago, I would've discounted the idea based on my limited knowledge and personal experiences. But I've had to rethink my position based on the research. Nuclear energy points to a clear path forward—and it's worth our attention.

The front entrance to Cheniere's facility at Sabine Pass. Courtesy of Cheniere.

Cheniere's facility at Sabine Pass. Courtesy of Cheniere.

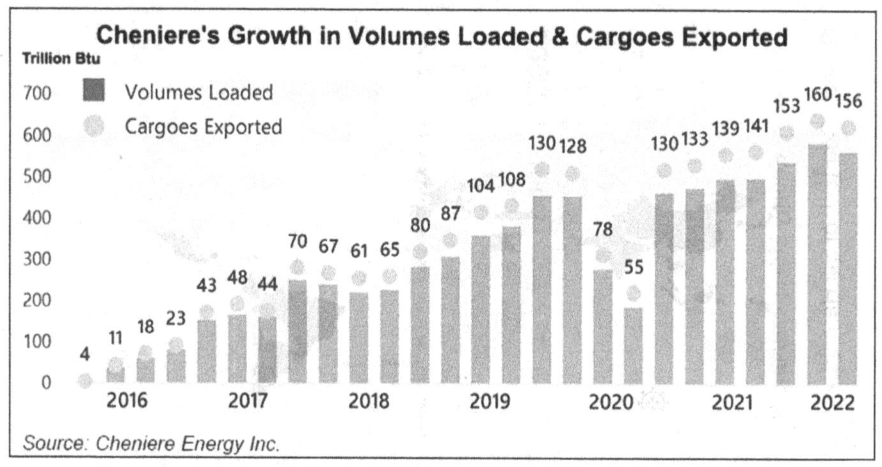

Cheniere's growth from 2016 to 2022 is shown in both volumes loaded and cargoes exported. Courtesy of Cheniere.

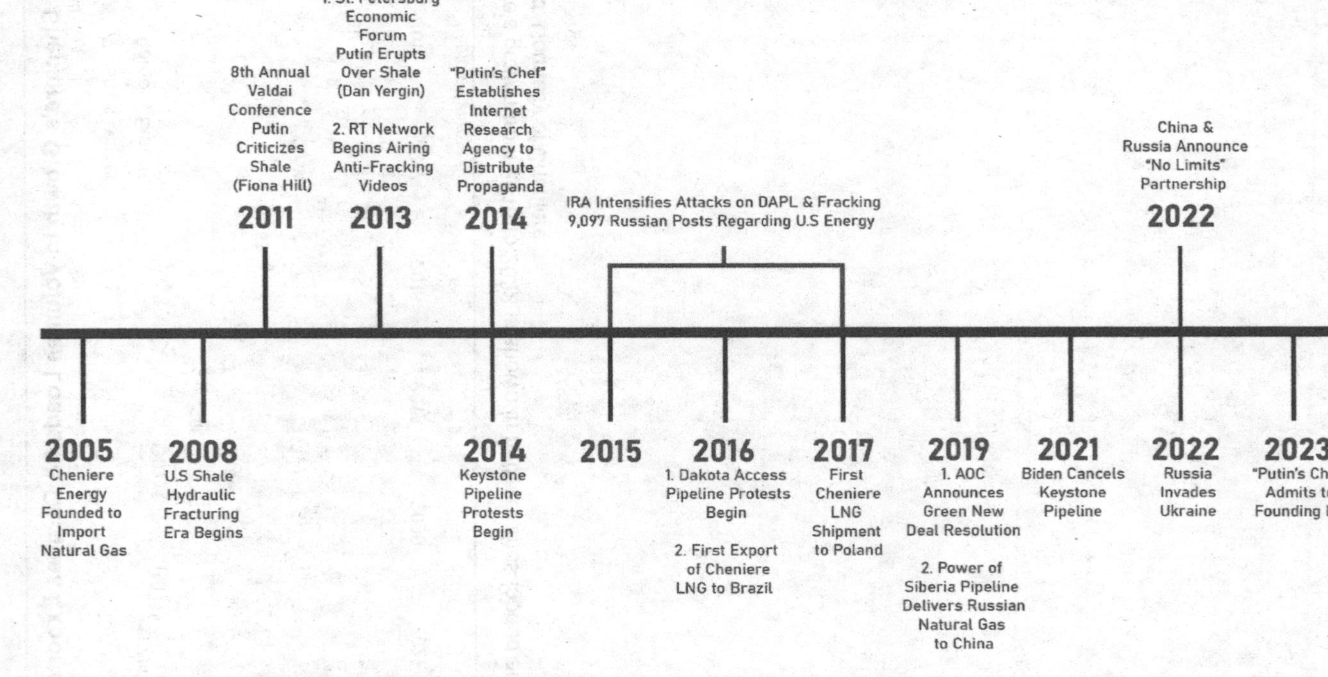
8th Annual Valdai Conference Putin Criticizes Shale (Fiona Hill)
2011
1. St. Petersburg Economic Forum Putin Erupts Over Shale (Dan Yergin)
2. RT Network Begins Airing Anti-Fracking Videos
2013
"Putin's Chef" Establishes Internet Research Agency to Distribute Propaganda
2014
IRA Intensifies Attacks on DAPL & Fracking
9,097 Russian Posts Regarding U.S Energy
China & Russia Announce "No Limits" Partnership
2022
2005
Cheniere Energy Founded to Import Natural Gas
2008
U.S Shale Hydraulic Fracturing Era Begins
2014
Keystone Pipeline Protests Begin
2015
2016
1. Dakota Access Pipeline Protests Begin
2. First Export of Cheniere LNG to Brazil
2017
First Cheniere LNG Shipment to Poland
2019
1. AOC Announces Green New Deal Resolution
2. Power of Siberia Pipeline Delivers Russian Natural Gas to China
2021
Biden Cancels Keystone Pipeline
2022
Russia Invades Ukraine
2023
"Putin's Chef" Admits to Founding IRA

Timeline of Energy Milestones and Russian Response

Source: Courtesy of Bill Herrington.

CHAPTER 8

NUCLEAR ENERGY

SHOULD WE GIVE NUCLEAR POWER A SECOND CHANCE?

"Failure is the opportunity to begin again, this time more intelligently."

– Henry Ford

When Bill Gates first learned about nuclear energy, the multibillionaire and founder of Microsoft was skeptical, but intrigued.

His initial skepticism is typical of many of us who have been negatively influenced by high-profile nuclear disasters. There's residual fear from memories of the 1979 Three Mile Island accident. The fear was exacerbated by a deadly 1986 disaster at the Chernobyl Nuclear Power Plant, where design flaws caused an explosion and graphite fire that rained radioactive material onto parts of the Soviet Union and other European countries.

However, a growing number of countries are interested in the potential of nuclear power as clean energy. There are 440 nuclear reactors around the world, and fifty-five are under construction. Like Gates, more and more Americans are intrigued.[265] A 2016 survey found that 75 percent of Americans feel nuclear energy will be important in meeting the country's future electricity needs, and 45 percent believe its importance will increase with time. Eighty percent of respondents favor renewing operating licenses for nuclear power plants that continue to meet federal safety standards, and 68 percent believe that nuclear power plants operating in the United States are safe and secure.[266]

Today, study after study by top scientific journals consistently come to the same conclusion: nuclear power plants are the optimal way to make reliable electricity. And the environmental benefits are clear. Nuclear energy is the cleanest, highest-density option that takes up the least amount of land.

Robert Bryce illustrates the enormous density advantage of nuclear energy with Indian Point Energy Center. This nuclear site provides as

---

265. "Plans For New Reactors Worldwide," World Nuclear Association, updated December 2022, https://world-nuclear.org/information-library/current-and-future-generation/plans-for-new-reactors-worldwide.aspx.

266. "Myths About Nuclear Energy," Center for Nuclear Science and Technology Information, http://nuclearconnect.org/know-nuclear/talking-nuclear/top-10-myths-about-nuclear-energy.

much as 30 percent of electricity to New York City. With a footprint of about 250 acres, the power density of the site exceeds two thousand watts per square meter. Compare that to the power density of wind turbines, which is only about one watt per square meter. Bryce estimates that we'd need to pave more than 770 square miles of land with wind turbines—an area about the size of Rhode Island—to generate as much electricity as Indian Point.

The density flaw of renewables and the amount of land they consume are hurdles impossible to dismiss and ignore. That's why some very smart people are taking another look at nuclear energy.

ADVANCED REACTOR TECHNOLOGY

Gates' skepticism yielded to intrigue when he read a paper about a new generation of nuclear reactors. He became convinced that nuclear energy is a vital part of the energy transition. In 2008 he founded TerraPower, a nuclear reactor design and development engineering company headquartered in Bellevue, Washington.

The first test plant was developed at a shuttered coal site and is slated to begin service in 2028. The vision is fully functional nuclear energy capable of complementing a grid of wind and solar power by 2050. It could position the United States as a dominant force in nuclear power and set the world standard. This initiative is necessary because the U.S. government and the U.S. nuclear industry are falling behind China and Russia. The two countries are building plants with advanced technologies and seek to export nuclear energy to countries around the world.[267]

Now Gates is working to turn the tide of public perception on nuclear energy—and he's starting with safety.

267. Catherine Clifford, "Bill Gates' Terrapower Aims to Build Its First Advanced Nuclear Reactor in a Coal Town in Wyoming" CNBC, November 17, 2021, https://www.cnbc.com/2021/11/17/bill-gates-terrapower-builds-its-first-nuclear-reactor-in-a-coal-town.html.

The Safest Option

Gates says advanced reactor designs guard against the accidents of the past. A new approach to cooling systems in "natrium plants" ensures greater safety measures: liquid sodium is used as a cooling agent instead of water. Liquid sodium absorbs more heat, reduces internal pressure, and prevents explosions. In the event of an emergency shutdown, the cooling system relies on its own natural circulation rather than outside energy sources.[268]

Even with the rare accidents in the past, nuclear power is linked to the fewest number of deaths per unit of electricity when compared to the other forms of energy generation. Michael Shellenberger, the president of Environmental Progress, says the Three-Mile Island incident caused more fright than actual cause for concern. If anything, it proved the relative safety of nuclear energy because nobody died.[269] Nuclear power has always been the safest way to generate energy.

Additionally, the risk of an uncontrolled nuclear reaction in the United States is particularly small. The industry is governed by diverse and redundant barriers, safety systems, trainings, testing and maintenance activities, and regulatory requirements and oversight of the U.S. Nuclear Regulatory Commission.

Yet the stigma impacts the progress of nuclear power. Researcher Joshua Goldstein and economist Staffan A. Qvist say that most countries' energy policies are shaped by long-standing phobias about radiation rather than hard facts. Here are two cases in point: a 1975 hydroelectric dam failure in China killed tens of thousands, and a 1984 Bhopal gas leak at a union carbide plant in India killed four thousand then another

---

268. Catherine Clifford, "How Bill Gates' Company Terrapower Is Building Next-Generation Nuclear Power,"CNBC, April 8, 2021, https://www.cnbc.com/2021/04/08/bill-gates-terrapower-is-building-next-generation-nuclear-power.html.

269. Shellenberger, "If Nuclear Power Is So Safe, Why Are We So Afraid Of It?"

fifteen thousand more over time, yet we don't fear those industries.[270]

In the United States, activists are celebrating the closure of the two nuclear reactors at California's Diablo Canyon Power Plant slated for 2025, even when it means the loss of more annual low-carbon electricity than its solar photovoltaics and wind plants cumulatively generated in 2016. Across the country, commercial reactors are facing shutdowns even as they provide one-fifth of the electricity produced in the nation. Ahmed Abdulla, an assistant research scientist for the Center for Energy Research at the University of California San Diego, chalks up the closures to the industry's "inability to convince policymakers that it can contribute to a low-carbon energy transition, forcing [the industry] to resort to other narratives; the difficulty and expense inherent in nuclear innovation; and the failure to improve public perception."[271]

Yet Shellenberger is optimistic that educating the public about the safety of nuclear energy will help it regain momentum as a viable energy source. A growing number of experts in radiation, climate, and public health are speaking up in favor of nuclear power plants.

Increased Storage and Capacity

The natrium reactor technology allows the conservation of large-scale energy storage for future use, similar to a battery. It increases a power plant's output from about 345 megawatts to 500 megawatts over five hours, but with less maintenance. And the capacity of nuclear power isn't contingent on other factors, like the long list of conditions affecting solar and wind facilities, including location, time of day, seasonal variations, climate, and weather conditions.

270. Joshua S. Goldstein and Staffan A. Qvist, "Only Nuclear Energy Can Save the Planet," NEI, January 11, 2019, https://www.nei.org/news/2019/only-nuclear-energy-can-save-the-planet.

271. Ahmed Abdulla, "The demise of US nuclear power in 4 charts," *The Conversation,* August 1, 2018, https://theconversation.com/the-demise-of-us-nuclear-power-in-4-charts-98817.

Even with massive land requirements, the capacities of wind and solar farms cannot compete with nuclear facilities. A typical nuclear facility in the United States only needs a little more than one square mile to operate. Wind farms require 360 times more land area to produce the same amount of electricity.[272] Solar farms require seventy-five times more space. In other words, it would take more than three million solar panels or more than 430 wind turbines to produce the same amount of power as a typical nuclear reactor.

Lower Cost

The advanced power plants are cheaper than conventional plants. The capital cost of traditional plants is in the multibillions. They are enormous customized plants that almost always generate significant cost overruns. But the TerraPower design allows for mass production of smaller units in a more efficient manufacturing environment. They operate at lower pressures and don't require the same construction materials. Because they're also smaller, they appeal to utility companies seeking to plug nuclear power into their existing grids without big risks.

A major step forward for advanced nuclear reactors is the modular movement. New reactors are safer, smaller, cheaper, and *modular*, a combination of attributes that is new for the nuclear industry. The small modular reactors (SMRs) are about one-third the size of current power plants and more flexible. The International Atomic Energy Agency calls SMRs among the most promising technologies in nuclear power.[273] In 2022, a tiny modular design by an industry leader based in Portland,

272. "The Ultimate Fast Facts Guide to Nuclear Energy," Office of Nuclear Energy, January 16, 2019, https://www.energy.gov/ne/articles/ultimate-fast-facts-guide-nuclear-energy.

273. Andy Knight, "Purdue, Duke Energy Study Could Provide Blueprint for Developing Future Power Source," *The Herald Bulletin*, June 11, 2022, https://www.heraldbulletin.com/news/local_news/purdue-duke-energy-study-could-provide-blueprint-for-developing-future-power-source/article_23b49784-e73b-11ec-b83f-ebe627070164.html.

NuScale, was approved by the U.S. Nuclear Regulatory Commission in 2022 on all but the final formalities. The groundbreaking technology took six years of work and involved multiple universities and government laboratories. Now the trade association for U.S. nuclear plant operators aims to double nuclear energy output over the next thirty years.[274,275]

The new technology is economically leading other fuel sources. Studies have found that nuclear plants provide substantial economic benefits to surrounding states and regions, including producing more jobs at higher pay than all other energy sources combined.[276] Also, the cost of fuel for a nuclear power station is significantly less than that of a coal-fired power station, enough to offset the high cost of constructing, managing, and decommissioning a nuclear plant. As gas prices inevitably rise and coal faces the prospect of economic constraints on its emissions, nuclear energy is a competitive alternative.

And, like LNG, nuclear energy supports the economic security of the United States as a superpower. One of the motives driving Gates' TerraPower is the fact that there is a great advantage to producing and storing years of fuel for electricity independently—and leading other nations in the initiative.[277]

---

274. Caroline Delbert, "This Tiny Nuclear Reactor Will Change Energy—and Now It's Officially Safe," Popular Mechanics, September 2, 2020, https://www.popularmechanics.com/science/a33896110/tiny-nuclear-reactor-government-approval/.

275. "MidAmerican Energy Wants to Study Small Nuclear Power Plants. How Would They Work?" Des Moines Register, June 27, 2022, https://www.desmoinesregister.com/story/news/2022/06/27/how-would-small-nuclear-reactors-work-midamerican-wants-know/7728527001/.

276. James Conca, "Nuclear Power Provides a Whole Lot More Than Just Energy," *Forbes*, January 16, 2018, https://www.forbes.com/sites/jamesconca/2018/01/16/nuclear-power-provides-a-whole-lot-more-than-just-energy/#27a113bd5e7e.

277. "Energy for the World - Why Uranium?" World Nuclear Association, December 2012, http://www.world-nuclear.org/information-library/nuclear-fuel-cycle/introduction/energy-for-the-world-why-uranium.aspx.

Less Waste

Advanced nuclear reactors produce less waste than conventional plants. At TerraPower, the radioactive fuel powering nuclear reactors is consumed more efficiently and completely than at conventional plants, leaving less byproduct. Spent fuel takes up two-thirds less volume than traditional reactors. And a game-changer is in the works: the first U.S. power plant is signed up to recycle spent nuclear fuel into new nuclear fuel. The recycled fuel will be optimized for fuel requirements.[278]

Nuclear power also has one of the smallest carbon footprints of any energy source. Because nuclear power plants do not burn fuel, they do not produce greenhouse gas emissions. They are approximately eight thousand times more efficient than plants that burn fossil fuels.

Also, in a 2022 technological breakthrough, the U.S. Department of Energy announced a scientific milestone hailed as "one of the most impressive feats of the 21st century." Government scientists at a California laboratory produced a nuclear fusion reaction that creates a net energy gain—the first time more energy is produced in a reaction than is consumed. Nuclear fusion combines two light atomic particles to form a single heavier particle, harnessing massive amounts of energy. The technology is a long way from powering the grid, but it has the potential to combat climate change by producing no greenhouse gasses or radioactive waste.[279,280]

Because it's clean and reliable, nuclear energy is recommended

278. Annette Cary, "Richland Nuclear Plant Could Be 1st in U.S. to Produce Power This Way Under New Deal," Tri-City Herald, Yahoo! News, July 18, 2022, https://www.yahoo.com/news/richland-nuclear-plant-could-1st-185857517.html.

279. Ben Adler, "Energy Department Announces Nuclear Fusion Milestone: 'Clean Energy Source that Could Revolutionize the World'," Yahoo! News, December 13, 2022, https://www.yahoo.com/news/energy-department-announces-nuclear-fusion-milestone-clean-energy-source-that-could-revolutionize-the-world-165844246.html?guccounter=1.

280. Bradford Betz , "US Scientists Make Major Breakthrough in 'Limitless, Zero-Carbon' Fusion Energy: Report," Fox Business, December 11, 2022, https://www.foxbusiness.com/energy/us-scientists-make-major-breakthrough-limitless-zero-carbon-fusion-energy-report.

by many scientists as required for a future sustainable energy system alongside other forms of low-carbon power generation. Nuclear power doesn't show up on lists of "clean" energy, but one country has accepted the risks and embraced the future of energy—with remarkable results.

Five Fast Facts About Nuclear Energy

1. The United States is the world's largest producer of nuclear power.
2. Nuclear energy provides half of America's carbon-free electricity. It's the largest domestic source of clean energy.
3. Nuclear power is the most reliable energy source in America. Plants operate at full capacity more than 92 percent of the time.
4. Nuclear fuel is extremely dense. All of the used nuclear fuel produced by the U.S. nuclear energy industry over the last sixty years could fit on a football field at a depth of less than ten yards.
5. Nuclear reactors help power homes and businesses in twenty-eight states. Of the ninety-two commercial reactors helping power homes and business, the most are in Illinois (eleven reactors), which receives more than half of its power from nuclear.[281]

GERMANY VS. SWEDEN

For an intriguing comparison of nuclear energy policy decisions, we can look at Germany and Sweden. In 2010, Germany introduced Energiewende, an energy transition program that eliminated nuclear power and doubled renewables. Meanwhile, Sweden took a very different path. It continued to develop the nuclear power that it started in the 1970s, when oil supply and prices were uncertain.[282]

281. "5 Fast Facts About Nuclear Energy" Office of Nuclear Energy, March 23, 2021, https://www.energy.gov/ne/articles/5-fast-facts-about-nuclear-energy.
282. "Nuclear Power in Sweden," World Nuclear Association, updated October 2022, https://world-nuclear.org/information-library/country-profiles/countries-o-s/sweden.aspx.

Today, the results are vastly different. Germany is experiencing what happens when a country focuses on renewables alone to address carbon emissions. In contrast, Sweden illustrates what might have been for Germany and our nation.

Germany

The Germans will tell you that the wind and sun are unreliable. They even have a term lamenting the resulting intermittency of wind and solar power: they call it *dunkelflaute,* which loosely translated means "dark doldrums."[283]

The problem is illustrated by Germany's energy transition program, Energiewende, which eliminated nuclear power and doubled renewables in its energy mix, particularly solar and wind energy. Solar and wind power are vulnerable to locations, times of day, seasonal variations, climates, and weather conditions, and Germany is no exception. Because the demand for power is required around the clock—and renewable energy is intermittent and unreliable—Germany was forced to add coal as a second energy source as a standby power.

A backup system can be either battery-based, which is costly and unproven on a large scale, or provided by traditional generating methods, which is both costly and inefficient. Because nuclear power had been eliminated, the country turned to dirty brown coal plants as its backup source. Energiewende depends on coal plants as well as increased imports of electricity from other nations, two energy costs not generally factored in the production costs of solar and wind energy.

Today, 40 percent of Germany's energy comes from coal plants, six of which make the list of Europe's ten most polluting power plants. Essentially, Energiewende traded nuclear for renewables—one carbon-free source for another—then dirtied the deal with coal. It is a global

283. "If You Think the U.S. Can Go 100% Renewables, You're Fantasizing," Natural Gas Now.

trade-off: the IER concluded in 2017 that emissions of carbon dioxide emissions and consumption of coal and natural gas all increased, despite record growth in wind and solar power. [284, 285]

Germany shows us what happens when a country focuses on renewables alone to address carbon emissions. In the past decade, Germany's "Operation Energiewende" program has roughly doubled its production of energy from renewables, which now accounts for a quarter of Germany's energy production. During this same period, carbon emissions per person has not declined.

Sweden

At the other end of nuclear energy policy spectrum is Sweden. At almost the exact same period that the United States rejected nuclear energy, Sweden strategically embraced it.

In the 1970s, Sweden followed France's lead by expanding its electrical supply in an unconventional way: developing nuclear power rather than fossil fuels. At the time, the motivation wasn't global warming; it was reliability. Hydropower was proving environmentally undesirable, and the oil crises of that decade made petroleum an unpredictable source. Over the next two decades, Sweden built twelve nuclear power plants, eight of which still operate today. Together, they supply 40 percent of Sweden's electricity, equal to its hydropower. Wind and biofuels supply the rest.

When Sweden built its nuclear reactors throughout the 1970s and 1980s, it was able to add new electricity production relative to its GDP at five times the speed of Germany. Sweden's carbon emissions dropped

---

284. Ariel Cohen, "California's New 100% Green Energy Target May Do More Harm Than Good."

285. Richard Rhodes, "A Sensible Climate Solution, Borrowed from Sweden," *New York Times*, February 5, 2019, https://www.nytimes.com/2019/02/05/books/review/bright-future-joshua-s-goldstein-staffan-a-qvist.html.

in half, even as its electricity production doubled.[286] As a result, electricity in Sweden is cheap, clean, and reliable. Goldstein and Qvist, the authors of *A Bright Future*, say the difference in outcomes is universal: "In every case where nuclear power was shut down, renewables have not filled the gap and CO_2 emissions have gone up, whereas in places… that expanded nuclear power, emissions went down."[287]

Today, Sweden is the most successful country at expanding low-carbon electricity and addressing GHG emissions. It has weaned itself off fossil fuels and simultaneously solved its carbon-emission problem. While Swedes use one-third more energy per person than Germans, they emit about half the carbon pollution per person versus Germans. Goldstein and Qvist estimate that it will take over a hundred years with Germany's Energiewende renewable plan to achieve the carbon reduction Sweden did in twenty years with nuclear.

Sweden shows us what might have been for our nation. The country is thriving. Along the way, it is debunking the stigma of nuclear power. Sweden demonstrates the promise of nuclear energy in solving energy and emissions issues for their nation—and for the rest of the watching world.

A WORLD OF DECISIONS

The contrast between Sweden and Germany is as stark as the contrast between developing and developed countries.

The carbon emissions of the thirty-eight high-income developed countries in the Organization for Economic Cooperation and

286. Joshua S. Goldstein and Staffan A. Qvist, "Only Nuclear Energy Can Save the Planet," NEI, January 11, 2019, https://www.nei.org/news/2019/only-nuclear-energy-can-save-the-planet.

287. Richard Rhodes, "A Sensible Climate Solution, Borrowed from Sweden," *New York Times*, February 5, 2019, https://www.nytimes.com/2019/02/05/books/review/bright-future-joshua-s-goldstein-staffan-a-qvist.html.

Development (OECD) have been declining for fifteen years. It's evidenced by the fact that Sweden is celebrating climate leadership and the United States is seeing progress by shifting from coal to natural gas. However, the carbon emissions of non-OECD countries have been significantly increasing, causing global carbon emissions to grow at the fastest rate in nearly fifty years.

The problem is two-fold. One aspect is the use of coal. It's being phased out now, but it was critical in the early development of OECD countries. Today, non-OECD countries are catching up and leveraging coal for their development because coal is abundant, relatively cheap, and easily transported.

Another aspect is population. The majority of the world's population lives in non-OECD countries. Around 60 percent live in the Asia Pacific region. Their standards of living are improving, which is a good thing. The hitch is that even a slight increase in energy consumption over a large population significantly impacts emissions. The carbon emissions of the Asia Pacific region are soaring—more than double the combined emissions of the United States and the United Kingdom. It's a problem across many non-OECD countries.

While Sweden's nuclear power results are impressive and our LNG supplies are promising for our individual nations, it'll take more to solve the problem of global GHG emissions. The data clearly indicates that the technological innovations of developing nations are only making a dent globally.

AN EMISSIONS GAME OF WHACK-A-MOLE

The sobering reality is that even if the United States reduces its emissions to zero, it wouldn't be nearly enough to reduce the upward trend of worldwide emissions. The worldwide emissions would continue to increase because of the explosion of CO_2 emissions in Asia, primarily in China and India.

China is key to global GHG emissions, but it won't quit coal as its main energy source. The country is relying on construction and other carbon-intensive energy to revive its economy, especially now after power shortages caused blackouts and shutdowns. The energy insecurity is worsened by the possibility of disrupted foreign oil supplies due to the war in Ukraine.[288] China has pushed back on Western pressure to reduce GHG emissions, arguing that its current emissions plan is the fastest time frame a country its size has proposed, which means global climate goals are also pushed back.[289]

A review of charts by BP illustrates the problem. Carbon emissions from the United States and Europe have declined since 2005 due primarily to replacing coal with natural gas.[290]

At the same time, China and India's emissions have increased by 50 percent and 88 percent respectively due to their increasing reliance on coal. In India, 281 coal plants are operating, 28 are under construction, and 23 are preparing to break ground. It's much worse in China—the top global coal miner, consumer, and emitter—where more than 1,000 coal plants are operating and another 240 are under construction or in planning phases.[291] China is promoting coal-fired power to revive its

288. Joe McDonald, "China Promotes Coal in Setback for Efforts to Cut Emissions," Associated Press, April 24, 2022, https://apnews.com/article/climate-business-environment-beijing-economy-8023a20303f690bda410c222c4a1a975.

289. Christian Shepherd, "With Coal Surge, China Puts Energy Security and Growth Before Climate Change," *The Washington Post*, April 22, 2022, https://www.washingtonpost.com/world/2022/04/22/china-coal-climate-change-xi-energy/.

290. Robert Rapier, "Yes, The U.S. Leads All Countries In Reducing Carbon Emissions," *Forbes*, October 24, 2017, https://www.forbes.com/sites/rrapier/2017/10/24/yes-the-u-s-leads-all-countries-in-reducing-carbon-emissions/?sh=78f1691d3535.

291. Sudarshan Varadhan and Aaron Sheldrick, "COP26 Aims to Banish Coal. Asia Is Building Hundreds of Power Plants to Burn it," Reuters, October 31, 2021, https://www.reuters.com/business/energy/cop26-aims-banish-coal-asia-is-building-hundreds-power-plants-burn-it-2021-10-29/#:~:text=Across%20India%2C%20281%20coal%20plants,not%20expected%20to%20attend%20COP26.

struggling economy. Citing "energy security," China is boosting its coal production capacity by 7 percent in 2022 after an increase of 5.7 percent in 2021.[292]

Of course, Western nations are not wholly innocent when it comes to emissions in China. While the United States and Europe have made strides in reducing domestic greenhouse gas emissions, the trends are not as impressive when trade is considered. Many wealthy countries import materials from Chinese factories rather than producing them domestically, thereby outsourcing a large portion of their carbon pollution overseas. After all, the Paris Agreement only holds countries responsible for emissions produced within their own borders.

For example, Britain reduced its domestic emissions by one-third over a twenty-five-year span, but only because many energy-intensive industries like steel and cement have moved abroad to factories with looser pollution rules. In truth, Britain's total carbon footprint increased slightly when the steel used to produce its skyscrapers and cars are factored in. The same holds true for Japan and Germany, who cut their domestic emissions but doubled or tripled the carbon dioxide outsourced to China. In the United States, the leading importer of "embodied carbon," our reported emissions would be 14 percent higher if we accounted for the imported cars, clothing, and other goods that cause pollution worldwide. Western countries are not making as much progress toward GHG emissions as reported when they're outsourcing emissions elsewhere.

Meanwhile, China and India are receiving the jobs—and the blame. And they're following the lead of Western nations: more recently, developing nations are the ones more frequently outsourcing carbon to other developing nations. China, for example, is moving some of its carbon-

292. Robert Rapier, "Carbon Emissions On Track To Reach An All-Time High," OilPrice.com, July 23, 2022, https://oilprice.com/The-Environment/Global-Warming/Carbon-Emissions-On-Track-To-Reach-An-All-Time-High.html.

intensive activities to Cambodia, Vietnam, and India. Steven J. Davis, a scientist at the University of California Irvine, compares it to a game of whack-a-mole.

It's a game dependent on the commitment of non-OECD countries to decrease their use of coal—the very nations that want the same economic power and prosperity enjoyed by developing nations. To solve the global problem, they must arrive there differently than by relying on coal. It also means that the United States must demand cooperation from countries like China to cut emissions. And Western nations must be honest about their total worldwide emissions, not just emissions within their borders. Worldwide carbon-emission levels cannot improve without addressing China, India, and other emerging Asian nations—and without acknowledging our impact on developing nations.[293]

Whether we like it or not, GHG Emissions cannot be solved by any one nation. The fate of emissions reductions rests in how well *all* nations come together to accomplish a global goal. And it starts with how well the people within our own nation come together to address American energy.

We must find the courage to reject short-sighted plans that over-promise but actually weaken our economic and national security.

293. Content throughout this section was derived from Brad Plumer, "You've Heard of Outsourced Jobs, but Outsourced Pollution? It's Real, and Tough to Tally Up," *New York Times*, September 4, 2018, https://www.nytimes.com/2018/09/04/climate/outsourcing-carbon-emissions.html.

King Coal Comes Storming Back
"China began construction on 15 gigawatts of new coal-fired power...The volume of new projects...amounts to almost one coal plant unit per week."
-- Global Energy Monitor, August 2022
The Iron Law Of Electricity Strikes Again: Germany Re-Opens Five Lignite-Fired Power Plants
India may delay coal plant closures amid crisis in blow to climate action
Asian thermal coal hits new record on soaring European demand
© Robert Bryce

Coal continues to be an apparent necessity in global energy production. Courtesy of Robert Bryce. Source material from media outlets: https://tradingeconomics.com/commodity/coal and https://time.com/6090732/china-coal-power-plants-emissions/.

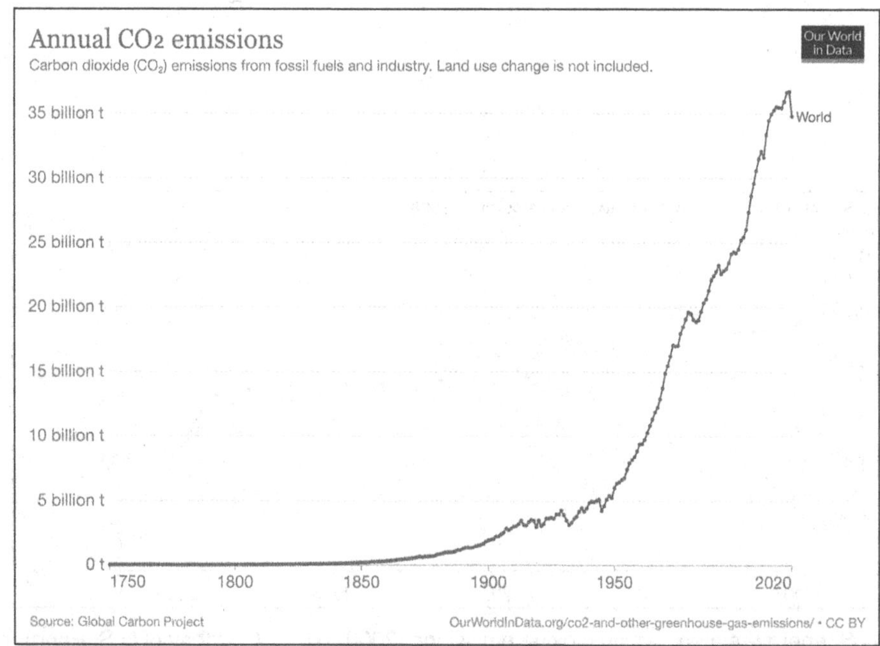

Annual CO_2 emissions by world region. This measures fossil fuel and industry emissions. Land use change is not included. Courtesy of Our World in Data based on the Global Carbon Project (2022) OurWorldInData.org/co2-and-other-greenhouse-gas-emissions CC BY-SA 4.0..

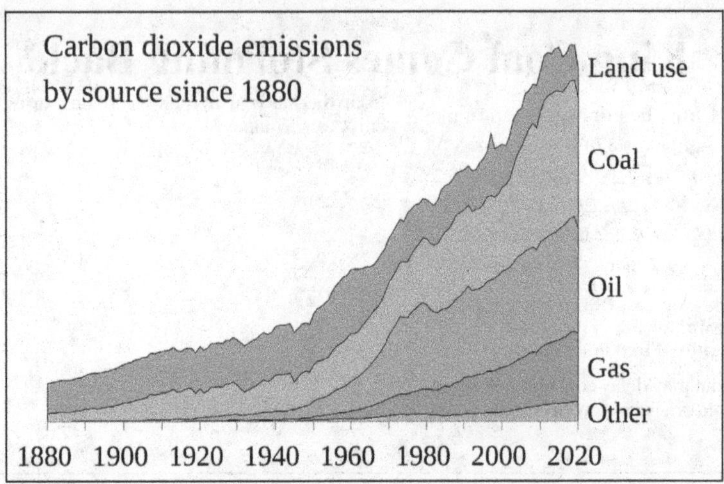

Carbon dioxide emissions by source since 1880 as calculated for the 2020 Global Carbon Budget. Carbon dioxide generated by land use changes (deforestation) has been added to as coal, oil, and natural gas consumption have each ramped up in turn. Courtesy of Efbrazil, CC BY-SA 4.0, via Wikimedia Commons.

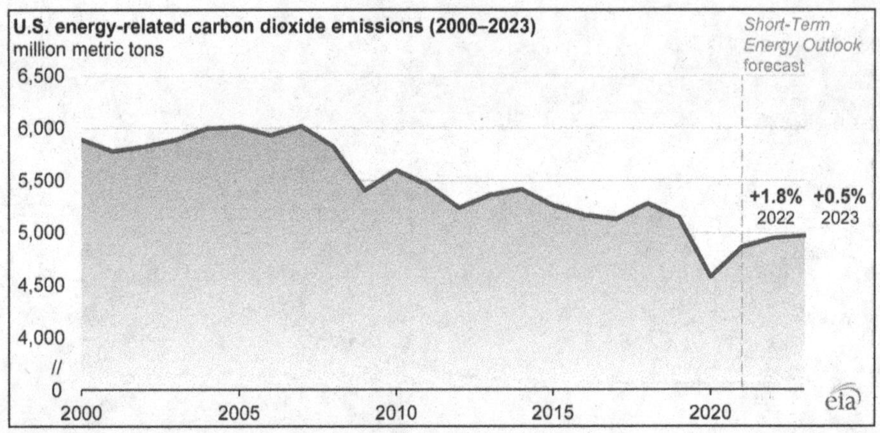

U.S. energy-related carbon dioxide emissions (2000–2023). Courtesy of U.S. Energy Information Administration, *Short-Term Energy Outlook* forecast, January 20, 2022.

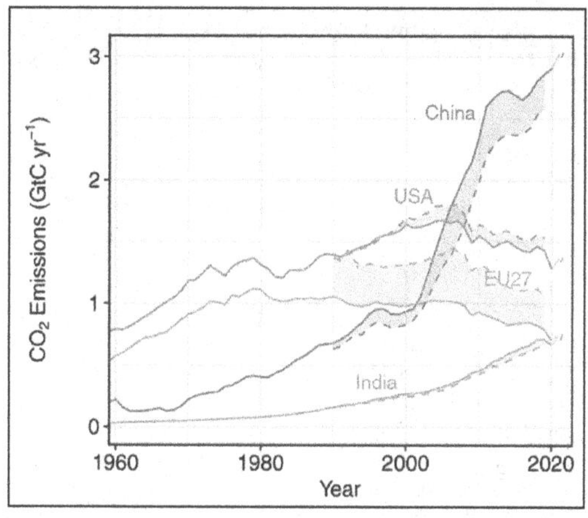

Fossil CO_2 emissions for (a) the globe; (b) territorial (solid lines) and consumption (dashed lines) emissions for the top three country emitters & EU27; (c) global emissions by fuel type and cement; (d) per capita emissions. Courtesy of Authors of the study: Pierre Friedlingstein1,2, Matthew W. Jones3, Michael O'Sullivan1, Robbie M. Andrew4, Dorothee C. E. Bakker5, Judith Hauck6, Corinne Le Quéré3, Glen P. Peters4, Wouter Peters7,8, Julia Pongratz9,10, Stephen Sitch11, Josep G. Canadell12, Philippe Ciais13, Rob B. Jackson14, Simone R. Alin15, Peter Anthoni16, Nicholas R. Bates17, Meike Becker18,19, Nicolas Bellouin20, Laurent Bopp2, Thi Tuyet Trang Chau13, Frédéric Chevallier13, Louise P. Chini21, Margot Cronin22, Kim I. Currie23, Bertrand Decharme24, Laique M. Djeutchouang25,26, Xinyu Dou27, Wiley Evans28, Richard A. Feely15, Liang Feng29, Thomas Gasser30, Dennis Gilfillan31, Thanos Gkritzalis32, Giacomo Grassi33, Luke Gregor34, Nicolas Gruber34, Özgür Gürses6, Ian Harris35, Richard A. Houghton36, George C. Hurtt21, Yosuke Iida37, Tatiana Ilyina10, Ingrid T. Luijkx7, Atul Jain38, Steve D. Jones18,19, Etsushi Kato39, Daniel Kennedy40, Kees Klein Goldewijk41, Jürgen Knauer12,42, Jan Ivar Korsbakken4, Arne Körtzinger43, Peter Landschützer10, Siv K. Lauvset19,44, Nathalie Lefèvre45, Sebastian Lienert46, Junjie Liu47, Gregg Marland48,49, Patrick C. McGuire50, Joe R. Melton51, David R. Munro52,53, Julia E. M. S. Nabel10,54, Shin-Ichiro Nakaoka55, Yosuke Niwa55,56, Tsuneo Ono57, Denis Pierrot58, Benjamin Poulter59, Gregor Rehder60, Laure Resplandy61, Eddy Robertson62, Christian Rödenbeck54, Thais M. Rosan11, Jörg Schwinger44,19, Clemens Schwingshackl9, Roland Séférian24, Adrienne J. Sutton15, Colm Sweeney53, Toste Tanhua43, Pieter P. Tans63, Hanqin Tian64, Bronte Tilbrook65,66, Francesco Tubiello67, Guido R. van der Werf68, Nicolas Vuichard13, Chisato Wada55, Rik Wanninkhof58, Andrew J. Watson11, David Willis3, Andrew J. Wiltshire62, Wenping Yuan69, Chao Yue13, Xu Yue70, Sönke Zaehle54, and Jiye Zeng55, CC BY 4.0, via Wikimedia Commons.

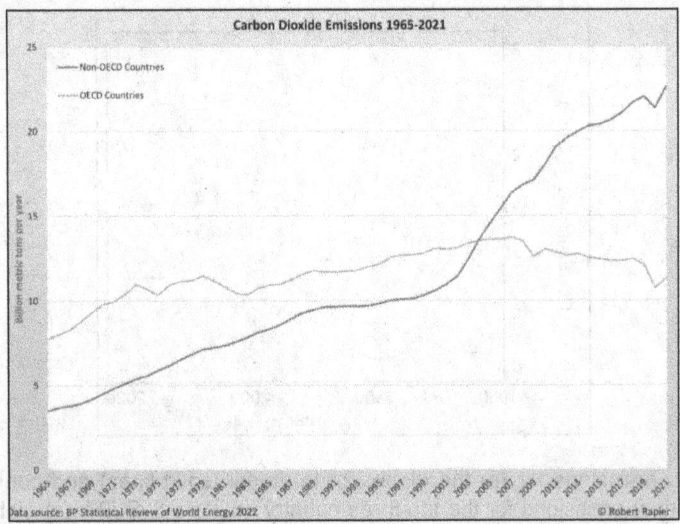

Global Carbon Dioxide Emissions 1965-2021 by OECD and Non-OECD countries. Courtesy of Robert Rapier, "Carbon Emissions On Track To Reach An All-Time High," OilPrice.com, July 23, 2022, https://oilprice.com/The-Environment/Global-Warming/Carbon-Emissions-On-Track-To-Reach-An-All-Time-High.html.

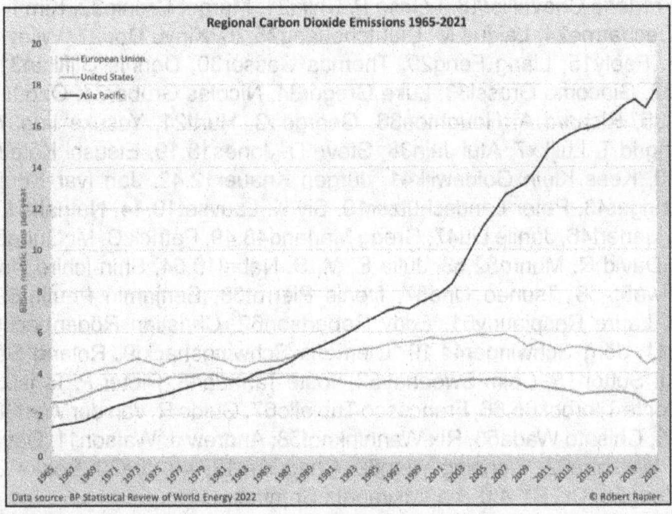

Regional Carbon Dioxide Emissions 1965-2021: European Union, United States, Asia Pacific. Courtesy of Robert Rapier, "Carbon Emissions On Track To Reach An All-Time High," OilPrice.com, July 23, 2022, https://oilprice.com/The-Environment/Global-Warming/Carbon-Emissions-On-Track-To-Reach-An-All-Time-High.html.

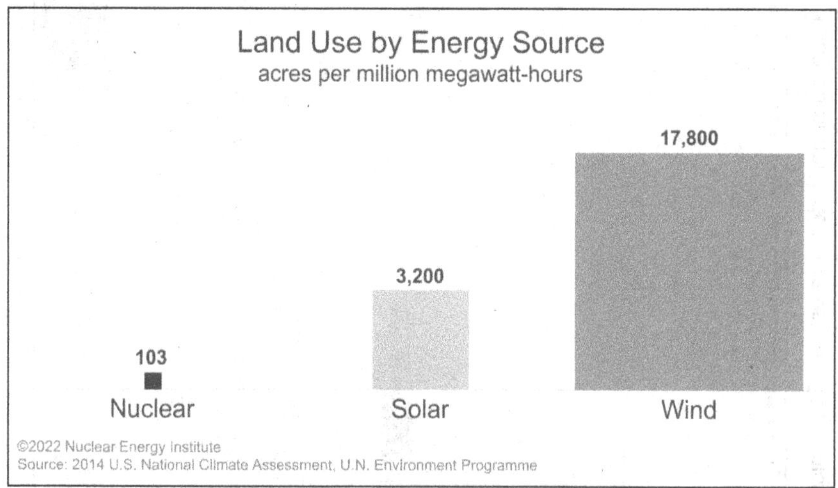

To generate the same amount of electricity as a 1,000 megawatt reactor, a wind farm would require over 140,000 acres, which is over 170 times the land needed for a nuclear reactor. Courtesy of Nuclear Energy Institute, "Nuclear Needs Small Amounts of Land to Deliver Big Amounts of Electricity," 29 April, 2022. Accessed at https://www.nei.org/news/2022/nuclear-brings-more-electricity-with-less-land.

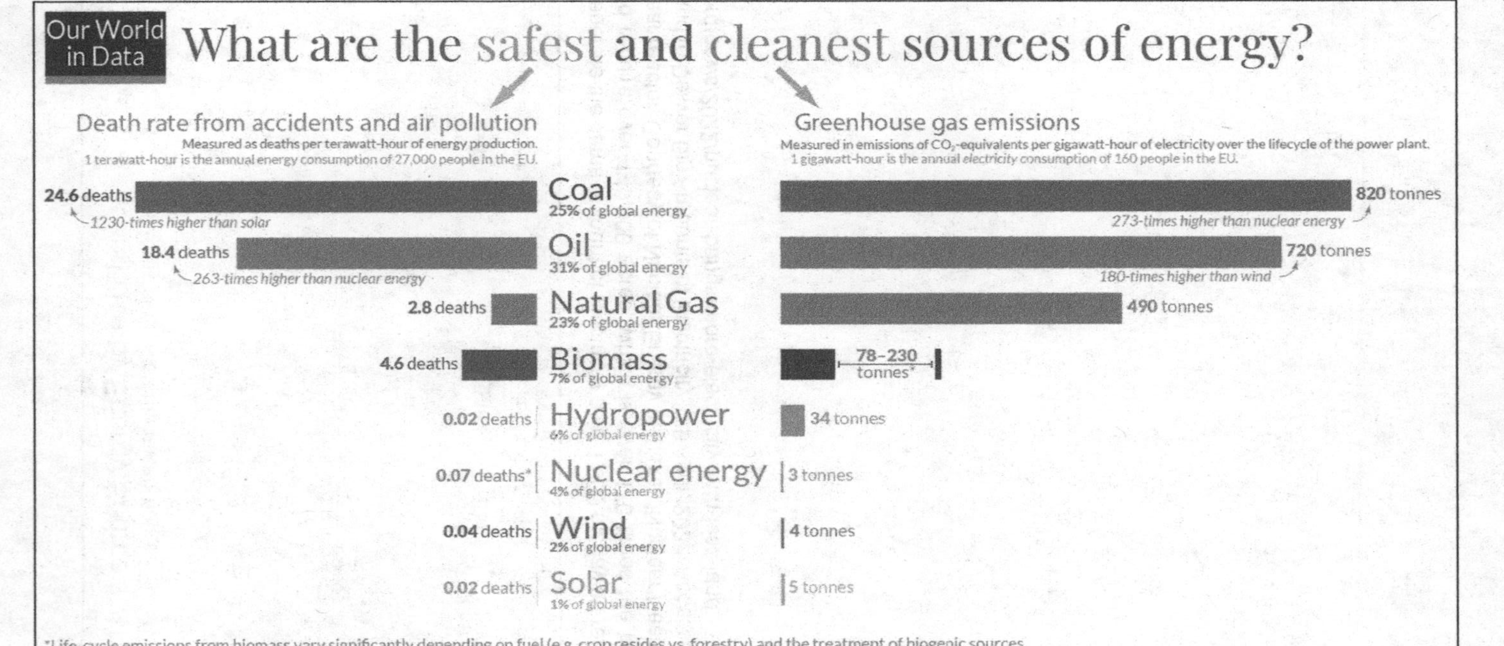
Our World in Data
What are the safest and cleanest sources of energy?
Death rate from accidents and air pollution
Measured as deaths per terawatt-hour of energy production.
1 terawatt-hour is the annual energy consumption of 27,000 people in the EU.
Greenhouse gas emissions
Measured in emissions of CO_2-equivalents per gigawatt-hour of electricity over the lifecycle of the power plant.
1 gigawatt-hour is the annual electricity consumption of 160 people in the EU.
24.6 deaths
1230-times higher than solar
Coal
25% of global energy
820 tonnes
273-times higher than nuclear energy
18.4 deaths
263-times higher than nuclear energy
Oil
31% of global energy
720 tonnes
180-times higher than wind
2.8 deaths
Natural Gas
23% of global energy
490 tonnes
4.6 deaths
Biomass
7% of global energy
78–230 tonnes*
0.02 deaths
Hydropower
6% of global energy
34 tonnes
0.07 deaths*
Nuclear energy
4% of global energy
3 tonnes
0.04 deaths
Wind
2% of global energy
4 tonnes
0.02 deaths
Solar
1% of global energy
5 tonnes
*Life-cycle emissions from biomass vary significantly depending on fuel (e.g. crop resides vs. forestry) and the treatment of biogenic sources.
*The death rate for nuclear energy includes deaths from the Fukushima and Chernobyl disasters as well as the deaths from occupational accidents (largely mining and milling).
Energy shares refer to 2019 and are shown in primary energy substitution equivalents to correct for inefficiencies of fossil fuel combustion. Traditional biomass is taken into account.
Data sources: Death rates from Markandya & Wilkinson (2007) in The Lancet, and Sovacool et al. (2016) in Journal of Cleaner Production;
Greenhouse gas emission factors from IPCC AR5 (2014) and Pehl et al. (2017) in Nature; Energy shares from BP (2019) and Smil (2017).
OurWorldinData.org – Research and data to make progress against the world's largest problems.
Licensed under CC-BY by the authors Hannah Ritchie and Max Roser.

Bar chart comparing death rates and CO_2 emissions from various energy sources. Courtesy of Hannah Ritchie and Max Roser, CC BY-SA 3.0, via Wikimedia Commons.

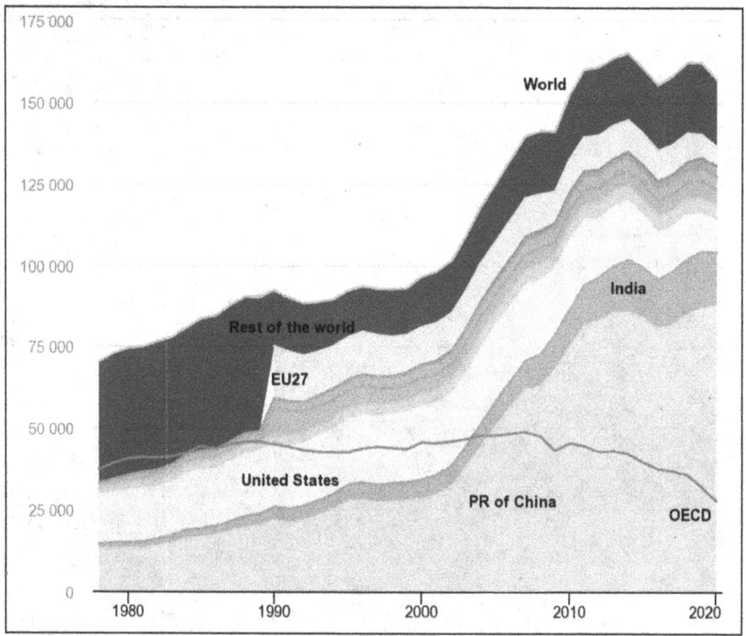

World coal consumption, 1978-2020. Courtesy of IEA (2021), Coal Information: Overview, IEA, Paris https://www.iea.org/reports/coal-information-overview.

Full-scale mockup of the upper one third of the NuScale Power Module.™ Photo courtesy of NuScale, via Oregon State University, CC BY-SA 2.0, via Wikimedia Commons

CHAPTER 9

AUTOPSY OF THE GREEN NEW DEAL

WHY THE SEDUCTIVE PROMISES OF THE GND ARE DANGEROUS FOR AMERICA

"Ending fossil fuel investments would be the road to hell in America."

– Jamie Dimon[294]

294. Joe Silverstein, "Top Bank CEOs Decline Radical Climate Demands from Rep. Tlaib: 'That Would Be the Road to Hell for America'," Fox Business, September 21, 2022, https://www.foxbusiness.com/media/top-bank-ceos-decline-radical-climate-demands-rep-tlaib-road-hell-america.

For all of the publicity and rhetoric surrounding the Green New Deal (GND), surprisingly few seem to know exactly what the GND really says or includes.

THE ORIGIN OF THE GND

The phrase "Green New Deal" has been around for years. Environmentalists, social activist Jill Stein and the Green Party, and even *New York Times* columnist Thomas L. Friedman have all had plans for addressing greenhouse gas emissions that they branded a Green New Deal. But after the U.S. 2018 midterm elections, a youth activist group named the Sunrise Movement promoted the catchy slogan by demanding environmental changes and holding a sit-in outside the office of Nancy Pelosi, the soon-to-be-speaker of the House of Representatives, to mandate action on climate change. NY Representative Alexandria Ocasio-Cortez attended the sit-in with the protestors, providing support to their proposal and setting the foundation for what ultimately became a joint congressional resolution.

The Green New Deal (GND) congressional resolution, born out of the Sunrise Movement sit-in, was formally introduced to Congress in February of 2019 by Ocasio-Cortez and Senator Edward J. Markey of Massachusetts. You can read it in its entirety in the Appendix (see Exhibit A). It was a co-sponsorship intended to benefit from the youthful exuberance of thirty-year-old Ocasio-Cortez and the sound experience of the seventy-four-year-old senior senator. The resolution laid out a grand plan to address greenhouse gas emissions, but it also included sprawling provisions to fix broader perceived societal problems including racial injustice, inequality, and poverty.

A BUNGLED ROLLOUT

Although the resolution was co-authored by Markey, the responsibilities of unveiling the plan to the public were largely assumed by the charismatic but inexperienced freshman legislator Ocasio-Cortez. The rollout of the plan was bungled from the very beginning when Ocasio-Cortez's office sent out a fact sheet detailing some controversial GND ideas, including guaranteeing economic security to those "unwilling to work" and "working collaboratively with farmers and ranchers in the U.S. to eliminate pollution and greenhouse gas emissions from the agricultural sector..." Ocasio-Cortez's office later disavowed the fact sheet, but the damage had been done.

Due to the resolution's overreach and botched rollout, even early Democratic supporters—it had over 100 co-sponsors initially—headed for the hills. On March 26, 2019, lawmakers in the Senate voted 57-0 against advancing the resolution, with forty-three out of forty-seven Democrats voting "present" to avoid taking a formal position.

The resolution itself steers clear of endorsing or rejecting specific technologies or sources of energy, something that Mr. Markey said was done purposefully to encourage broader support for the plan. It acts more as a set of principles and goals rather than as detailed policies.

FIVE SWEEPING GOALS

The proposal, although remarkably vague in terms of specifics, calls on the federal government to wean the United States from fossil fuels and curb planet-warming greenhouse gas emissions across the economy. But you'll see in Exhibit A in the Appendix that it includes much more than that, boldly outlining an enormous list of duties they expected the federal government to address beginning in the very first section.

Following the preamble, which assigns blame for climate change to human activities, the initial Resolution "GND Goals" are stated as follows:

Resolved, That it is the sense of the House of Representatives that—

(1) it is the duty of the Federal Government to create a Green New Deal—

(A) to achieve net-zero greenhouse gas emissions through a fair and just transition for all communities and workers;

(B) to create millions of good, high-wage jobs and ensure prosperity and economic security for all people of the United States;

(C) to invest in the infrastructure and industry of the United States to sustainably meet the challenges of the 21st century;

(D) to secure for all people of the United States for generations to come—

(i) clean air and water;

(ii) climate and community resiliency;

(iii) healthy food;

(iv) access to nature; and

(v) a sustainable environment; and

(E) to promote justice and equity by stopping current, preventing future, and repairing historic oppression of indigenous peoples, communities of color, migrant communities, deindustrialized communities, depopulated rural communities, the poor, low-income workers, women, the elderly, the unhoused, people with disabilities, and youth (referred to in this resolution as "frontline and vulnerable communities");

After a careful reading of only this first section, I stared in disbelief at the sweeping vastness of the broad federal government action that Markey and Ocasio-Cortez were promoting. Two of the most influential members of Congress were proposing that it is the duty of the federal government not only to control CO_2 emissions but also to make far-reaching legislative changes that would impact almost every aspect of American lives, redress almost every challenge in society, and promote justice and equity to…well, almost everyone. One of the few things missing was a provision to cure cancer. It was enough to take a capitalist's breath away.

OVERREACH

The overreach didn't stop in the first section. Some of the other more noteworthy provisions are as follows:

…The Goals of the GND should be accomplished through…a 10-year national mobilization (referred to in this resolution as the "Green New Deal mobilization") that will require the following goals and projects—

…guaranteeing universal access to clean water;

…ensuring that any infrastructure bill considered by Congress addresses climate change;

…upgrading all existing buildings in the United States and building new buildings to achieve maximum energy efficiency, water efficiency, safety, affordability, comfort, and durability, including through electrification;

…spurring massive growth in clean manufacturing in the United States and removing pollution and greenhouse gas emissions from manufacturing…

…a Green New Deal must be developed through transparent and inclusive consultation, collaboration, and partnership with frontline and vulnerable communities, labor unions, worker cooperatives, civil society groups, academia, and businesses; and

…ensuring that the Federal Government takes into account the complete environmental and social costs and impacts of emissions through—

(i) existing laws;

(ii) new policies and programs; and

(iii) ensuring that frontline and vulnerable communities shall not be adversely affected;

... providing resources, training, and high-quality education, including higher education, to all people of the United States, with a focus on frontline and vulnerable communities, so that all people of the United States may be full and equal participants in the Green New Deal mobilization;

... guaranteeing a job with a family-sustaining wage, adequate family and medical leave, paid vacations, and retirement security to all people of the United States;

... strengthening and protecting the right of all workers to organize, unionize, and collectively bargain free of coercion, intimidation, and harassment;

... ensuring that public lands, waters, and oceans are protected and that eminent domain is not abused;

... obtaining the free, prior, and informed consent of indigenous peoples for all decisions that affect indigenous peoples and their traditional territories, honoring all treaties and agreements with indigenous peoples, and protecting and enforcing the sovereignty and land rights of indigenous peoples;

... ensuring a commercial environment where every businessperson is free from unfair competition and domination by domestic or international monopolies; and

- providing all people of the United States with—

- affordable, safe, and adequate housing;

- economic security; and

- clean water, clean air, healthy and affordable food, and access to nature.

Some of the earliest critics of the GND claimed it was a Marxist socialist plan. I dismissed this early criticism and attributed the condemnation to our current divisive political climate. But, after reading provisions "guaranteeing a job" and providing "economic security" to all people of the United States, I reconsidered my opinion.

The New York Times claimed that the GND was a plan for tackling climate change.[295] But they were wrong, and the conservative critics were right. The GND in fact reads like a Marxist socialist manifesto wrapped in a cloak of a climate change resolution.

Although there isn't any direct attack on fossil fuels in the GND, it was cleverly written so that future critics of fossil fuels and pipelines could draw from the language, including the reference to "eminent domain," in the resolution. Even though the document calls for protecting our forests, lands, and water, my guess is the writers weren't thinking about the thirty thousand acres of land per day that may have to be prepared for a 100-percent solar and wind mobilization for the U.S. They likely were also not thinking about the pollution caused by mining for seventeen rare earth minerals—or about the disposal of solar panels and windmill blades.

FUNDING

There's also the issue of how to fund such an ambitious overhaul of the U.S. economy.

Advocates of the Green New Deal who promote an unorthodox macroeconomic framework called Modern Monetary Theory (MMT), including Ocasio-Cortez, believe the government shouldn't be too concerned about the cost.

295. Lisa Friedman, "What Is the Green New Deal? A Climate Proposal, Explained," New York Times, February 21, 2019, https://www.nytimes.com/2019/02/21/climate/green-new-deal-questions-answers.html.

"The federal government can spend money on public priorities without raising revenue, and it won't wreck the nation's economy to do so," a group of prominent MMT supporters wrote in an op-ed for *The Huffington Post*. "The U.S. government can never run out of dollars, but humanity can run out of limited global resources. The climate crisis fundamentally threatens those resources and the very human livelihoods that depend on them."[296]

Alarmed at the breadth of the GND, the initial one hundred co-sponsors deserted the GND resolution, and it officially died on March 26, 2019.

THE GND LIVES ON

The GND may have died on paper, but its spirit lives on. Some of the principles of the GND were included in the Inflation Reduction Act (IRA) of 2022.

It didn't matter that the IRA act doesn't actually have much, if anything, to do with reducing inflation. As we learned with the Water Protectors and the GND, branding is what's important. Elements of the GND that made it into the IRA act include, according to a release from the Biden administration, "historic investments in environmental justice, including establishing several new environmental justice grant programs. The law will improve public health, reduce pollution, and revitalize communities that are marginalized, underserved, and over-burdened by pollution while increasing access to affordable and accessible clean energy."[297]

296. Stephanie Kelton, Andres Bernal, and Greg Carlock, "We Can Pay For A Green New Deal," November 30, 2018, HuffPost, https://www.huffpost.com/entry/opinion-green-new-deal-cost_n_5c0042b2e4b027f1097bda5b.

297. "The Inflation Reduction Act," EPA, last modified November 21, 2022, https://www.epa.gov/green-power-markets/inflation-reduction-act#:~:text=The%20Inflation%20Reduction%20Act%20of,emissions%2C%20and%20advance%20environmental%20justice.

True to their word, in September 2022 the Biden administration, through the Environmental Protection Agency (EPA), "created a new national office of environmental justice to address the disproportionate harm that pollution and climate change has caused in low-income areas and communities of color."[298]

The new office will oversee the implementation and delivery of a $3 billion climate and environmental justice block grant program created by the Inflation Reduction Act. The office is expected to be staffed by two hundred people in Washington and across the EPA's ten regional offices.

At the same time, the attention on the Green New Deal has put new pressure on Republican critics to come up with their own plan for cutting greenhouse gasses. And that's exactly why our nation needs a Green *Real* Deal: a balanced path forward for America that depends on five must-have tenets.

298. Sonnet Swire, "EPA Launches New Office Dedicated to Environmental Justice," CNN, September 24, 2022, https://www.cnn.com/2022/09/24/politics/epa-new-office-environmental-justice/index.html#:~:text=The%20Environmental%20Protection%20Agency%20will,color%2C%20the%20agency%20announced%20Saturday.

Representative Alexandria Ocasio-Cortez (center) speaks on the Green New Deal with Senator Ed Markey (right) in front of the Capitol Building in February 2019. Courtesy of Senate Democrats, CC BY 2.0, via Wikimedia Commons.

CHAPTER 10

A PATH FORWARD

THE FIVE TENETS OF A GREEN REAL DEAL

"Get all the education you can, but then, by God, do something. Don't just stand there, make it happen."

– Lee Iacocca

LOOKING BACK, THE 2016 protest in downtown Houston that originally sparked my interest in researching energy solutions was not a grassroots gathering of concerned citizens. Today, I understand it was a collection of "useful idiots" organized by a professional group and likely funded by dark money—the same dark money that's funding environmental protests across the country and influencing the American psyche and Washington policymakers.

Fossil Fuels have long been a crucial source of affordable and dependable energy that has sparked innovation and economic growth in America. Rational energy strategists have assumed that good judgment would eventually prevail and restore a sound and comprehensive American energy policy. However, the runway for such complacency is shortening.

Disruptive environmental activism is accelerating and intensifying, and it's being normalized by the media. The 2021 eco-terrorism book *How to Blow Up a Pipeline* has been made into a movie, and *Rolling Stone* magazine reviews have irresponsibly recommended it for a date night.

In the backdrop of this climate hysteria, our country and the rest of the world are at a crossroads with respect to making long-term strategic energy choices.

The options available today resemble those in 1979 after the Three Mile Island incident. That's when our nation rejected nuclear power in favor of domestic coal and imported oil. Since that fateful decision, the U.S. steadily increased its consumption of coal. Only after the U.S. perfected horizontal hydraulic fracturing techniques in the last decade or so has the consumption of coal declined in favor of cleaner natural gas. This energy revolution has reversed our increasing over-reliance on imported oil from the Middle East, allowing the U.S. to once again become the world's largest oil producer.

Forty years after Three Mile Island, more than 80 percent of U.S.

energy is produced by fossil fuels, which is a diminishing non-renewable resource. Regardless of how you or I feel about GHG emissions, it is inevitable that our future will be less dependent upon fossil fuels.

Meanwhile, the impact of increased carbon emissions can no longer be ignored. It only accelerates our need to progress toward a lower-carbon future. Those who dismiss the issues of carbon emissions make a serious miscalculation, but those who advocate an entirely renewable energy path for the U.S. make a similar mistake, one that could undermine our country's economic and national security. We don't want to cause a worldwide economic depression or destroy ourselves in the process while addressing GHG Emissions.

And we don't have to.

Passionate and idealistic plans like the Green New Deal (GND), the energy plan proposed by many environmental activists, are a reminder of our country's previous rejection of nuclear power in favor of fossil fuels. The plan underscores the threat of ill-conceived solutions. Decrying fossil fuels and nuclear energy, proponents of the GND advocate solar and wind as adequate and environmentally friendly energy substitutes. They want to shut down nuclear power and replace it with so-called renewable energy.[299]

But the math and the evidence don't support this perspective.

Solar and wind are among the least efficient forms of energy: they could require the development of over 267 million acres of land. And they require dependable backup energy from coal, oil, nuclear, or LNG because the wind doesn't always blow, and the sun doesn't always shine. There's plenty of evidence to prove that renewable energy lacks the reliability, efficiency, and density to meet our needs.

It doesn't take a nuclear engineer to understand the shortcomings of

299. Sammy Roth, "One Way to Combat Russia? Move Faster on Clean Energy," *Los Angeles Times*, February 26, 2022, https://www.latimes.com/business/story/2022-02-26/one-way-to-combat-russia-move-faster-on-clean-energy.

a plan like the Green New Deal, which promotes a transition to 100-percent renewables. Even Elon Musk says "civilization will crumble" unless we keep using oil and gas until better solutions are in place.[300]

The irony with the current environmental protests against pipelines and fossil fuels is that environmentalists are the reason for the current dependence. Forty years ago, American environmentalists demanded a rejection of nuclear energy and a return to conventional sources. The California governor at the time, Jerry Brown, called nuclear energy a "pathological addiction" of President Jimmy Carter.

I can't say I blame them or Governor Brown. Like most Americans, when I left Harrisburg, Pennsylvania, in 1979, I shared their fear of nuclear power. Fear clouded facts and judgment.

Making decisions rooted in fear had enormous political, economic, and military implications. Consider the wars and conflicts related to oil and gas over the last forty years, such as the Kuwaiti Gulf War and others that required an increased U.S. military presence in the Middle East. Fear is the sentiment that drives environmentalists to demand renewables today.

We can see in Germany what happens when a country focuses on renewables alone to address carbon emissions. In the past decade, Germany's "Operation Energiewende" program has roughly doubled its production of energy from renewables, which now accounts for a quarter of Germany's energy production. But during this same period, carbon emissions per person have not declined. Germany has simply replaced one carbon-free energy source (nuclear) with another, much-less efficient carbon-free source: renewables. Now, after Russia's invasion of Ukraine, Germany's economy is vulnerable to collapsing because it is overly dependent on Russian natural gas.

300. Paul Best, "Elon Musk Says 'Civilization Will Crumble' Unless We Continue Using Oil and Gas in the Short Term," Fox Business, August 29, 2022, https://www.foxbusiness.com/economy/elon-musk-says-civilization-crumble-continue-using-oil-gas-short-term.

With current technology, renewables cannot meet energy needs on their own. Protesting to keep fossil fuels in the ground without a suitable replacement is an oversimplified and nonsensical response. It is a cause hijacked by people who are well-intentioned but misguided—or who are enemies of our country. Some protestors of fossil fuels exaggerate claims about alternative energy sources because their Russian backers benefit from a less-efficient America. It is unpatriotic and wrong and should be considered eco-terrorism.[301]

In contrast, we see in Sweden what might have been for our nation. At almost the exact same period that the United States rejected nuclear energy, Sweden strategically embraced it as the most efficient of the ten prevailing sources of energy in the world. In doing so, Sweden has mostly weaned itself off fossil fuels and has solved its carbon-emission problem. Today, Sweden uses one-third more energy per person than Germany but emits about half the carbon pollution per person as Germany. Estimates are that it will take over a hundred years with Germany's Energiewende renewable plan to achieve the carbon reduction Sweden did in twenty years with nuclear power.[302]

Sweden asserts it has solved the issue of energy and GHG emissions and advocates the same solution for the rest of the world. The authors of *A Bright Future* even coined a term for it: "nuables," a combination of nuclear and renewable energy.

Some American leaders are embracing a solution that includes "nuables." For example, political leaders like former presidential candidate Andrew Yang promote studying thorium to utilize the benefits of nuclear

---

301. Craig Timberg and Tony Romm, "These provocative images show Russian trolls sought to inflame debate over climate change, fracking and Dakota pipeline," Washington Post, March 1, 2018, https://www.washingtonpost.com/news/the-switch/wp/2018/03/01/congress-russians-trolls-sought-to-inflame-u-s-debate-on-climate-change-fracking-and-dakota-pipeline/?utm_term=.0484f709629e.

302. Richard Rhodes, "A Sensible Climate Solution, Borrowed from Sweden," New York Times, February 5, 2019, https://www.nytimes.com/2019/02/05/books/review/bright-future-joshua-s-goldstein-staffan-a-qvist.html

energy without the danger of nuclear weapons. His stance is an encouraging, unconventional approach. However, Virginia's recent shuttering of the biggest uranium mine in the country proves that the acceptance and development of nuclear power in America will take a long time.[303]

A thoughtful decision for the United States is more complicated than the plan outlined in Sweden. Fossil fuels are not a part of Sweden's proposed long-term global solution. The country glosses over the importance of fossil fuels with respect to national defense, shipping, construction, world order, and a multitude of other needs. They mostly dismiss the progress that has been made in carbon capture and storage by the energy industry.

Regarding national defense, Sweden may be unaware of Operation Paukenschlag in 1942, when German U-boats sank or damaged seventy-four tankers in an era dubbed by the Germans as "The American Shooting Season." The United States triumphed over Hitler's Nazi Germany only after pipelines delivered oil to the northeast that was refined into crucial products for the Allied forces. Perhaps national defense is not as important to the Swedes due to their traditional stance of neutrality in world conflicts. Their policy of neutrality provided cover for the Swedish decision to sell iron ore to the Nazis during World War II, which fortified the Germans, extended the war, and cost many lives. This highlights the importance of making thoughtful long-term choices, not emotional ones like we made after 1979.

America has not had—and will not have—the luxury of declaring neutrality against future tyrants. We will be expected to lead the effort against them. Like it or not, future conflicts will be heavily dependent upon reliable fossil fuel energy, including our ability to protect our nation from Russia and China.

---

303. Richard Wolf, "Supreme Court Allows Virginia to Block Mining of Nation's Largest Uranium Deposit," *USA Today*, June 17, 2019, https://www.yahoo.com/news/supreme-court-allows-virginia-block-152609189.html.

As a world leader, our future hinges on the energy conversation our country is having today.

THE AMERICAN ENERGY CONVERSATION

Worse than fake energy protests is the fact that so few Americans recognize the danger of being influenced by people and entities who do not have our best interests in mind. The reports of Russian interference in our social media should serve as a wake-up call. Russia is threatened by our economic strength and stands to benefit when we make inefficient energy decisions.

The disappointing truth is that we are losing an information war to Russia through state-backed and social media. It's undermining our energy industry and our economy, including American jobs. We become weaker when we lose sight of the fact that energy from fossil fuel resources gives America power over and protection from other countries. The truth is that strengthening our flow of oil and gas loosens Russia's grip on the world.

Clemson professor Patrick Warren said, "There were more tweets in the year *after* the election than there were in the year before the election. I want to shout this from the rooftops. This is not just an election thing. It's a continuing intervention in the political conversation in America."[304]

Intervention by the Russians will continue as long as Moscow feels threatened by the competition from Western democracies. They know they cannot compete with a united America. Therefore, their economic future is dependent upon dividing the West against itself.

The political conversation and the economic security in our country is—and will remain—under attack. Wrapped in the guise of good

304. Oliver Roeder, "Why We're Sharing 3 Million Russian Troll Tweets," *ABC News*, July 31, 2018, https://www.google.com/amp/s/fivethirtyeight.com/features/why-were-sharing-3-million-russian-troll-tweets/amp.

causes, Americans are blindly accepting so-called truths from Russians and environmentalists. Ours is now a culture in which much debate is based on intentionally misleading news stories that are interspersed with truth. Opinions and ideas are being formed not by facts but by repeated, emotional talking points. According to Harvard professor Tom Nichols, our discourse has become characterized by ignorance and unreason.

In his book, *The Death of Expertise: The Campaign Against Expertise and Why it Matters*, Nichols says he has observed "a new and accelerating—and dangerous—hostility toward established knowledge. People [are] no longer merely uninformed…but aggressively wrong and unwilling to learn. They actively [resist] facts that might alter their preexisting beliefs."

Such is the case for "water protectors" and environmentalists. They are clutching a moral high ground about nuclear energy, pipelines, and fossil fuels even if it means destroying American jobs, threatening national security, and trading a working solution for an unreliable renewable one. They are insisting on a renewable solution that relies on the mining of as many as seventeen different nonrenewable minerals from the earth and that in some cases is polluting the land, air, and water across the globe—facts that get in the way of their preexisting beliefs. It's much more acceptable and idealistic to stand with American Indians and engage in a malignant, deliberate attack against laborers, welders, truckers, and their working-class families.

But there's nothing "morally high" about environmentalists throwing people out of work, not without considering the possibility that natural gas can replace coal or that other technologies like carbon capture and storage can work. There is nothing reasonable about the fact that working-class Americans have become collateral damage in the environmentalist war against fossil fuels.

The result is energy solutions that feel good but are reckless. It has somehow become okay for dedicated blue-collar workers to lose their jobs because of specious arguments by environmentalists and political activists. It's shocking that more attention is not paid to the people impacted by activities related to environmental activists. Pipelines may provide the only good careers a one-armed dozer operator or a dyslexic welder can find. It matters especially now: manufacturing jobs once plentiful in the post-World War II era are being eliminated or moved overseas, killing American jobs and decimating previously vibrant cities. Rather than moving our nation forward, said former Energy Department officials Ernest Moniz and Andy Karsner, these feel-good, reckless solutions are only "magical thinking" that moves us sideways and threatens to derail climate progress.[305]

While we have been arguing about fossil fuels in the United States, other countries are advancing their own plans that include nuclear and LNG. In 2018, there were fifty-three nuclear reactors under construction around the world, including twenty-one in China, five in Russia, and four in India. The U.S. has three, just one more than Pakistan. Russia is building a new reactor every year with the goal of producing 75 percent of its energy from nuclear by the end of the century. Additionally, Russia leads the world in exporting fourth-generation turnkey plants that it will design, build, and operate. While Americans (inventors of nuclear energy) are debating a Green New Deal based on inefficient energy sources, Russians are exporting their natural gas for cash flow and preparing for the future with nuclear energy. Russia and China are poised to win the economic race while we consider stalling like Germany, which focused on renewables. It is an American tragedy that Americans have ceded the leadership of nuclear development to Russia and China.

305. Ernest Moniz and Andy Karsner, "What America Needs is a 'Green Real Deal': Obama/Bush Energy Policymakers Say," *CNBC,* March 11, 2019, https://www.cnbc.com/2019/03/11/what-america-needs-is-a-green-real-deal-top-energy-experts-say.html.

True climate progress and leadership begin with an honest conversation. When we are willing to acknowledge the shortcomings of each of our energy sources, we can form a realistic energy solution. Consider these limitations:

- Fossil fuels are nonrenewable resources that will eventually run out. They contribute to carbon emissions, particularly coal.
- Renewables like solar and wind energy are unreliable technologies because of their inherent intermittence. They require a reliable backup source. They can't meet our current or projected needs, and they can't shoulder the task of national security. Regarding batteries, they provide storage over hours, not weeks or seasons, and are nowhere near capable of the energy density necessary for air travel. Also, batteries leave consumers with a difficult decision: should they buy electric vehicles to minimize their carbon footprints? Or should they avoid electric cars because of their association with human suffering, environmental damage, and, as Bryce put it, the "squandering" of vast areas of land?
- Nuclear power may have helped us avoid the climate situation that we have today if environmentalists hadn't destroyed its viability forty years ago. However, uranium introduces global safety concerns.

Just as pipelines disrupted the business of teamster-driven horses over 150 years ago, another disruptive energy solution will one day render fossil fuels obsolete. When that occurs, the world may not need fossil fuels and pipelines. But that's not today or in the foreseeable future. Today, we need diverse sources of energy that can both meet our needs and be transported in the safest way possible.

From our homes to our hygiene products to our automobiles, energy is essential to modern life. In the book *How the World Really Works,* Professor Emeritus Vaclav Smil explains that modern societies require four pillars of civilization: cement, steel, plastics, and ammonia.

Cement is the key ingredient in concrete, without which there are no modern cities, tunnels, dams, roads, runways, or ports. Without steel, there would be no skyscrapers or cars—including electric vehicles. Plastics are found in everything from computers to furniture to clothes; moreover, they are indispensable in nearly every aspect of health care, from incubators to artificial hearts. Ammonia is the basis for all nitrogen fertilizers; without the food produced with modern fertilizers, billions of people would starve.[306]

These four pillars of civilization require the burning of fossil fuels. Smil says, "There's no credible path, no physical chemistry or energetics, to significantly replace these materials on a global scale."

That's why the protest by "water protectors" against any interference with the environment is theoretically ideal but destructive in practice for a modern society such as ours. All our current energy options have been proven to be insufficient and imperfect on their own in some way.

In an effort to mobilize our nation to fight GHG emissions, Senator Cory Booker, an advocate of the Green New Deal, said, "When the planet has been in peril in the past, who came forward to save the Earth from the scourge of Nazis and totalitarian regimes? We came forward. Who came forward to save the planet, or continents, from financial ruin? We came forward with the Marshall Plan," he said. "Our history is standing up and saying, 'look, humanity is in crisis, America is going to be the light and the hope.'"[307]

It is an ironic battle cry for the dwindling number of Americans who still remember who truly did "come forward to save the Earth

306. Kevin Killough, "Why Modern Civilization Isn't Possible Without Fossil Fuels," Cowboy State Daily, February 10, 2023, https://cowboystatedaily.com/2023/02/10/modern-civilization-isnt-possible-without-fossil-fuels-say-energy-experts/.

307. Gregg Re, "Ocasio-Cortez contradicts herself on role of government in massive and unprecedented 'Green New Deal'," Fox News, February 8, 2019, https://www.foxnews.com/politics/ocasio-cortez-hours-after-introducing-green-new-deal-contradicts-herself-on-governments-role.

from the scourge of Nazis and totalitarian regimes." The government and private industry unified and strengthened an entire nation in crisis by building the Big Inch and Little Inch pipelines.

AMERICAN ENERGY POLICY: A GREEN REAL DEAL

Indeed, our history reveals who—and what—has enabled America to be "the light and the hope." It reminds us of what we are capable of. Together, we can move forward to create a better energy strategy and policy framework to protect our national interests and reduce CO_2 emissions.

Today, we need a common-sense approach that is based on practicality, not ideology, which means admitting our need for a more diverse solution than 100-percent renewables. A balanced path forward depends on the following five tenets:

1. **Accept that fossil fuels and the pipelines that transport them are critical to our national and economic security.**

- Acknowledge the lessons of World War II and the 2022 Russian invasion of Ukraine. Namely, traditional oil & gas is critical for American economic and national security. Opposition to pipelines undermines our national security.
- Examine the motives of those demanding to "keep it in the ground." The demand is not just naïve. It is unpatriotic and perpetuated by nations unfriendly to America and our Western allies. Given the fundamental importance of national defense, pay attention to evidence of conflicts of interest or subversive intent.
- Understand that technology improvements related to hydraulic fracturing are a gift to the United States and a threat to other producers, particularly Russia. Stop vilifying an innovative industry that supports America and millions of workers and families.

- Recognize the charade of halting pipelines and other traditional energy projects in the name of water protection. American Indians are among the country's biggest oil producers, with many owning their own pipelines. Energy royalty payments made to American Indians totaled $975 million in 2021 alone.
- Support environmental terrorism legislation that safeguards our energy infrastructure. Groups or individuals who cross the line and use targeted violence—no matter how noble their intent—should be held accountable.

2. Protect our forests from irresponsible destruction.

- Recognize the impracticality of a 100-percent "renewable" energy policy of wind and solar. Such a policy could require the development of up to 267 million acres of forest and land in the United States, according to a 2021 Princeton study.
- Stop the absurd destruction of American forests to produce wood pellets for Europe. Understand that switching from coal to wood-burning pellets hurts the planet. Our forests and trees are the lungs of the planet, and the protection of this resource was the original intent of the founding of the Sierra Club by John Muir.

3. Sensibly expand renewables and rare earth mineral supply chain.

- Utilize wind and solar power using the least amount of land and water. Rooftops of homes, parking lots, barns, commercial buildings, government facilities, bridges, roads, and oil production facilities are all rational places for solar and some wind installations.
- Realistically forecast how much energy these low-density sources can provide. Until the storage capacity of batteries improves, solar and wind energy will require reliable backup power from nuclear or fossil fuels and will have a limited role in solving the world's energy needs.

- Incentivize battery research and development.
- Invest in renewable energy initiatives like the groundbreaking graphite plant in Vidalia, Louisiana, so that we can establish responsible processing of minerals needed to expand renewables and supply chains in the United States.
- Hold the renewable industry accountable for solving its own troublesome environmental risks, including the mining of rare-earth minerals and the disposal of batteries, solar panels, windmill blades, and related toxic materials. With their relatively short lifespans, it's easy to predict a "renewable" environmental crisis on the horizon.
- Develop domestic control of rare earth minerals to mitigate national security concerns and our over-reliance on China, which controls most of the world's specialized minerals used to build weapons, electronics, and parts for wind turbines and solar panels.

4. Make coal cleaner and discourage new coal plants where feasible.

- Accept that, when it comes to producing electricity, developing countries are increasingly reliant on coal due to its abundance, affordability, and reliability.
- At a minimum, and for the foreseeable future, coal will serve as a backup energy source when other cleaner energy supply disruptions occur, as is now occurring in Europe, Pakistan, India, and China.
- Recognize that renewables cannot—will not—meet soaring global energy demand. Their limitations include intermittency, land constraints, lack of sufficient high-voltage transmission capacity, and the staggering quantity of necessary commodities such as concrete, copper, steel and rare earth elements.[308]

308. Robert Bryce, "Soaring Demand for Electricity and Coal Shows Why We Need Nuclear Energy," The Hill, July 7, 2022, https://thehill.com/opinion/energy-environment/3548160-soaring-demand-for-electricity-and-coal-shows-why-we-need-nuclear-energy/.

- Convert existing coal plants to natural gas wherever practical, here and around the world, and discourage new coal plants wherever feasible.
- Invest in carbon capture and storage and other "clean coal" technologies wherever coal is used.

5. Commit to increased nuclear research and development.

- Recognize the viability of nuclear energy. It is a carbon-free source of energy that requires the least amount of land.
- Embrace a new view of nuclear energy informed by realities and benefits rather than forty-year-old fear rooted in the Three Mile Island incident. As Sweden has shown, nuclear energy stands to benefit an expanding worldwide population who all wish and deserve to enjoy energy and electricity.
- Recommit ourselves to nuclear in a smarter way with newer, smaller, modular technology along the lines of the molten salt design proposed by Terra Energy and the design by NuScale.
- Develop emerging technologies like nuclear fusion, which requires years of dedicated attention to support our power needs.

The battle by environmentalists against one of America's oldest industries—a battle that threatens to impede our advancement and renders us vulnerable to other countries—is not the way forward. To address our energy challenges, we must act differently.

We can partner with people with whom we haven't partnered before, collaborating with industry to improve greenhouse gas emissions and protect the environment. We can unleash visionaries, cultivating bold business ideas and developing technological innovations.

We can remember where we came from. In a history threatened by the Nazis and totalitarian regimes, we came from people like Harold Ickes and the pipeliners. Our nation was strengthened by the unification of government and private industry. We were victorious because of the Big Inch and Little Inch pipelines that delivered oil in time for the greatest generation of Americans to defeat Hitler. And we can rely on our natural resources to withstand oppressive countries today, too.

Some are now suggesting that we battle Russian and Chinese aggression by moving even faster on wind and solar energy.[309] But they are wrong. The best way to battle Russia and other future enemies of democracy is to responsibly invest in oil and natural gas, as well as the infrastructure to move it, including pipelines and LNG export and import terminals. This strategy, combined with the development of cleaner coal and nuclear energy to reduce CO_2 emissions and protect the environment, will strengthen America and our European allies and crush Putin and his future army of followers.

Indeed, our history reveals who—and what—has enabled America to be the light and the hope. It reminds us of what we are capable of. Together, we can move forward to create a better energy solution and a Green Real Deal.

309. Sammy Roth, "One Way to Combat Russia? Move Faster on Clean Energy," *Los Angeles Times*, February 26, 2022, https://www.latimes.com/business/story/2022-02-26/one-way-to-combat-russia-move-faster-on-clean-energy.

APPENDIX

Exhibit A: The Green New Deal

RESOLUTION[310]

Recognizing the duty of the Federal Government to create a Green New Deal.

Whereas the October 2018 report entitled "Special Report on Global Warming of 1.5 °C" by the Intergovernmental Panel on Climate Change and the November 2018 Fourth National Climate Assessment report found that—

(1) human activity is the dominant cause of observed climate change over the past century;

(2) a changing climate is causing sea levels to rise and an increase in wildfires, severe storms, droughts, and other extreme weather events that threaten human life, healthy communities, and critical infrastructure;

(3) global warming at or above 2 degrees Celsius beyond preindustrialized levels will cause—

310. "H.Res. 109 — 116th Congress: Recognizing the duty of the Federal Government to create a Green New Deal." www.GovTrack.us. 2019, https://www.govtrack.us/congress/bills/116/hres109

(A) mass migration from the regions most affected by climate change;

(B) more than $500,000,000,000 in lost annual economic output in the United States by the year 2100;

(C) wildfires that, by 2050, will annually burn at least twice as much forest area in the western United States than was typically burned by wildfires in the years preceding 2019;

(D) a loss of more than 99 percent of all coral reefs on Earth;

(E) more than 350,000,000 more people to be exposed globally to deadly heat stress by 2050; and

(F) a risk of damage to $1,000,000,000,000 of public infrastructure and coastal real estate in the United States; and

(4) global temperatures must be kept below 1.5 degrees Celsius above preindustrialized levels to avoid the most severe impacts of a changing climate, which will require—

(A) global reductions in greenhouse gas emissions from human sources of 40 to 60 percent from 2010 levels by 2030; and

(B) net-zero global emissions by 2050;

Whereas, because the United States has historically been responsible for a disproportionate amount of greenhouse gas emissions, having emitted 20 percent of global greenhouse gas emissions through 2014, and has a high technological capacity, the United States must take a leading role in reducing emissions through economic transformation;

Whereas the United States is currently experiencing several related crises, with—

(1) life expectancy declining while basic needs, such as clean air, clean water, healthy food, and adequate health care, housing, transportation, and education, are inaccessible to a significant portion of the United States population;

(2) a 4-decade trend of wage stagnation, deindustrialization, and anti-labor policies that has led to—

(A) hourly wages overall stagnating since the 1970s despite increased worker productivity;

(B) the third-worst level of socioeconomic mobility in the developed world before the Great Recession;

(C) the erosion of the earning and bargaining power of workers in the United States; and

(D) inadequate resources for public sector workers to confront the challenges of climate change at local, State, and Federal levels; and

(3) the greatest income inequality since the 1920s, with—

(A) the top 1 percent of earners accruing 91 percent of gains in the first few years of economic recovery after the Great Recession;

(B) a large racial wealth divide amounting to a difference of twenty times more wealth between the average white family and the average Black family; and

(C) a gender earnings gap that results in women earning approximately 80 percent as much as men, at the median;

Whereas climate change, pollution, and environmental destruction have exacerbated systemic racial, regional, social, environmental, and economic injustices (referred to in this preamble as "systemic injustices") by disproportionately affecting indigenous peoples, communities of color, migrant communities, deindustrialized communities, depopulated rural communities, the poor, low-income workers, women, the elderly, the unhoused, people with disabilities, and youth (referred to in this preamble as "frontline and vulnerable communities");

Whereas, climate change constitutes a direct threat to the national security of the United States—

(1) by impacting the economic, environmental, and social stability of countries and communities around the world; and

(2) by acting as a threat multiplier;

Whereas the Federal Government-led mobilizations during World War II and the New Deal created the greatest middle class that the United States has ever seen, but many members of frontline and vulnerable communities were excluded from many of the economic and societal benefits of those mobilizations; and

Whereas the House of Representatives recognizes that a new national, social, industrial, and economic mobilization on a scale not seen since World War II and the New Deal era is a historic opportunity—

(1) to create millions of good, high-wage jobs in the United States;

(2) to provide unprecedented levels of prosperity and economic security for all people of the United States; and

(3) to counteract systemic injustices: Now, therefore, be it

Resolved, That it is the sense of the House of Representatives that—

(1) it is the duty of the Federal Government to create a Green New Deal—

(A) to achieve net-zero greenhouse gas emissions through a fair and just transition for all communities and workers;

(B) to create millions of good, high-wage jobs and ensure prosperity and economic security for all people of the United States;

(C) to invest in the infrastructure and industry of the United States to sustainably meet the challenges of the 21st century;

(D) to secure for all people of the United States for generations to come—

(i) clean air and water;

(ii) climate and community resiliency;

(iii) healthy food;

(iv) access to nature; and

(v) a sustainable environment; and

(E) to promote justice and equity by stopping current, preventing future, and repairing historic oppression of indigenous peoples, communities of color, migrant communities, deindustrialized communities, depopulated rural communities, the poor, low-income workers, women, the elderly, the unhoused, people with disabilities, and youth (referred to in this resolution as "frontline and vulnerable communities");

(2) the goals described in subparagraphs (A) through (E) of paragraph (1) (referred to in this resolution as the "Green New Deal goals") should

be accomplished through a 10-year national mobilization (referred to in this resolution as the "Green New Deal mobilization") that will require the following goals and projects—

(A) building resiliency against climate change-related disasters, such as extreme weather, including by leveraging funding and providing investments for community-defined projects and strategies;

(B) repairing and upgrading the infrastructure in the United States, including—

(i) by eliminating pollution and greenhouse gas emissions as much as technologically feasible;

(ii) by guaranteeing universal access to clean water;

(iii) by reducing the risks posed by climate impacts; and

(iv) by ensuring that any infrastructure bill considered by Congress addresses climate change;

(E) upgrading all existing buildings in the United States and building new buildings to achieve maximum energy efficiency, water efficiency, safety, affordability, comfort, and durability, including through electrification;

(F) spurring massive growth in clean manufacturing in the United States and removing pollution and greenhouse gas emissions from manufacturing and industry as much as is technologically feasible, including by expanding renewable energy manufacturing and investing in existing manufacturing and industry;

(G) working collaboratively with farmers and ranchers in the United States to remove pollution and greenhouse gas emissions from the agricultural sector as much as is technologically feasible, including—

(i) by supporting family farming;

(ii) by investing in sustainable farming and land use practices that increase soil health; and

(iii) by building a more sustainable food system that ensures universal access to healthy food;

(H) overhauling transportation systems in the United States to remove pollution and greenhouse gas emissions from the transportation sector as much as is technologically feasible, including through investment in—

(i) zero-emission vehicle infrastructure and manufacturing;

(ii) clean, affordable, and accessible public transit; and

(iii) high-speed rail;

(I) mitigating and managing the long-term adverse health, economic, and other effects of pollution and climate change, including by providing funding for community-defined projects and strategies;

(J) removing greenhouse gases from the atmosphere and reducing pollution by restoring natural ecosystems through proven low-tech solutions that increase soil carbon storage, such as land preservation and afforestation;

(K) restoring and protecting threatened, endangered, and fragile ecosystems through locally appropriate and science-based projects that enhance biodiversity and support climate resiliency;

(L) cleaning up existing hazardous waste and abandoned sites, ensuring economic development and sustainability on those sites;

(M) identifying other emission and pollution sources and creating solutions to remove them; and

(N) promoting the international exchange of technology, expertise, products, funding, and services, with the aim of making the United States the international leader on climate action, and to help other countries achieve a Green New Deal;

(3) a Green New Deal must be developed through transparent and inclusive consultation, collaboration, and partnership with frontline and vulnerable communities, labor unions, worker cooperatives, civil society groups, academia, and businesses; and

(4) to achieve the Green New Deal goals and mobilization, a Green New Deal will require the following goals and projects—

(A) providing and leveraging, in a way that ensures that the public receives appropriate ownership stakes and returns on investment, adequate capital (including through community grants, public banks, and other public financing), technical expertise, supporting policies, and other forms of assistance to communities, organizations, Federal, State, and local government agencies, and businesses working on the Green New Deal mobilization;

(B) ensuring that the Federal Government takes into account the complete environmental and social costs and impacts of emissions through—

(i) existing laws;

(ii) new policies and programs; and

(iii) ensuring that frontline and vulnerable communities shall not be adversely affected;

(C) providing resources, training, and high-quality education, including higher education, to all people of the United States, with a focus on frontline and vulnerable communities, so that all people of the United States may be full and equal participants in the Green New Deal mobilization;

(D) making public investments in the research and development of new clean and renewable energy technologies and industries;

(E) directing investments to spur economic development, deepen and diversify industry and business in local and regional economies, and build wealth and community ownership, while prioritizing high-quality job creation and economic, social, and environmental benefits in frontline and vulnerable communities, and deindustrialized communities, that may otherwise struggle with the transition away from greenhouse gas intensive industries;

(F) ensuring the use of democratic and participatory processes that are inclusive of and led by frontline and vulnerable communities and workers to plan, implement, and administer the Green New Deal mobilization at the local level;

(G) ensuring that the Green New Deal mobilization creates high-quality union jobs that pay prevailing wages, hires local workers, offers training and advancement opportunities, and guarantees wage and benefit parity for workers affected by the transition;

(H) guaranteeing a job with a family-sustaining wage, adequate family and medical leave, paid vacations, and retirement security to all people of the United States;

(I) strengthening and protecting the right of all workers to organize, unionize, and collectively bargain free of coercion, intimidation, and harassment;

(J) strengthening and enforcing labor, workplace health and safety, antidiscrimination, and wage and hour standards across all employers, industries, and sectors;

(K) enacting and enforcing trade rules, procurement standards, and border adjustments with strong labor and environmental protections—

(i) to stop the transfer of jobs and pollution overseas; and

(ii) to grow domestic manufacturing in the United States;

(L) ensuring that public lands, waters, and oceans are protected and that eminent domain is not abused;

(M) obtaining the free, prior, and informed consent of indigenous peoples for all decisions that affect indigenous peoples and their traditional territories, honoring all treaties and agreements with indigenous peoples, and protecting and enforcing the sovereignty and land rights of indigenous peoples;

(N) ensuring a commercial environment where every businessperson is free from unfair competition and domination by domestic or international monopolies; and

(O) providing all people of the United States with—

(i) high-quality health care;

(ii) affordable, safe, and adequate housing;

(iii) economic security; and

(iv) clean water, clean air, healthy and affordable food, and access to nature.

ABOUT THE AUTHOR

Bill Herrington worked as a laborer on pipeline construction crews during the summers of 1979 and 1980. His first pipeline job was in Harrisburg, Pennsylvania, three months after the nuclear accident at Three Mile Island, just south of Harrisburg.

After graduating from Louisiana State University, Herrington began a 35-year career in corporate banking, which included a focus on the energy service industry in south Louisiana and Texas. He has completed the Harvard Business School general manager program and is now a private equity and private credit investor based in Houston, Texas.

Herrington's first book, *Contraflow*, won the 2017 Independent Publisher Bronze Medal for Best Regional Nonfiction (South U.S.).

Connect with Herrington at his website at billherrington.com or join the conversation on Twitter: @bherrington713.

ALSO BY THE AUTHOR

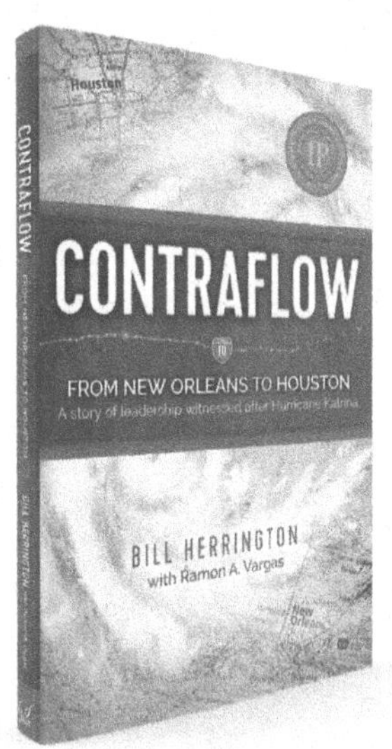

CONTRAFLOW

From New Orleans to Houston. A story of leadership witnessed after Hurricane Katrina.

2017 Independent Publisher Bronze Medal Winner

Best Regional Nonfiction South U.S.

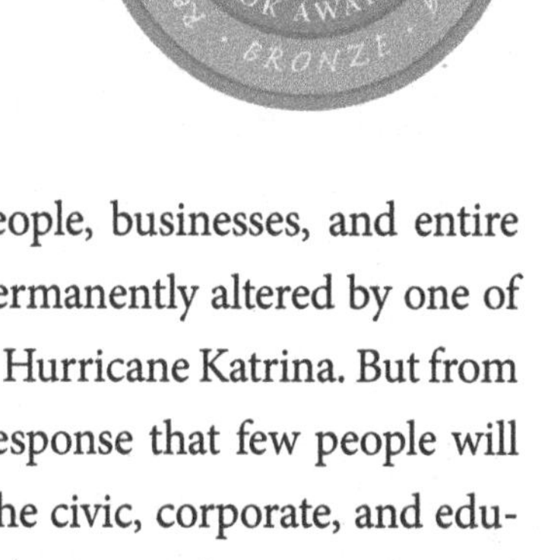

Herrington weaves together the lives of people, businesses, and entire cities that were temporarily reversed and permanently altered by one of the most catastrophic storms in U.S. history, Hurricane Katrina. But from the destruction emerged a humanitarian response that few people will ever experience. *Contraflow* is a tribute to the civic, corporate, and educational leaders who stepped up to show leadership and compassion and to provide critical resources and hope in the aftermath of a devastating storm. Connect with the author on Twitter @bherrington713.

"In a gripping and well-informed account of the aftermath of Hurricane Katrina, Herrington shares inspiring stories of everyday heroes who overcame adversity, helped others do so, and who turned individual tragedies into a community triumph."

– Bill White, former Houston mayor,
chairman of Lazard Houston

AVAILABLE IN PAPERBACK, HARDCOVER, OR E-BOOK FORMAT.

INDEX

www.ingramcontent.com/pod-product-compliance
Lightning Source LLC
Chambersburg PA
CBHW011536260326
41914CB00007B/1170
* 9 7 8 1 9 5 9 6 7 7 1 3 0 *